Austin -

Best Wishes

[illegible]

Business Is Our Business

But Whose Blood . . . . .

. . . . . And On Which Carpets

Business Is Our Business

was written and created by
Malcolm C Miller
and is distributed by the
Australian Consulting Group
Strategic Management Specialists

This book is dedicated to my children
that one day they may know

and
understand

Copyright

Intellectual Property Rights

Disclaimer

ISBN

0 - 646 - 27190 - 3

Date of Publication

First Edition
June, 1996

Contact Address

Australian Consulting Group
PO Box 36
Baulkham Hills, Sydney, Australia, 2153
Price in Australia : $40 plus $4 postage, packaging, and handling.

WARNING

this book may be classified as

Faction

it is a blend of

Fact and Fiction

[being the believable and the unbelievable]

but it is all

TRUE

this is both a serious and a controversial book
it addresses vital but almost invisible drivers of our society
being those of
corporate governance and fundamental accountancy
consequently any whimsical punctuation
which may be encountered amongst its pages
is included for my entertainment

About The Author

Malcolm C Miller

is a strategic-thinker and has been a management consultant for some twenty-five years. He was born in York, England, and holds both British and Australian citizenship. He is a Certified Management Consultant and a Fellow of the Institute of Chartered Accountants in England & Wales and in Australia. He graduated from the University of York with a Bachelor of Arts honours degree majoring in Economics and was also awarded a Masters Degree from the School of Business Leadership at the University of South Africa. During his career he has worked for, and consulted to, numerous large, medium, and small business enterprises, in many industries, and in several countries.

Comment

Between the covers of this book, and in the author's own highly readable, basically chatty, sometimes philosophical, occasionally entertaining, but always inimitable style, are important messages for our society. These multi-faceted messages call out for action by the Accountancy Profession in Australia, the Australian Stock Exchange, Australian Financial Institutions, Corporate Australia, and others. This book is, itself, underwritten by an intellectually demanding leading-edge work that exceeds four hundred pages and which is written in a very different style to this offering. That state-of-the-art work, which was also written by the same author, underpins the practical yet philosophically attractive approach which is taken by the boutique management consultancy practice of the author and which firm specializes in strategic management.

This book embraces corporate governance, strategic management, and the accountancy profession whilst, at one and the same time, it focuses on certain moral, ethical, and intellectual dimensions. Initially it is set amongst, and identified with, various pillars of the business world and whose behaviour, in the public interest, is challenged relative to the needs and values of our society. The accountancy profession is then, and in a similar vein, discussed in its own right, at an individual, a firm, and an industry level. This book is unusual, for contained amongst its pages is a hint, no it is more than a hint, it is a taste of the soiled reality of that profession, its collective lack of competence, its neglect, and its failure, and which collective lack of competence, neglect, and failure has cost our society dearly. Like no other book before, it dares to openly address, confront, and provide insight into the leadership, and certain behaviour, of that somewhat ethereal and almost invisible pillar of the business world, the accountancy profession. The crucifixion and the resurrection of the profession is handled, some would say with sensitivity, as the pain of its truth is cut open (and blood is spilt all over the carpet) prior to the revelation of what is a fundamental contribution to the future well-being of that most vital of professions.

This counter-culture perspective provides a warts and all view of professional reality when seen from the perspective of society. It does, indeed, provide very interesting reading !!!!!

Business Is Our Business

Content

Preamble

If ever there was a profession that has failed society, and in such a glorious way, it is the accountancy profession, for that profession is, indeed, unfit for our times. This book looks at the accountancy profession relative to the world of business and concludes that that profession, despite its efforts, is incestuous in nature, feeding on itself, whilst damaging society in an invidious way. This book, in fact, questions the very value of that profession to society, for it is clear that if the laws which support its existence were different, such mediocrity, in its present form, would struggle to survive.

This book, as it challenges the accountancy profession, sets aside the endless detail in which that profession has become lost and, more appropriately, it focuses upon the big picture, and the broad sweep of things, as it provides knowledge, understanding, and insight into the basic fundamental failings of what is one of the respected pillars of the business community. The substance of the book, which is written in easy-to-read business-type language, unequivocally addresses, and head on, the issue of professional relevance or, more correctly, professional irrelevance. It openly condemns the accountancy profession for what has, historically, been its intellectual ignorance and gutless conviction whilst, and at one and the same time, it castigates its recent leadership for its present remoteness from business reality. It also provides a future direction that is based on matters fundamental and of substance.

The messages in this book are, without doubt, for you, being the shareholders, whether direct or indirect, of business enterprises (being indirect through, for example, your superannuation fund or a unit trust) company stakeholders, being customers, suppliers and employees; as well as every member of society. Its contents reach over and beyond the established institutions and the respected organizations, such as the regulatory bodies, the stock exchange, the commercial banks, the securities institutes, the many business organizations, the boards of directors of powerful companies, and those bodies which represent the accountancy profession, and speaks directly to individuals for, without doubt, the images and the reputations of the aforementioned foundations of our society far surpass the reality of their actions; for those established institutions and respected bodies have, both jointly and severally, failed our society . . . . and they continue to do so.

Business Is Our Business . . . . .

. . . . . Well I suppose it had to strike some time !!!!!

Chapter One

Unfit For Our Times

It never fails to amuse me when I see laughing John Prescott, the chief executive of BHP, on television. I can't work out whether the world has done him a grave injustice or whether, in fact, he's had a humour by-pass. As he growls his way through his interviews his whole body, so as to say, takes part. His bear-like physique (as it appears to be when presented through such a medium . . . . for I have never actually seen him in real life) typically engulfs the whole screen. His monotone delivery is, without doubt, so exciting that it would send the dead to sleep. Whilst his dower facial expressions are almost guaranteed to make any baby cry. Yet, as managing director of 'The Big Australian' being the biggest and, in the past decade, the most successful company in Australia, both he and this massive multi-national have done very well.

But has society done well . . . . and what about the future ?!!!!

Obviously (since its awakening as a result of the shock-waves which were rendered to that then 'corporate sloth' by the takeover bids of Robert Holmes a Court and, as some would say, rescue by John Elliott) BHP has contributed greatly to the economic well-being of Australia. BHP is, today, truly a world class blue chip company. Time, however, marches on and, in order to be relevant and to remain at the leading-edge of contemporary developments, and indeed to be leaders, things must change.

Today the big issue is corporate governance. It is essential to the future development of our society. It is fundamental. And it is of substance. Its tentacles spread everywhere and they entangle everything. Appropriate corporate governance (apart from the dimensions of serendipity and misfortune) in the end determines both business success and business failure. The problem is that although corporate governance is, in contemporary terms, only embryonic in its development, it has already been abducted (and at birth) by those who have, historically, done so much damage to our society : *The Establishment.* The establishment are those bodies in our society who are (so as to say) acceptable, who are high on self-interest and prestige, and who also wield much power. The establishment controls, it influences, and it directs perceptions. Being all sorts of perceptions. Corporate governance, however, is too important to our future. We cannot abdicate responsibility for that activity and so leave it in the hands of the establishment; for they have already failed us too many times. Too many people have already suffered due to their fundamental failures and their amazing ineptitudes. Shareholders have been ruined and their life savings have been unjustly lost. Stakeholders have lost their jobs, their families, and their health. Whilst parts of our society have been absolutely debilitated. The establishment has, indeed, and without doubt, built up a very large debt, and to all Australians.

The establishment is, in fact, unfit for our times !!!!!

As the age of republicanism beckons, Australians must embrace a whole new epoch. We are a young, a fresh, and an invigorating country. We have vision. We have opportunity. We have intellect. We have energy. We have multiculturalism. We have decent and down to earth values. We have humanity in abundance. And we want a society, not only now but also in the future, of which we are proud. The new order is, indeed, dawning. And it is dawning all around us. And it touches almost every aspect of our lives. There is an air of expectancy. An eager anticipation. New values are emerging. Values that are people-based. Values which exude quality of life. The golden dollar, as such, is no longer paramount. It's role is being reassessed and its importance is being placed in perspective. Economic rationalism is dead. It must die its death. And business must embrace its new role. Business must be a means to an end and not an end in itself. It must serve society as never before. The environmental movement, as a major issue, is already with us; and in its many forms. It has changed both the political and business agendas. Technology, the communications boom, and access to and the ability to create information, is empowering the individual. Whilst democracy, whether of the Westminster variety or otherwise, is now sweeping the world; and people, as people, are once again important.

So why would anyone look to the old order, the neo-classical Australian establishment, to embrace the future? Its incumbents are mediocre. They pretend to acknowledge change, but they cling to the values of the past, modifying that past to meet the needs of *their* future as they basically continue to apply their old mindsets, and specifically for their own advantage. They are steeped in self. They lack vision. And they are remote from reality. Such a move could only be retrograde. What would make anyone think that the neo-classical establishment will do anything to protect and enhance the interests of shareholders, stakeholders, and society in general. Only delusion. For their actions coincide overwhelmingly with their own interests and underwhelmingly with the interests of our society. And they are motivated by miserably outdated and irrelevant paradigms and philosophies. God, nobody did anything worthwhile, for so long, to stop the inhumanities which were being inflicted by ruthless forces, and on so many, in Bosnia; and that was when real and horrible human mutilation and slaughter was involved, and such terrible physical events were presented each day, and day after day, on television, and on current affairs programs; and over two hundred thousand people, including some seventeen thousand children, were murdered or just died. Shareholders, stakeholders, and society are, in media terms, only concepts. They, unlike the victims of Bosnia, don't lose arms and legs, except proverbially; there are no blind or mutilated children to be seen on television and rescued; and the bloodbaths, being merely financial, do not capture the personal agony of their victims. We are anaesthetized, and along whatever dimensions we may consider, to wrongdoing and to cruelty, and to reality; and we are too inert to stand up and help ourselves. But it is vital that the real values of our society, being those values which are important to the quality of our lives and those values that are now unfolding as being of importance thereto, are reasserted or are, in all truth, created and established.

No, the future is too important to leave to the establishment. They got it wrong before and they'll get it wrong again. This time round society must take a hand in its own future. Society must determine the values. And society must set the ground rules. Society must change the equation, and the balance of power. And it must be active in the management of that power. For society is composed of individuals. For society is you and it is me. And you and I must be heard. The abdication of responsibility is over. You have got views and you have got opinions. And they count. The future belongs to me and the future belongs to you. And we must create that future. We must not leave it to others who care less.

But for the future to belong to society and thereby to us (and not, by abdication or by default, to the neo-classical establishment) then individuals themselves must be active. The information age, and the age of communication, is here and it is providing members of society with the ability to speak out and to do things. Do not tolerate the mediocre but, rather, embrace the future. Time and again, in the business world, those who have cost society dearly have gone on to hold even more important and even more influential positions, as though they were being rewarded for their failures; and meanwhile we pay their price. Time and again the same individuals turn up on the boards of directors of major companies, and on government bodies, as the myth of their contribution is perpetuated, and its reality is delivered. These people must be challenged. Their motives must be questioned. And their contribution to society must be examined. And if that contribution is deficient then they, and not we, must pay the price. Australian citizens have paid too much, in personal and in family terms, and too often, to allow incompetence to thrive and to prosper. A change is dawning. This is our society and it must be accountable to us; and it must satisfy our values . . . . not theirs.

So who is this neo-classical, non-contemporary, establishment that lacks competence? The neo-classical establishment is composed of human being who are shielded by conceptual structures which are created by the public and private sectors. It is those persons in our society who hold key positions of power and authority, and who, potentially, have a profound effect on our lives. They are the faceless people cloistered away in bodies or in institutions and which bodies and institutions have, in themselves, and with our support, created an image of honour, respectability, and prestige. The establishment have the trappings of office and significant access to the media to present and to reinforce their viewpoints. BHP is part of the neo-classical establishment or, rather, its top management, and its 'unknown' board of directors, are part of the establishment. So are those who wield power at the Australian Stock Exchange. And so are those who, in effect, control the Institute of Chartered Accountants. Each of these organizations, and its people, are different, but each has a part to play as we, in our society, together address and embrace the future. Each would tell us that 'Business Is Our Business' but we know that for our society to function, and function as we would wish, then business itself must perform; and it must perform in accordance with the new moral and the new ethical order of life in the world.

Relatively early in 1995, and in relation to an acquisition offer made by a major mining company listed on the Australian Stock Exchange, a judgement was handed down in the Federal Court of Australia and which judgement required more information to be provided for the benefit of shareholders in order that they may consider, more appropriately, the matters which were set before them and on which they were to make a decision. The level of knowledge and understanding for ordinary shareholders was, in effect, not to be assumed to be equivalent to that of institutional investors. This ruling, although not necessarily intended to be path-breaking, was indicative of a basic change in attitude within our society. In response to that judgement a letter from myself was published in the Australian Financial Review (AFR) an extract of which letter reads as follows:

Dear Sir

The article (AFR, April 4th, 1995) which addressed the judgement handed down by Federal Court Judge Justice Tamberlin in the Renison Goldfields case was indeed admirable for it drew attention to the fact that the courts have now recognized the growing need to look after the interests of small shareholders.

Small shareholders are those people who put important parts of their life savings into financing companies, but they are also often the people who do not have the capacity (unlike major investment companies) to understand the consequences of their actions. They also typically do not have the financial and legal capability to ensure that wrongs committed against them, by the directors and officers of their own companies, are rectified; or, alternatively, that they are paid adequate damages by those parties.

Let us hope that the aforementioned judgement is built upon by the courts for the principles involved are fundamental to the future development of our society. The judgement shows a sensitivity to the wants and needs of the ordinary citizens of our country whilst, at one and the same time, it provides a sound basis (legal judgements) upon which to counter the seemingly endless onslaught of powerful bodies . . . .

. . . . Let us hope that the judgement will set the direction for a more just, fair, and equitable treatment of small shareholders by the very people, being auditors, directors, and advisers, who are suppose to look after their interests.

Best Wishes

Recently there has been a great deal of turmoil at Coles Myer, being a major corporate which has a market capitalization of five billion dollars ($5b) or thereabouts. Coles Myer owns, amongst other retail interests, Coles Supermarkets, K-Mart, Target, and Myer-Grace Bros. The aforementioned turmoil was very fortunate for BHP as it was both more 'sexy' and a more rapidly developing story for the media than was that of the Ok Tedi mine whilst, in any case, Ok Tedi was off-shore and in what some may describe as a third world backwater. Accordingly, the various media paid much attention to the Coles Myer saga and, at the time, somewhat less attention to the problems at BHP.

Although both Coles Myer and BHP had fundamental challenges to embrace and to address, it was evident that the immediate problems at Coles Myer were different. Corporate governance is, to say the least, a deficient dimension at that company. But that was not unusual. This is the case with the overwhelming majority of companies around the world. It is not a situation peculiar to Australia. This observation, incidentally, does not make corporate governance deficiencies acceptable, or even any less disagreeable. What attracted attention to the Coles Myer situation, however, was the perception of wrongdoing. This perception (in relation to which there were, and are, several dimensions and not least of all a particular share transaction which had taken place in 1990, and which became known as the Yannon affair, as well as a significant dollar amount of related-party transactions) may be seen by various parties as having illegal connotations and/or it was viewed as being not desirable on a moral or an ethical basis. Time will, no doubt, reveal any illegalities. The Coles Myer situation also had the element of intrigue, with the removal in September,

1995, of Philip Bowman, the Finance Director of that company, allegedly for investigating various sensitive matters including the aforementioned Yannon share transaction. This action, being his removal from office, seemed to be the trigger for the fiasco which was to then unfold. Laurence Gruzman QC had previously, and over the preceding years, put some significant personal effort into endeavouring to highlight the related-party transactions and, it may be stated, with a fair degree of success; but the removal of Philip Bowman as the Finance Director of the company was to lead to crunch time, and considerable changes to the board of directors of this well known and publicly quoted retail company, Coles Myer.

If only people could see the future, or at least use some common sense, they may do things differently; but that's not the way things happen. People don't really think strategically. After all, its far easier to be reactive and expedient. And this is particularly so if you consider yourself, or yourselves, to be invulnerable; or at least well protected.

By the way, this unfolding that I referred to will have some very interesting outcomes and may well go on for a good year or two; or even longer. And I aren't merely referring to the immediate and obvious events but, rather, the triggering of significant matters known, unknown, and unknowable. The Coles Myer affair will, however, and almost for certain, ensure that the business world will, both for good and for bad, never be the same again in Australia.

To hold a different view or a different opinion, or to disagree with someone or something, does not make it either wrong or illegal. Poor judgement is an occupational hazard of business life and executives may well be required to resign, or even be removed, for exhibiting poor judgement. These observations are not at all intended to refer to the specifics concerning the removal of the aforementioned Finance Director but are stated in order to ensure that it is understood that the world of business, at least at the top level, is not mechanistic or deterministic in nature but is, rather, overwhelmingly based on judgemental decision-making and that, at times, such judgemental decisions and actions will need to give way to decisions and actions that are, in essence, inspirational.

Those judgements, and that inspiration, must not, however, be exercised recklessly, careless of the consequences, but rather, decision-making of that type, to be non-negligent, must be based on appropriate corporate governance; being a matter which will be addressed later.

Coles Myer and BHP were, at that time, in the second half of 1995, being portrayed as the 'terrible twins' of Corporate Australia; whether or not that term was actually used. As the nature of their basic managerial and leadership ineptitudes and, in essence, the basic way in which each of those companies handled their respective crises, was revealed, it also became evident that the fundamental shortcomings of those two companies were being used as a vehicle to promote the political agenda of other players in that most incestuous of environments, the business world.

The Australian Investment Managers Association (AIMA) whose views on corporate governance seem to be very similar to those of the Australian Stock Exchange (ASX) in reality turned the Coles Myer issue into the personification of why their particular view on corporate governance should become the de facto standard in Australia. AIMA, the umbrella body of the institutional investors, has unfortunately clutched at the shadows and has failed to grasp the substance of corporate governance. But it was hell-bent on ensuring that the views of the major institutions were to be adopted by the business world. The main movers and shakers behind the AIMA initiative were AMP Investments, State Superannuation Corporation of New South Wales, and Bankers Trust. [It's almost like, as the old saying goes, the pot calling the kettle black.] AIMA got ample media exposure for its absolutely average corporate governance philosophy and practices, with this being not only at the expense of shareholders, in total, but also to the detriment of stakeholders, including employees, suppliers, and customers, as well as society in general. What a surprise !!!!

The managing director of the ASX, as one of the participants on the 'Lateline' programme on ABC television one evening, stated that the recently introduced ASX listing rule on corporate governance is world's best practice. This statement was laughable and his opinion was immediately contradicted, in no uncertain way, by Professor Bob Walker of the Australian Shareholders

Association. And even if, for one fleeting moment, we were to believe that the new corporate governance rule is truly world's best practice, then it is evident that world's best practice isn't good enough. The listing rule is toothless and abysmal . . . . and no amount of continuous reporting will help improve that situation.

Given the substance of the new corporate governance listing rule it is evident, at least in my opinion, that the ASX is more concerned with maintaining favour with the large institutional investors and managers than it is with looking after the interests of all shareholders in total; being those parties who are the very essence of both the ASX and Corporate Australia. One can only wonder how many more times establishment bodies in our society, such as those of the ASX and the Institute of Chartered Accountants in Australia, are going to focus on the wishes of powerful sub-sets or secondary and tertiary interest groups whilst, at one and the same time, failing to look after the essential well-being of their primary reference groups and which groups, in total, they are suppose to serve. Whilst the Institute of Chartered Accountants in Australia has shown (through its joint task force activities) that, rather than representing the profession in total, it is little more than an instrument of the large accountancy firms (endeavouring to protect them, not least of all through its immoral and unethical championing of the capping of negligence awards, being an initiative which is detrimental to the very shareholders who paid the fees and salaries of their delinquent members whilst they were busy committing their gross acts of 'negligence' against shareholders) we find that the ASX, with its corporate governance rule, has also whimped-out with regard to its onerous responsibility to shareholders. The eight topics which the ASX suggests should be addressed by companies when complying with the listing rule are, indeed, underwhelming, there being little or no cutting-edge in their application, whilst its focus on the identification and management of business risks once again panders to that most debilitating of business diseases, being that of entrepreneurial impoverishment.

I know that, as a management consultant, I would be most ashamed to have provided any company with such a limp hand to address the fundamental and the far reaching challenges of corporate governance. With such an ineffective listing rule and which rule will, no doubt, need to be taken into account by the auditors of Corporate Australia when they form their opinions (being the very same Big Six accountancy firms who so ably sold shareholders down the river during the debacles of the 1980s) we, I am sure, can only look forward to an equally interesting performance during the next round of corporate delinquency. When, one can only wonder, will large corporates, institutions, and leading professional bodies get real about their fundamental responsibilities to society !!!!!

The corporate governance rule of the ASX, together with its accompanying guidelines, should be truly condemned for the sham that it is in practical terms. The views of AIMA and the ASX in relation to corporate governance are remote from reality and that includes, not least of all, their views on executive and non-executive chairpersons. AIMA may be sincere in its endeavours in the area of corporate governance . . . . but it is sincerely wrong. Categorically stated . . . . AIMA has got it wrong on corporate governance . . . . and so has the ASX. The purpose of business enterprises is not to spend an inordinate amount of time and effort on accountability. The 'watchdog' dimension may, indeed, be valid and vital . . . . but it is not business. The 'watchdog' role, whether or not it is carried out in a positive vein, is essentially a negative dimension. Executives (whether or not they are board members and whether, as board members, they are executive or non-executive in status) are there to lead, action, and manage. AIMA, in its June, 1995, publication on corporate governance, apart from coming out with a smorgasbord of what are little more than motherhood statements, endeavours to portray itself as representing the interests of all shareholders; being large through to small. That contention by AIMA is, itself, a deception for it conceitedly subsumes all small shareholders, and of all types and descriptions, under the umbrella of the large investors; and it goes on to equate their interests with those of the large institutions. [Twenty-two percent of the market value of all equities that are quoted on the ASX are held by two point five million small shareholders; the equivalent figure for superannuation and life offices is twenty-four percent.] Shareholder abdication of responsibility has been a debilitating problem for many decades. How common is it, however, for institutions to vote non-establishment shareholders onto the boards of large corporates. It is an essential part of corporate governance that all shareholders (as non-subsumed owners and, therefore, in contradiction to the views of AIMA) should have the ability to be effectively active in ensuring that their company is both led and managed appropriately, and that this is done in the best interests of all of its shareholders, in total.

We would, of course, all agree (or at least most of us would probably agree) that management practices should be improved. Hopefully such improvement occurs on a continuous basis. But the astounding statement in the aforementioned AIMA document which claims that 'adoption of these guidelines will also enhance the competitiveness of the Australian economy' is ludicrous, at least in terms of the fundamental AIMA corporate governance philosophy, whilst the additional statement that the 'booklet should provide both management and investors with the criteria upon which to anticipate and base . . . decisions and votes' fails to point out the implications, or consequences, of a world as seen by AIMA and which view of life is, to say the least, pedestrian.

The fundamental difference in philosophy in relation to world views of corporate governance is encapsulated in the basic dichotomy 'Management v Accountability' for those competing philosophies determine the focus and the emphasis of corporate governance. That choice provides a mindset. No !!!!! It provides a whole mindscape on which to base the design, development, implementation and utilization of corporate governance practices, procedures, and systems. Of course the choice of one philosophy does not exclude the use of aspects of the other philosophy. They are not mutually exclusive. AIMA, however, successfully used the Coles Myer affair to promote its own dysfunctional view of corporate governance; being overwhelmingly that view which is captured in the 'accountability' perspective and which particular perspective, when deconstructed, is the least relevant and the least productive of the alternative philosophies !!!!!

Have we still not learnt that progress is secured by achieving things. Real things. Worthwhile things. In simple terms, what counts in business, basically and ultimately, is entrepreneurship, leadership, management, and action !!!!! Coles Myer was seen as a god-send by AIMA for as far as AIMA was concerned it was a glorious technicolour example of the convergence of all things bad in corporate governance. It could not have suited AIMA's political agenda more perfectly. AIMA, accordingly, climbed into the board of Coles Myer . . . . and the media didn't have the wherewithal to seek out alternative views and opinions, and alternative philosophies, to those being applied by AIMA. After all, they represented the big investors, the big end of town, so how could they have got it wrong? Easy !!!!! A report by the City Research Group in London, England, indicated that eighty-four percent (84%) of institutional investors and seventy-six percent (76%) of merchant bankers believed that audit committees are vital to, or provide assistance in, achieving sound corporate governance. Presumably they didn't respond in a trivial way and, accordingly, it is assumed that they viewed the contribution of an audit committee in terms of a material, non-trivial, contribution; being a contribution of significance to the corporate governance of a business enterprise. When surveying the FTSE-100 companies in the UK only twenty-two percent (22%) of executives who responded had similar beliefs to those which have just been indicated. Incidentally, every one of these leading one hundred (100) companies have audit committees, as do some ninety-eight percent of the next two hundred and fifty (250) leading companies in the UK, but their views on the contribution of audit committees with regard to contributing in a significant way to good corporate governance is obviously at variance to those of the institutions.

The institutional investors, the merchant bankers, the investment bankers, the corporate advisory firms, and the other members of the establishment may well do 'big' deals around town, but basically they're wet behind the ears when it comes to the real practicalities of business. The problem is, they don't know any better !!!!!

The redeeming factor for Australia, of course, is that the above percentages refer to the absolutely pure, blue-blooded, untouched by human hand, give me a girl in kinky black leather underwear, have you got your whip, the trouble is, Charles, there's three of us in this marriage, classical English establishment . . . . whilst our lot here in Australia are only the all singing, all dancing, humming like a bee, I couldn't agree more with myself, neo-classical variety.

So there is hope for us after all.

Meanwhile, back at BHP, an even more challenging problem existed. But where was AIMA? The alleged issues of pollution on a massive scale, support for the undermining of democracy, and a four billion dollar damages claim may pale into insignificance when those matters are compared with the real issue, being basically that of impoverished corporate governance at BHP.

The bottom line was that the directors of that company made expedient decisions in relation to the Ok Tedi debacle and in so doing they have, so as to say, sold their shareholders down the river. The board of BHP had, in reality, given its shareholders short-term tactical benefits in exchange for long-term strategic problems; being on-going strategic problems beyond that of Ok Tedi. When the BHP ineptitudes were uncovered its management and leadership bungled the handling of the issues and, in the process, revealed the real values of that company; compounding the problems that had been exposed by the 'Iron Baron' and the 'Moura Mine' disasters. BHP even endeavoured to hide behind the iniquitous laws of Victoria, as passed by its State government, whereby the right of its citizens to bring contempt of court proceedings has been abolished and basically placed in the hands of a politician. [By the way, we know that politicians always make decisions that are in the best interests of citizens (even though they may not be in their own best interests) so no-one should lose any sleep; well not much anyway. After all, you may never need the protection of the law.] The politician, the Attorney-General of Victoria, refused to bring such an action, even if only to reveal that *no contempt* occurred; and this despite the contrary findings of a judge. In the end the moral and the ethical considerations will condemn BHP and they will do so all the more for its use of anti-democratic laws in a miserable attempt to protect itself.

The following letter, which again was written by myself, was published in the Australian Financial Review (AFR) in mid 1995 and in relation to the BHP Ok Tedi debacle. It addressed BHP and Democracy. BHP initially denied any involvement in the affair.

Dear Sir,

Further to your article entitled 'BHP confesses to role in PNG law' (AFR, 18th August) which stated that BHP has admitted that it helped to prepare a draft of controversial legislation that would impose fines of up to $100,000 on people who pursue legal action in relation to the Ok Tedi mine, one can only wonder where our society is heading.

Not only have we had the Institute of Chartered Accountants pressuring state and federal governments for legislation to cap negligence awards made against their members for damage inflicted on the clients of their members; being a most immoral and unethical initiative. Not only have we had the ASX failing to act in the best interests of shareholders, being the parties who are the very essence of the stock exchange, by adopting miserable corporate governance requirements which fail to protect shareholders in any significant way. We now have BHP, with all its might and power, failing to act morally and ethically in its business transactions.

The extent to which BHP was involved with the PNG authorities in actually putting the finishing touches to this most iniquitous bill (and thereby potential act of parliament) is of less immediate concern than is concern with regard to what action is now going to be taken by BHP. It is quite clear that BHP could, at any time, walk away from the agreement that it has, or will enter into, with the PNG authorities. This junking of the settlement terms, which terms would not be accepted in Australia, could be taken on the basis that the act of parliament, when it is passed, will deprive the citizens of PNG of their basic democratic right to look to the courts for a resolution of their dispute with BHP. This draconian legislation, which supports the BHP agreement in relation to the Ok Tedi mine compensation claim, also includes a $10,000 per day fine on persons for assisting any party objecting to the agreement, giving evidence against the agreement, or challenging the law when it is enacted. Further, any Australian (or any other party for that matter) who commits any of those offences outside PNG will also be subject to the rigours of this obnoxious legislation were they ever to visit PNG.

Why, given the anti-democratic nature of this legislation, would BHP want to be seen spearing democracy? Could it be for a few dollars ?!!!

Best Wishes

The cartoon that was published with this letter was rather comical and stated 'How dare you suggest that BHP would trifle with democracy over a few dollars . . . . Its for lots, and lots, and lots of dollars !!!!!' The message contained in the cartoon by Clement speaks for itself and, no doubt, encapsulates the views of many of those who are appalled at the behaviour of BHP.

BHP, as is indicated above, initially (that is, after they had, for a prolonged period of time, denied any involvement in the drafting of a part of that most iniquitous legislation) blamed the inclement weather conditions at the mine site for their problems, rather than their own intentions, and their value system. They claimed that they had tried but that they could not successfully construct a most expensive tailings dam at that location due to the impact of the weather. No doubt the weather does have a fundamental impact on the construction of a tailings dam. Their real problems, however, were moral and ethical, and had little to do with the weather. Given their own justification for their actions, which justification typically focused on the problems with the tailings dam, it may be pointed out that even that most quintessential of Australian characters 'Blind Freddy' could see what the weather conditions are like in that part of the world; and this was so even before embarking upon the venture. Funnily enough the weather hadn't changed much, at that particular location, in over one hundred years. It had always rained cats and dogs. Rumour, in fact, had it that the weather had tended to be somewhat inclement there for an even longer period of time . . . . but that, of course, was only a rumour !!!!!

Given the BHP excuse for its actions, one can only ponder on why 'The Big Australian' couldn't see what our very own Australian genius 'Blind Freddy' could see so clearly; even in the rain. The reality, of course, was that if BHP could focus attention on specifics, such as the weather and its many state-of-the-art efforts to overcome the insurmountable challenges produced thereby, it could deflect attention from the underlying principles that would affect activities both at their mine site in PNG as well as away from their other mining and exploration activities elsewhere in the world. Every activity could then be agonized separately. The big questions could be broken down and reality could be hidden from sight. Meanwhile, of course, the profits would continue to flow; even to the detriment of those natives who had never seen a white man before 1963 but who, unfortunately for them, lived near a mountain that contained four or five billion dollars worth of mineral wealth. [Those natives must have been so pleased that civilization had at last arrived.] Also, if BHP could identify some of the good things which they were providing in PNG then these things, either one at a time or in small parcels, could be presented to the relevant audiences as being far more important than any negative impacts and consequences which their activities may, so as to say, pour down on the natives.

Setting aside specifics for a moment (and the enormity of their transgressions) one must wonder how good corporate governance practices are at BHP. That is, cutting-edge corporate governance, and not the remote AIMA variety. The handling of the Ok Tedi debacle, together with the botching of a major investment in Vietnam (irrespective of how that may turn out) together with what would seem to be a deficient flow of information within and without the company, could well indicate that there are problems in that area. This glimpse into what is basic mismanagement, and basic mismanagement which emanates from the top, may only be the tip of the iceberg. The response to that comment, within the walls of world headquarters, naturally, may well be titanic in proportions ['What tip ?!!!! .... What iceberg ?!!!!'] for after all it is the victors and the powerful who gain the right to write history; and not some strategic management specialist who is merely observing reality.

BHP had directed much effort, early in the Ok Tedi mine affair, at endeavouring to show, legally, that moral and ethical wrongs committed by that company are, in law, right. Apart from the fact that legal success can never prove that moral and ethical values are wrong (for the two are evaluated along somewhat different dimensions) a legal success in that area would, in itself, prove to be counter-productive and very very empty indeed for BHP. In addition, one can only wonder whether the behaviour of BHP would have been different had this mine been located in America. After all, BHP backed-off at at the speed of light when Uncle Sam whispered, ever so quietly in its corporate ear, something about a pipeline to Iran. Perhaps this is just another signal revealing weaknesses in cutting-edge corporate governance at BHP.

BHP has, unlike most companies and many major corporates, massive resources on which to ride out its problems in the area of corporate governance. It is almost a forty billion dollar ($40b) company in terms of market capitalization. The juggernaut will undoubtedly role on and, hopefully, from one success to another. And its mistakes will be buried amongst its achievements. This does not mean, however, that poor corporate governance will not have its toll. There are many levels of corporate governance and each with varying degrees of tolerance. The breathing space that is available to this company (for that is all that it is) has been created, whether consciously or otherwise, by years of success upon success. Relative debilitation, nonetheless, will eventually take its toll (as it did with CSR throughout much of the 1980s and early 1990s) and reality will then start to crystallize. A change in both values and practices and, indeed, in fundamental corporate governance philosophy is, in accordance, on the agenda for BHP. The announcement of an overhaul of management at BHP was made in December, 1995. It was made just after the disclosure of its massive multi-billion dollar take-over bid for copper company, Magma Corporation, of the USA. The reorganization is to focus on growth, globalization, and the preparation for a generational change in leadership. Even at that time John Prescott was still stating that they, BHP, had not taken their eye off the ball in PNG, although he did recognize that the Ok Tedi affair had been a catalyst for change at BHP. He contended that there had actually been what he called a 'retrospective' adjustment of community standards. [Retrospective. That's a funny turn of phrase. I suppose it's a bit like re-writing history. I guess what happened in essence was that they didn't care less and looked after what they thought were their own best interests . . . . but instead they got bogged down in their own sludge.] It's not clear whether the head of BHP meant that there had been a change in community standards here in Australia, or in PNG, but with the hostile attitude of the authorities in PNG to anyone who has a different view of the Ok Tedi affair compared with that of their own, it may be correct to assume that the so called 'retrospective' change had occurred in Australia. He then went on to state that there is a limit to how quickly engineering adjustments could be actioned. But he failed to acknowledge even a half decent compensation arrangement and preferred to concentrate on reducing any compensation by the cost of a tailings dam; after all, the natives would be benefiting from such a dam. [That's a good idea . . . . BHP could transfer the costs of doing what they should have done anyway, to their victims. Paying for the benefit of not being raped is a really good concept. My goodness, just another advantage of civilization.] Before long such a strong case will have been constructed in relation to the benefits which are being provided to the villagers from the presence of the mine that, before long, those very same villagers will be paying compensation to BHP.

Let us just step aside for a moment.

When a major mine is established in some remote location (and remember, these mines are often around for ten and twenty years or more) all sorts of costs and benefits flow, both to the local communities and to the mining company. Its all part and parcel of being in the mining business. You cannot, accordingly, separate out, for your own purposes, all the satellite benefits which may come with the main game, being the mine itself . . . . for no-one was building roads, houses, schools, and hospitals without the mine and its anticipated profit flows. To argue that the benefits are, in fact, benefits that are remote from the establishment of the mine is farcical. They are no more and no less than costs to the mining company and they are costs that are incurred for the right to make the aforementioned profits; and this is so whether or not those profits are, in the end, realized. They form some of the costs of establishing, and then operating, a mine.

Justifying, or endeavouring to mitigate, absolutely wrong behaviour (being that of environmental pollution on a massive scale and which pollution impacts communities in a significantly adverse way) with the contention that the parties damaged are themselves obtaining benefits is deceptive. Such a contention is both morally and ethically wrong. The essence of this type of damage is that the lives of people are changed dramatically, and sometimes fundamentally, and in a way which is uninvited, not welcome, and simply traumatic. The damage can be tremendous.

It is also wrong to endeavour to reduce the amount of damages payable by the cost of the construction of a tailings dam as a tailings dam was already an essential part of the mine. Nowhere in Australia would that type of pollution have been knowingly tolerated. It is massive. By not constructing a tailings dam the company was gaining an advantage (whether or not, in reality, it turned out to be an advantage) and the cost of that advantage is, in the end, at least the amount of the compensation settlement.

It is also not a valid argument for the company to claim that it endeavoured to construct a tailings dam, and failed, but that the company will now undertake a further attempt, this time at the cost of the villagers; and with that cost being the amount of the reduction in the total of the compensation payout. All that the company is doing in this situation is transferring the business risk (which the company took upon itself when it obtained its right to build a mine, including a tailings dam) from the company to the villagers; being its victims. The villagers were never in the mining business and they never ever took the risks of mining upon themselves. Those risks correctly belong to BHP. In addition, of course, there is the mistake of believing that what is promised will, in reality, be delivered. Time and again in the business world what is agreed to is, at one and the same time, viewed as having already been accomplished, and with only the reality being required to be actioned. The achievement of reality may then be treated as something incidental and, therefore, almost a foregone conclusion; and with much less of substance being delivered. Sometimes there is no intention to deliver anything at all. In any case a whole new approach to the problem or, indeed, to the mine itself, needs to be embraced. Thinking along the same type of dimensions (no matter how advanced may be that thinking or those dimensions) will not necessarily, and of itself, produce a very satisfactory solution or resolution to the exceptional or, as some may believe, insurmountable challenges which face BHP.

Whatever the final settlement may be let us not be fooled by the superficially valid and intuitively appealing arguments that are put forward by BHP. Let me remind you. More copper waste than you could ever possibly imagine is being tipped into the river system, each and every day of each and every year, together with zinc, lead, and cadmium mine waste, and for which waste there is no natural mechanism for detoxification. BHP claims these levels are low but there will be a reservoir of toxic heavy metals hanging around the river system and its environments for centuries after the money has been made and the mine has ceased its operations.

BHP got it wrong. It was as simple as that. And when they endeavoured to justify their wrongful actions they revealed to the world their true values. Worse, however, and unknown to them, they had also inadvertently revealed the existence of important corporate governance problems at the company. It is no use John Prescott making the statement that 'within the context of the scale of the company's operations the vast majority of our operations have been carried out without adverse impact' for that, by implication, merely rationalizes the wrongdoing. No doubt Shell could also make a similar statement with regard to its activities and its particular behaviour in Nigeria. But the brutalization of parts of the population of that country, including the callous murder and vicious mutilation of helpless inhabitants and their subsequent lifelong agony, not to mention extreme large scale pollution, and all this in the interests of the nation (according, at least, to the government of Nigeria) do not make matters any better for those people. Gains made on some dimensions are absolutely obliterated by losses inflicted on other dimensions. Would you exchange a real arm or a real leg for a hospital to care for your mutilation? The same 'national interest' reasons could, of course, be applied to events in PNG. On that basis, damaging the few for the benefit of the many can always be justified. We could all then be picked off, one at a time or in small groups, by the powerful. No, its not the average performance but, rather, what happens at the cutting-edge, the marginal reality, which reveals the real values of a company or a body; provided of course that such things are ever revealed for scrutiny. Given this brief insight into the problems of porous and inept corporate governance at 'The Big Australian' then perhaps a top level generational change will, in truth, be beneficial to the shareholders of BHP !!!!!

In relation to the Coles Myer fiasco [which is being used here to highlight different dimensions of corporate governance than those which are being illustrated by the use of the BHP Ok Tedi debacle and, in the case of Coles Myer, being that there are perfectly valid, although fundamentally different, approaches to corporate governance available to a company, and not just the one version which is practiced and pushed by AIMA and which accords with that most dysfunctional of corporate governance versions, being that of the 'accountability' philosophy] the managing director of the ASX is reported to have stated that 'we would only suspend (a share) to protect the integrity of the market', whatever that means. It is also reported that he went on to say that 'the sooner these issues are dealt with the better' as everybody will be running around 'wanting to bring in rules which won't be effective in changing the environment' . . . . at least, that is, according to his view of life. He is then reported as going on to state that this type of event, being the Coles Myer affair, could not help the international reputation of Australia in financial markets.

Paraphrased, this may of course be read as, the sooner we get this mess off the front pages the sooner we can get back to doing what we don't do very well. Damn it, its drawing attention to some of the fundamental inadequacies of the business world; being both our own inadequacies as well as those of our cronies. Sooner or later someone will cotton-on and then the media will go to town on us. We'd better bring in the old red herring issue, international reputation, to divert attention. It always seems to work. After all, who remembers the screw-ups in Japan with their bank and non-bank financial institutions and their property market loans, the Lloyds debacle in the UK, the Barings issue and its Singapore connections or, for that matter, US Junk Bonds, and the myriad of other cock-ups that keep occurring despite the pathetic efforts of our mates in the different arms of the establishment. Yes, push the damage to the international reputation angle, no-one will ever remember that that lot overseas are just as incompetent and that they have just as many problems as we do here in Australia.

The trouble, of course, is that these crises do, in fact, keep popping up. Unfortunately, however, they are viewed as 'one-offs' or, at least, they are often portrayed as such by the establishment and, in accordance therewith, are presented as being abnormal or extra-ordinary happenings that must be dealt with expeditiously; and by suitable members of the establishment. In reality all these debacles and fiascos are, of course, and at least in the big scheme of things, normal business events. Only the plots, the characters, and the scenes are different. Trying to prevent them is about as successful as attempting to stamp out alcohol, drugs, prostitution, or gambling. The basic idea behind introducing specific corporate governance reporting requirements is the improvement of the management of at least the major quoted companies and those business enterprises which are controlled by those companies and, in particular, to improve management at the top of those companies and those business enterprises. The improvement of corporate governance practices should not, however, carry with it an implicit denial of the inevitability of problems either at the time they arise or when they unfold. Pretending that problems, and not least of all major problems, are extra-ordinary events and which events are, therefore, a surprise (as was evidenced, early in the piece, by the almost daily agonizing of the Coles Myer affair by at least one or other member of the establishment including both AIMA and the ASX) only means that the establishment, including AIMA and the ASX, reside in fairyland.

Yes, there are problems at Coles Myer. Real problems. But we must, for present purposes, differentiate problems of illegality, if any, from the problems and challenges relating to the corporate governance of that company. And these problems of corporate governance must, themselves, be differentiated from the farcical 'corporate governance' standards which are presently being promoted around the business world and in Australia. These so-called standards, for they are indeed laughable, will eventually be seen for what they are, being basically flawed and remote from reality, for they will not achieve what they should achieve. AIMA can then remove its vested interests and make room for those with more wherewithal and with less capacity to retard progress; and who have a more relevant contribution to make to society.

AIMA, it will be recalled, represents institutional shareholders. This fact, however, does not endow AIMA with any great insight into corporate governance; after all, much of the output from the establishment is developed from incestuous consultations with one another . . . . whilst, at this very time and in the UK, there are serious concerns being expressed with regard to the type of approach to corporate governance that is peddled by AIMA. Accordingly, and whilst the establishment (and not least of all AIMA and the ASX) dictate corporate governance requirements, and which requirements are being misguidedly supported by the business media, then Australia couldn't possibly lead the world in this most important area of business practice, for those bodies themselves, being AIMA and the ASX, have a follower mentality. And, it is noted, we have no need to look any further afield for an illustration of this very point than that of their own attitude and approach to that of corporate governance: they basically followed.

Generally, and with regard to the establishment, there seems to be so many amateurs in its ranks who, due to their positional power, insist on giving what seem to be important opinions; and this includes some of the supporters of AIMA. [This charge may well be made against myself concerning the content hereof but, there again, I'm not part of the establishment (I personally don't mix with the 'right' people . . . . that's one of the reasons that I can write this book) and, in any case, you need only watch the news, or various business programs, to see what I mean.] Real members of the establishment (such as directors of certain major companies, or certain partners of large professional firms, or the heads of various high profile business bodies, and so forth) seem to consider that their views and opinions are true and correct; and of importance. Such views and opinions are indeed important. But they are important because others (and not least of all other members of the neo-classical establishment) listen to them and, like lemmings, act in relation to those views and opinions. But such views and opinions are not necessarily underpinned by real knowledge, real understanding, real insight, and real substance. These people are not immortal. And nor are they invincible. In fact, they're often pretty ordinary people once you strip them of their pin-stripped suits and their positions of authority and power. Sometimes they're not even that bright. We've only got to recall the many establishment screw-ups to appreciate that fact. No, let's get AIMA and the ASX into perspective. Although the establishment may well think of itself as leaders, and as being progressive, the truth of the matter is that often the establishment leads from behind. Those corporates which actually introduce leading-edge state-of-the-art corporate governance practices (and with regard to which matters I would be most pleased to advise) will typically be non-establishment companies; being those with energy and vision. They are the real business leaders of Australia.

A more significant problem in the Coles Myer debacle was, of course, that the media, just as it did in the 1980s shambles, shed its real responsibilities. Seemingly oblivious to the fact that the fundamental victim of the Coles Myer affair was indeed corporate governance itself, the media (and of all types) having got the scent of blood, prostituted itself as it once again became an actor in the play. By presenting the institutions as the 'goodies' and the board of Coles Myer as the 'baddies' the media unquestionably adopted the opinions of the institutional investors as being the correct view of corporate governance. The media has thereby established that view, warts and all, as the de facto standard in Australia. It is sad, but all too often insight and wisdom is wrongly equated with authority and power. This has been the case with regard to AIMA.

As we listen to the grunts of agreement that a just, a fair, and an equitable outcome has resulted from the events of recent times, both in relation to Coles Myer and BHP, let us focus on the fact that sound corporate governance was the real victim and that the media has now potentially bequeathed our society to yet another generation of mediocre management. Those without vision, but with deep pockets, are back. The same players who, with gay abandon, wasted billions of dollars of shareholders monies, and who destroyed or depleted the savings and the superannuation of millions of Australians as a result of their incompetence in the 1980s, are once again presented as responsible corporate citizens.

The corporate governance rules are a farce. Those same parties whose incompetence in the 1980s devastated many businesses, their shareholders, and their employees, are once again looking after our interests. How comforting !!!!! It is patently evident that the corporate governance rules serve neither shareholders nor business enterprises. The rules were basically designed by the institutions to serve themselves. They were adopted by the ASX in its own best interests. And compliance will, in the end, be addressed by the very auditors, the ever so able members of the Institute of Chartered Accountants who, in the 1980s, couldn't spot a corporate disaster when it was staring them in the face. It is stated here that there is no reason to believe that the pillars of the business world (including the institutions, the stock exchange, and the professions) are relatively any more responsible today than they were in the past. Wisdom, knowledge, understanding, and insight does not reside with those bodies. Given this, it is also noted that the ethos of 'greed is good' somehow invariably seems to survive each and every generation of business endeavour. In accordance therewith, those wolves who so ably control the money have merely changed their sheep-like clothing (perhaps from fleece to super-fleece) in order to continue *their* success !!!!!

To put corporate governance in perspective, an article that I wrote, and which was included in the July, 1995, copy of a newsletter which is circulated by one of the leading legal publishers, CCH, is set out below. The article is presented in a somewhat different form when compared with that of the aforementioned version. For those of you who take time out, and reflect upon the article, it may well leave you wondering what really has been achieved by the members of the establishment and in this most vital of emerging fields, corporate governance.

The Black Hole Of Corporate Governance

The Issue

The Australian Stock Exchange recently produced its new listing rule which was introduced on the 1st July, 1995, and which rule [3C(3)(j)] requires 'a statement of the main corporate governance practices that the company has had in place' during annual reporting periods ending on and after 30th June, 1996. Given this ASX earth shattering announcement then I trust that you will be well disposed to travel with me on this most interesting of journeys to discover the black hole of corporate governance.

The History

One may wonder why, and on a world-wide basis, stock exchanges, professional bodies, and multi-national companies have become so interested in what has become known as 'corporate governance' being a term which, one may add, is about as exciting as a cold shower. Why, it may be asked rhetorically, has this rush of ethical adrenalin to the corporate brain occurred at this point in time. The answer, put simply, is fear .... being the fear of being sued .... for there is nothing like a good dose of fear to induce action.

The trigger for this action (some, like myself, may say deficient action) was, of course, the stock market crash. In 1987 the world changed. The bottom fell out of the stock market and millions of investors, world-wide, lost billions of dollars. The flow-on effect, however, was staggering. Some companies that appeared to be substantial in nature, collapsed. They in turn brought down other companies. Millions of people around the world lost their jobs. And 'the recession we had to have' was aggravated beyond all belief, both in severity and duration. Australia, in my view, as both a direct and an indirect consequence, eventually lost something of the order of fifty billion dollars ($50b) of value. Society was changed for ever. And corporate governance was on the agenda.

The real cancer had, however, commenced its ubiquitous journey years earlier and, in all probability, some ten years before the stock market crash of 1987. The preconditioned environment for this deadly cancer had developed in the years from 1970 through to 1977. The cancer had, in fact, crystallized, not in Australia, but in the United Kingdom. (Alas, then as now, Australia was only a follower . . . . its own management visionaries having to depart these wonderful shores if they are to make any progress with their creative ideas.) In the early to mid 1970s certain of the trend setters of the accounting world (being sponsored by all of the then six major accountancy bodies in the United Kingdom) had applied some considerable intellect and had spent a significant amount of time developing what was without doubt, at that time, a state-of-the-art proposal for radical change in the way that quoted companies should report their results. This state-of-the-art proposal was rejected by the ordinary membership of those bodies in 1977. It was all too difficult. Despite a well fought rear-guard action, the battle for a quantum shift in the management practices of major corporates was lost. Mediocrity had won. The cancer had crystallized.

The social, political, economic, and technological environments of that time were in a hiatus. The business world wanted to be raped but it hadn't yet decided by whom. In Australia Cambridge Credit Corporation, Gollin (previously one of the most respected companies in Australia) and Poseidon, had all come and gone. In fact, just a glance at Trevor Sykes six hundred page book entitled 'Two Centuries Of Panic' with its subtitle 'A History Of Corporate Collapses In Australia' and which book documents two hundred years of corporate debacles through to 1979, may well convince any reasonable person that nothing much has changed. And the rape of the 1980s still lay ahead. Given the inhibited propensity of the business world to learn from its experiences it would seem that the future will, in essence, be much the same as the past. Shareholders will be ripped off.

The Action

So what can be done about it?

The ASX has now played its hand. It has followed, to some extent, the approach which was adopted in the United Kingdom, but with no mandatory prescriptions beyond the rule itself. It is argued in the official ASX news release that doubts were expressed about the effectiveness of a checklist-based approach. Some of the seventy-six respondents to the request for submissions, it is stated, argued that a requirement to explain deviations from a prescribed set of practices would promote form over substance (this is the latest turn of phrase in the world of accountancy; I wonder what will be next) whilst a reference to prescription inhibiting the continuing development of 'best practice' in this area (the term 'best practice' should never be omitted as it is meant to convey that appropriate and profound consideration has been given to all possible matters of relevance) was also made. The new rule, it is stated, will focus on the function rather than the form of disclosure and with specific corporate governance matters being identified in an indicative, rather than a prescriptive, list. The ASX believes 'that this will result in more information of greater relevance being disclosed' than would otherwise be the case.

The ASX goes on to state that a non-prescriptive approach will also facilitate the introduction of the codes of best practice that are now being developed by several organizations representing market participants.

The Purpose

Nowhere in the ASX news release does it tell us what is the purpose of the new listing rule. Shareholders, it would appear, are the essence of both the ASX and Corporate Australia. Bearing this in mind let us look at what the new non-prescriptive listing rule is perhaps endeavouring to achieve. It could be argued that the new rule is being introduced to help prevent shareholders from losing their investments though corporate debacles. Corporate-debacle companies are not the rule (despite rumour to the contrary) but are, in fact, the exception. Corporate debacles occur at the margin; at the cutting-edge. In order, however, that the effort involved in complying with the new listing rule is not redundant with regard to non-corporate-debacle companies (being the vast majority of companies whose corporate governance deficiencies are never laid bare for all to see) it could also be argued that the new listing rule is being introduced to significantly improve management practices across all quoted companies and their derivatives.

The Debacles

Given that one of the purposes of the new listing rule is the optimal avoidance of corporate debacles, and given the non-prescriptive requirements of the listing rule, then one must consider when anything was ever voluntarily divulged by a major company, and in an open and honest manner, when the company did not wish to divulge the particular matters at issue. The answer, of course, is never.

Just imagine an entrepreneur during the hay-days of the last decade when profits were apparently flowing as though they were going out of fashion (funnily enough they went out of fashion and actually turned into losses) and when all and sundry, including accountants, auditors, lawyers, and business journalists, actually became actors in the play, rather than objective contributors; revelling in the thrill of high profile take-over bids and record profit announcements, whilst dreaming about their own ambitions for wealth beyond belief. Now let us transport that scenario to a post 'new listing rule' environment. How many years of negotiation will it take the ASX to actually persuade the board of an evidently delinquent company to comply, beyond that of apparent compliance, with the new listing rule? Put simply. A virtual eternity.

History tells us clearly that when oodles of money, and powerful combatants, are involved in a difference of opinion, nothing is resolved quickly. If nothing is resolved quickly (and a major point of the focus on corporate governance is to facilitate swift action to secure fundamental advantage) then there is not much point in having the new rule. The potential corporate debacles, which the new rule is designed to avoid, will actually have happened; and this before anyone knew much (as a result of information produced under the new listing rule) about the real problems of corporate governance in the delinquent company. It would seem, therefore, that corporate debacles will not be prevented or, indeed, not even be mitigated by the new listing rule. Worse than this, however, even when the new rule is actually applied in practice its requirements are so remote from the cutting-edge of reality that the listing rule will, to all intents and purposes, be ineffective in helping to avoid corporate debacles.

The Delusion

The ability of the new listing rule to bring about a significant improvement in management practices generally is also questionable. It is evident that a new listing rule of this nature will, indeed, bring about change. The concern, however, is whether that change will be fundamentally beneficial to shareholders in total, and then to stakeholder, and then to society in general.

Of the eight matters that the ASX includes in its list of indicative items which may be taken into account, most are administrative or merely hygienic in nature. In fact, every one of the eight matters included in the indicative list are either negative avoidance procedures, or they are neutral in nature; whilst the rule itself is an invitation to any board of directors to disclose what they consider to be favourable to the company; and with other matters being discretely overlooked.

Motherhood is back in fashion !!!!!

Let us look at some of the matters which are included in the indicative list. It may, indeed, be useful for a shareholder to know whether individual directors are executive or non-executive in status and, in practice, shareholders should be made aware of those facts. Is that knowledge, however, going to alter the fundamental well-being of a corporate enterprise. It may or it may not. One would never know.

This issue tends to infer that there is some predetermined mix of executive and non-executive directors which will bring success to a company. Who knows whether or not the executives who are excluded from the status of executive director, because of the inclusion of non-executive directors on the board of a company, would not have brought more value to the company than the non-executive directors who are actually appointed in their place. There is no a priori reasoning which can be relied upon to resolve this predicament but, rather, there is only the certainty of shifting sand on which to build reality. The point is that the issue of executive and non-executive directors is a 'flavour of the month' management fad. Perhaps in years to come, when the current trend towards non-executive directors has been recognized as an empty initiative, and not the source of business success, the pendulum will swing again and the skills and the abilities of 'close to the action' executives may once more be applauded.

My view is that the composition of a board of directors, per se, tells us little or nothing with regard to the future success of a company and that statistics which support one case or the other are spurious in nature. What is important for fundamental business success lies well below the superficial question of the mix of executive and non-executive directors on the board of a company. Business success resides, rather, in the very foundations of sound business management; plus a good dose of serendipity.

The Contention

The point in relation to the aforementioned issue, as well as in relation to each of the other matters that are identified by the ASX, is that many of those matters do not address the fundamental well-being of a corporate enterprise. Yes, I hear the howls of complaint, and yes, I agree with your point of view; on the balance of probabilities benefit will hopefully flow. But let us not fool ourselves that the ASX has, in any fundamental sense, addressed the issue of corporate governance. Do we, for example, really believe that by devising criteria for board membership that such an initiative will, in total, produce a more appropriate array of people who hold directorships of quoted companies. Is there some oracle out there. Someone who has a list of the chosen ones; being people we need only seek out in order to secure business success. Let us be quite clear, in any list of the most successful company directors in the past fifty years there would be included therein the most unexpected people; being people who arrived in their positions from diverse directions, and from a variety of backgrounds, and whose brilliant success, before the event, could not have been predicted. And there are equally brilliant disappointments. The implication of this initiative, that Australia has a very limited supply of talented people who have the capacity to sit on the boards of major corporates and contribute in a significant way to their success, is an absolute myth. [Oh, and by the way, I am available for board appointments.] Likewise the review of remuneration arrangements and the adequacy, or otherwise, of the external audit are also important matters, but they are not the essence of good corporate governance. High ethical standards too, are to be applauded, but looking back over my thirty plus years as a professional person I have never seen ethics, per se, fatally flaw a highly motivated executive. A good dose of psychological rationalization always wins.

The Black Hole

The real issue, of course, is that corporate governance has been badly defined. The literature is wishy-washy. It misses the point. The fuzzy-wuzzy thinkers who have grabbed the issue will cost shareholders dearly. The indicative list of matters for disclosure, as produced by the ASX in its news release, are mere satellites orbiting reality. The corporate governance rule is way off target. Corporate governance has, through the process of group think, drifted off into outer space. It is critical that it is retrieved and brought back down to earth, and soon, for when the first round of legal actions are brought in relation to corporate governance disclosure, the gaping holes in the new listing rule will be revealed; and many shareholders and many company directors will be devoured forever by the black hole of corporate governance !!!!!

It is evident, bearing in mind the content of the preceding article, that the philosophy which underpins corporate governance must be carefully considered and appropriate paradigms developed if we are to harness and harvest any fundamental advantages from this present era of improvement in the management of business enterprises. The positive, rather than the passive, approach must be adopted, developed, and actioned. Corporate governance must address the very essence of business activity and not some remote satellites which are three or four times removed from practical relevance. Corporate governance is, accordingly and for sure, far too important to leave in the hands of the fuzzy-wuzzy thinkers and those who have abducted it at birth.

In order that you don't think that Coles Myer and BHP are the only two companies in Australia that have or have not, according to one's view, behaved badly in recent times, other companies with problems are also identified. These companies are household names in the business world, and are also supposedly respectable, yet they are somehow deficient in their corporate governance. It may be stated that not long ago three major Australian corporates, Pioneer, Boral, and CSR, where fined, in total, the sum of twenty-one million dollars ($21m) for what was, in effect, price rigging in the concrete industry. The managing director of CSR stated that he greatly regretted that CSR had been involved in these illegal activities, which wasn't at all surprising, after all, his company had been caught; whilst Boral placed a tomb-stone announcement in the print media apologizing to customers and shareholders for their behaviour. In another case TNT, Ansett, and Mayne Nickless were fined about eleven million dollars ($11m) for price fixing in the express freight business. Whilst in yet another case AMP, a massive financial services company, had to repay some fifty million dollars ($50m) for making misleading and deceptive representations in relation to the marketing of its products to its customers whilst, in another court decision, it was found that its treatment of one of its own top performing agencies was harsh, unfair, unconscionable, and against the public interest. Three builders, Multiplex Construction, Leighton Contractors, and Holland Stolte, together paid out millions in repayments and fines in relation to collusive tendering. And in the chicken market share and price fixing business Inghams and Steggles, which latter firm is part of Goodman Fielder, also incurred fines. Whilst, in the petrol business, Ampol was also fined three point five million dollars ($3.5m) for price fixing efforts. These firms were penalize under the law, as well as having their moral and ethical standards exposed, and their respective reputations correctly dented. Some of these companies will also face multi-million dollar civil damage claims through the courts.

The moral and ethical boundaries are much wider than are the purely legal boundaries, whilst the consequences of wrongdoing in the moral and ethical arena can be far more lethal in nature; and for all parties. The cutting-edge for assessment is not whether the aforementioned pillars of the business world, and others, have behaved legally or illegally in their activities (for the law itself requires specific proof, and under certain strict conditions, in order to prove wrongdoing) but, rather, the issue is whether or not their behaviour meets the emerging moral and ethical values of today's society. The general question, therefore, is more concerned with whether or not the behaviour of bodies, institutions, and major corporates is at least acceptable and, beyond that, whether or not their behaviour can be viewed as being exemplary. What the business bodies, institutions, and business enterprises identified herein did not seem to realize is that the world has changed. Values have altered. And the power of the individual has increased tremendously. Even the smallest of shareholders (and stakeholders) can now tell the world of their concerns, and someone somewhere out there will be listening !!!!! Technology, together with a significant change in social values, has ensured that outcome. Today almost anyone located almost anywhere can be contacted in one way or another. The telephone (and not least of all the mobile variety) the fax, and the computer, amongst other things, have joined forces to shift the balance of power away from the traditional sources and towards the ordinary person. Major reference works, as well as mere books like this one, can be produced by individuals directly from a personal computer and a laser printer; and their contents can impact the world in a way that was previously almost impossible. This fact alone should send a shiver, perhaps two shivers, or in fact a whole host of shivers, down the proverbial spines of those who have (whether justly, fairly, or otherwise) traditionally wielded power; for they, in many cases, have been unfit to have the sometimes unfettered power which they once possessed.

The preceding comments will probably leave no doubt in the minds of those they address, and the business world in general, that the game has indeed changed. By calling a spade a spade, this book will hopefully help to bring about a far greater sense of responsibility amongst those who wield power and authority in the business world and, in so doing, it may also assist in the introduction of an improved level of corporate governance and in terms of a different philosophy.

This book is cutting . . . . but true !!!!!

There is no longer any place for the mediocre to hide, for the propensity to exercise power has, on a continuum, shifted away from the traditional sources of power and authority (being, in Australia, the neo-classical establishment in its various forms) and it has moved towards that of shareholders and the individual. This move has been facilitated by the will of the people or, to put that in what may be more palatable terms for some people, the telecommunications and information technology revolutions. In what is merely a matter of minutes, or even in only a few seconds, views and opinions can now be transmitted around the globe. In a very short time indeed the content and the critiques of this book can be sent from Sydney, Australia, to appropriate sources in London, New York, and Tokyo; and from, and to, other centres all over the world. The 'anything, anytime, anywhere' information revolution, as facilitated by state-of-the-art telecommunications, is with us. There is no hiding place. Those who are not performing, and who are damaging society, can be exposed, on a worldwide basis, in just moments. The gagging, or the attempted gagging, of communications in one country is, today, easily circumvented by the simultaneous release of information in a more receptive, or at least in a less hostile, environment in one or more other countries. Instantaneous worldwide communication is here to stay. The message for those whose incompetence, or lack of competence, is no longer protected by ignorance and the inhibited ability of their victims (and others) to communicate their displeasure is simply, *transform yourself*, for a new age of democracy has emerged. And with this emergence has come a real and more effective ability to address problems, opportunities, and challenges in a way which has never been known before. The very foundations of our society are about to be shaken, and by a whole range, and a whole series, of proverbial earthquakes; and the business world is not exempt. A new era of success is, indeed, dawning. And the impacts, the consequences, and the outcomes thereof will be truly amazing.

Chapter Two

A Bankrupt Profession

One year the President of the Institute of Chartered Accountants in England and Wales visited Sydney, Australia. I had never actually met a President of the English Institute. I assumed that Presidents must be people of great knowledge, understanding, insight, intellect, and wisdom. As a member of both the English and the Australian Institutes I decided that I would seize the opportunity and personally provide him with a selection of my written material from over the years. Some material reflected on where we had been as a profession. Other material referred to my observations concerning the future well-being of the profession. Whilst yet other material addressed fundamental contemporary issues faced by the profession. This was all mind-bending stuff. Profound thoughts indeed. How he would treasure this material. And all this from just an ordinary member who actually cared !!!!!

Several weeks later he sent me a letter in which, amongst other things, he described my writings as *venomous*.

What wisdom this man must possess.

Presumably, from his choice of words, he was expressing concern and with regard to my views and opinions in relation to the accountancy profession. Or was he expressing his concern that I had actually expressed alternative views and opinions compared with those of the Institute? The mind can only boggle !!!

The attitude expressed in his letter was, however, no more than had been the implied attitude of the accountancy profession for many years for it has been a long time since any real expression of dissent had been made publicly, and on a sustained basis, by any ordinary member of that profession. In fact, now I come to think of it, in my more than thirty years in that profession (initially as an Articled Clerk, then as a Chartered Accountant, and later as a Fellow of one or more Institutes) I cannot recall any occurrence of that nature. Vibrant and invigorating interaction, it would seem, has never been a vital and distinguishing trait of the accountancy profession, with those in positions of power and authority in that profession having much preferred the establishment's golden rule, being 'I couldn't agree more with myself' and which rule, after all, is far safer than many of the alternatives .... Or is it ?!!!!

Incidentally, this was not the only expression of displeasure at my articulation of alternative views and opinions. Amongst others was that of an Executive Director of the Institute of Chartered Accountants in Australia who condemned me by name, in a letter to a national newspaper, for, as he asserted, 'attacking' my fellow professionals. This was a farcical contention for it implied that all members of the profession hold one view, being that which is espoused by the so-called leadership of the profession, and that detractors therefrom are somehow deviant or delinquent. The espoused assertion, however, was in keeping with what could be described as the characteristic 'group think' processes of the Institute and its various committees, and which 'group think' characteristics, in general, include the negative stereotyping of people who dare to speak out or hold different views or opinions to the power coalition, the applying of pressure to conform, the rationalizing of contrary facts or of evidence, the ignoring of the moral or ethical consequences of actions, mind-guarding and, amongst other things, the unspoken illusion of invulnerability.

How interesting it is that it was this same Executive Director of the Institute (who, it would appear, is not a Chartered Accountant himself) who wrote in the February, 1996, issue of Charter, the Australian Institute's official magazine, that 'The Institute has had a long history of active member involvement in all levels of Institute activities. The Institute is only as strong as it currently is because of this member involvement.' He then continued, 'We have been reflecting on the traditional way [don't I know about their traditional ways] in which members have been involved' but 'we have not always been able to involve some of those people with *new perspectives* to contribute.' .... What verbal diarrhoea !!!!! [This, of course, is Institute-speak for we've been cocking it up for so long now that even the all-powerful ones are getting a bit pissed off with having to bear the work-load for all those members who couldn't care less what the Institute did once they've got their ticket to ride; after all, many members of the profession probably have the 'If you don't bother me then I won't bother you' attitude, and have left the power-hungry to their own ends.] But who knows, perhaps the all-powerful ones down at the Institute have, so as to say, been 'born again' and are, indeed, out there singing and clapping and dancing and hallelujah-ing till the cows come home (or at least until they manage to get some more, so as to say, *active* members) and perhaps the chief 'knower of all' down at the 'all knowing and all wise' Institute is genuinely welcoming all of us 'god-forsaken' members back into their (or is it our) congregation.

But I don't think so.

Do you?

In addition I also received correspondence from the chairman of a large accountancy practice whose lack of tolerance for alternative views and opinions on fundamental issues was unmistakably obvious. He had a way with words !!!!! One can only wonder about the calibre of the people who lead these large firms. Whilst the then President of the Institute of Chartered Accountants in Australia took it upon himself to write to me and, in his role as President, suggested, in effect, that I get my thinking straight.

This was all 'riveting stuff' and was generated by the misguided determination of the accountancy profession (under the guidance of a joint accountancy profession task force which was dominated by an array of partners from the Big Six firms and their cohorts) to, in my opinion, immorally and unethically ensure that damage for professional wrongdoing, as determined by a judge, remained well and truly with the victims of the profession and that it was not shifted to its rightful place, being to the delinquent members of that revered profession. Attention was diverted from the real issues by the protestation that some of the threatened litigation was vexatious, frivolous, or an abuse of process, thereby trying to imply (by the use of that tactic) that the profession was the innocent party. The capping of damage awards, it is noted, was only the apparent issue at hand. The real issue was profits and, beyond that, the actual survival of individual firms; and not least of all the large firms. This effort may also have been motivated in relation to ensuring the survival of individual partners in those firms. Anyone who, in reality, objected to the institutionalizing of this most immoral and unethical behaviour was, accordingly, not welcomed by the establishment. It was not, after all, professional to get excited and voice a dissenting opinion compared with that of the established power coalition for it should be realized that another of the abiding rules of that profession is that 'around here son we don't get excited' so stop creating waves. I am in favour of introducing proportional liability (to replace joint and several liability for damage of the relevant type) but the act of capping is inherently iniquitous and has many vile consequences. In any case the 'brain power' down at the Institute soon began to state, in the media, that the introduction of proportional liability would not, in itself, be sufficient to ease the negligence burden. [Doing the job properly could help.] I wonder what they are trying to secure by such statements. Do they want our delinquent members to be able to damage clients with impunity and with absolutely no fear of retribution. What is the profession trying to achieve? Is it focused purely on the protection of its deviant members ?!!!!

In 1994, and in relation to the preceding matter, I wrote a trilogy of what I called my 'Shakespearian Snippets' to several dozen members of the profession. These were mainly partners, and the chairmen, chief executives, and managing partners, or whatever they call themselves, of the Big Six firms, as well as to some of the second tier partners. Others also received copies of the snippets. The three snippets were 'To Cap Or Not To Cap . . . . That Is The Question' 'Beware MacBeth's Dagger' and 'Then Take Thy Pound Of Flesh' and with each being distributed, from memory, to similar recipients. I won't bore you with the words of all three of those snippets. The gist of the matter can be obtained from the second snippet in the series. It went out in July, 1994. I actually received a few interesting responses from some Big Six partners. Perhaps some of them had, after all, been reminded of something.

The snippet, which is slightly altered, read as follows.

'Beware MacBeth's Dagger'

. . . . . *MacBeth, Act II, Scene I*

In my previous snippet 'To Cap Or Not To Cap . . . . That Is The Question' the capping of negligence awards was unequivocally condemned. In that snippet it was stated in relation to proven acts of negligence (as well as other delinquent acts perpetrated by members of our profession) that the amount of the damage recoverable from the accountancy profession should be that *proportion* of damage which was inflicted by the member. This is a just, fair, and equitable basis upon which to award damages. It would seem that, as a result of the deliberations of the Federal and State Attorneys General, the time is approaching for the introduction of the aforementioned concept of 'proportional liability' and which concept will replace the manifestly unjust, unfair, and inequitable concept of 'joint and several liability' as we know it today.

This most welcome anticipation is, however, still debased by the misguided efforts of the leaders of our profession, and those in positions of authority, who insist on undermining our ethical well-being by continuing their insistence on the capping of that portion of damage awards which members of our profession actually inflict on their victims. I remind you that the courts do not award damages against innocent parties and that the capping of damages is no less than institutionalized robbery. Capping is, without doubt, obnoxious for, by design, it unequivocally transfers damage from the wrongdoers and to their victims. It would appear that not only do the deviants in our profession rape their victims (for their behaviour is most unwelcome) but we as a profession, it would seem, connive (as cowards) to construct arbitrary arguments in an effort to allow such parties to escape the fulness of their punishment; thereby aggravating the damage imposed on victims by members of our profession.

Is the crime of our deviants, one may ask, merely that of being caught?

We, as a profession, seem able to wrestle with technical problems and to grapple with certain matters of principle, but when we are faced with fundamental dimensions of substance, our resolution fails us . . . . and we seem to pale into insignificance. We as a profession are, indeed, unable to grasp and address, adequately, the major issues of the day. Our strategic thinking is moribund. Our high ideals, conceived as youthful professionals and practised, year after year, as high-minded members of our profession, melt like snow in the first heat . . . . to drain down the gutter of expediency and on a journey to who knows where; for if we, as a profession, are to pursue capping (under the concept of proportional liability) then it will be clear, to ourselves and to the world at large, that we, the accountancy profession, are both morally and ethically bankrupt. Yes, as I reflect upon my thirty-odd years in our profession I find that we are indeed at the lowest of all ebbs. By failing to change in substance, and at the correct pace relative to the wants and needs of society, we have become a profession unfit for our times; and capping is just a symptom of our decline.

One may ask, rhetorically, are there no intellectual giants amongst our ranks whose strategic foresight and ethical underpinnings can embrace the wants and the needs of our society? Is there not one person who is gallant and brave enough, and worthy to lead our profession? Is there no-one out there who can grasp the mantle of visionary leadership and then boldly address the fundamental challenges of our future? Or, may I ask, is our profession destined for mere survival, and an abundance of mediocrity?

Turning now to more specific matters. In a recent television program the chairman of the National Joint Limitation of Liability Task Force (and senior partner of one of the Big Six professional firms) in promoting the capping of negligence awards, stated:

"And people have to understand an auditor has to work within a specified time. He can't take all the time in the world to reach his opinion. There is a need for a capping of liability, but only for very major cases, so that the cap on liability would be set at a figure very likely that would cover probably ninety-five percent of all claims." He then went on to say . . . . "Management and directors, of course, are the ones making the primary decisions, it's not the auditor. The auditor is reporting about the results of those decisions, but he's not the decision-maker."

The implications of both of these quotations are mind-boggling.

In the first case, and amongst other things, it would seem that time (and, dare I say it, perhaps even money) is being used as an implied excuse for not doing the job properly. Let us be quite clear, no audit should be signed-off where there is any doubt whatsoever with regard to the going concern basis or, for that matter, with regard to any other issue of fundamental importance; a lack of time or money is no excuse for negligence . . . . and that is what we are addressing.

Further, the statement goes on to categorically require the introduction of capping, but endeavours to mitigate such a stand by implying that ninety-five percent of claims would be unaffected by a cap; once again reinforcing that the cap is being introduced to, in reality, protect the big firms from having to pay out to the full extent of *their* negligence. Here a sectional interest is being protected (probably a mere one percent of the accountancy profession) by transferring the impact of damage from the wrongdoers to their victims.

These people (to reduce *their own miserable loss* and one for which *they themselves were responsible*) are quite prepared to transfer their damage to other people, including the mums and the dads of Australia who are shareholders in companies; to young people who, whilst saving for their first home, invested their savings in deposit-taking institutions; and to the superannuation funds upon which senior citizens, and those approaching retirement, rely for security in their old age; each of which class have suffered loss.

How debased are we?

Are each and every one of the one hundred thousand members of our profession, including those who prepare accounts and those who audit accounts, really prepared to countenance such self-interest? Are we really prepared to allow a relative handful of our membership to pursue their own selfish ambitions? Is a loss of say fifty million dollars ($50m) which is redistributed to innocent parties, and away from wrongdoers, any less painful because it was caused by the *capping* of a negligence claim (which excess may well have been paid) rather than by the *inability* of a firm, whether large or small, to actually pay the fifty million dollars of damages. The answer to this question is simple : No !!!!! So why would we wish to limit damage awards, especially under proportional liability, if it were not merely to pursue the selfish ambitions of a subset of members of our profession? Members who, I may add, embraced their assignment, acted negligently, took the fee, and willingly accepted the profits !!!!!

The second of the above quotations, it would seem, tries, amongst other things, to imply that the auditors of a business enterprise have less responsibility than they indeed have and this implication is so because it is claimed that it is the management and the directors of a company who make the primary decisions.

This is a red herring.

The auditor's responsibilities are one hundred percent the responsibilities of the auditor. Auditors have a clear duty to the shareholders to whom they report to categorically inform those shareholders with regard to any matters that should be drawn to their attention; and these matters would include whether or not their company is a going concern. *The fact that auditors do not make the primary decisions with regard to the management of a company is irrelevant.* Auditors are duty bound to report in relation to the decisions of management. There is, therefore, no secondary responsibility (and which responsibility is subservient to the primary decision-making powers of the management of a company, as is implied in the above quotation) there is only a primary responsibility; and that primary responsibility is to conduct the audit properly and on a non-negligent basis.

The editorial which appeared in the Australian Financial Review on 22nd July, 1994, was indeed stinging for in that editorial it is stated 'But while auditors should welcome the move to wind back joint and several liability, they want to introduce another doctrine that is equally unjust. This time, however, it is in their favour.'

The deeds of our profession are indeed selfish, for irrespective of whether our actions are aimed at benefiting our profession as a whole (which they are not) or a select sub-group thereof (which they are) we are, without doubt, intent upon depriving others of what truly belongs to them. Let us remember MacBeth's dagger, for that ethereal manifestation (whilst dripping with the blood of its unsuspecting victim) led MacBeth, the spineless wretch, along the path to disaster in much the same way that capping will lead our profession to even lower levels of debasement for, in relation to the moral values of society and the ethics of our profession we, like MacBeth, whilst clutching at the issues, seem unable to grasp the substance.

MacBeth, because he was weak and because he harboured confused ethics, was able to be led astray, and thereby to disaster, by the selfish ambitions of Lady MacBeth. Likewise our profession, and its ethics, are also being sacrificed to achieve the selfish ambitions of, in our case, the National Joint Limitation of Liability Task Force.

It would seem that we too have our very own Lady MacBeth !!!!!

The preceding snippet affords an interesting symptomatic insight into the many multi-dimensional problems which are faced by the profession. On the one part it is of much concern that the question even needs to be asked 'are there no intellectual giants amongst our ranks whose strategic foresight and ethical underpinnings can embrace the wants and needs of our society' whilst on the other part one has truly got to wonder what is going on when the senior partner (chairman, chief executive, or managing partner) of a Big Six accountancy firm, and a Past President of the Institute, can get it so wrong in relation to the responsibilities of auditors; and with that wrongness being in relation to their responsibilities now and not in relation to what those responsibilities may be, or should be, in the future. There are, in truth, many problems and challenges within the accountancy profession, each of which are separately identifiable but which problems and challenges, in total, are amazingly intertwined and entangled; and which problems and challenges are well and truly complicated by the practicalities of self-interest and power.

This comment, in itself, suggests that the profession is effectively ensnared by at least one multi-faceted dysfunctionality, an appreciation of which situation may well be enhanced by a flirtation with another symptomatic episode or two, and which episodes are related below. Before I do this, however, I would like to make it quite clear that not until 1992, thirty years after first commencing work in the office of a Chartered Accountant, did I get involved in publicly expressing my views and opinions in relation to the accountancy profession. Prior to that point in time I had never placed any small adverts postulating my particular position; I had never written a full page (or any other size) article for inclusion in a national or non-national newspaper; I had not written letters to the media in relation to business or accountancy issues; I had never, other than in the ordinary course of business (and possibly not even then) written to any fellow accountancy professionals (whether they were the chairmen, chief executives, managing partners, or any other member of the profession) in relation to developments in the profession; I had never made a submission to any exposure draft or to a report that was issued by the profession; and I had never written a book . . . . and definitely not a book like this book. Something had happened. Something, indeed, had happened. As a mature and competent professional, and although it had been coming for some years, I had finally had enough of the immoral, the unethical, and the incompetent, as well as those who lacked competence, being well and truly rewarded for their efforts, and at the expense of the moral, the ethical, the competent, and society itself. The rules are set by the mediocre so that the mediocre win. The pen, however, is mightier than the sword, and so my computer keys will keep on tapping and tapping and tapping; and those with power, but with little competence, will be challenged. Let this flirtation with revelations of professional life, and the profession, continue and let another symptomatic episode or three be related, if only for purposes of immortality (in the form of this book being lodged with the National Library and which book contains a counter-culture commentary on the profession in the latter part of the twentieth century) and, of course, let it roll on for your edification. Yes, let the flirtation roll on . . . . And let me tell you about democracy.

Once upon a time, as the fairy tale goes, I stood for elected office at the Institute or, rather, I should say that once I nearly stood for elected office; being that of a member of the State Council of the Institute. What happened, in essence, was that I submitted my nomination form together with my allocated write-up with regard to myself and in which write-up I indicated that, if elected, I would be a 'breath of fresh air' blowing through the Institute; after all, I am a creative, highly intelligent, independent thinker.

Shock !!! Horror !!!

This was all too much for the establishment, or at least for one or other of the power coalitions. Perhaps on reflection there was only one coalition and they ruled the Institute as despots. I don't know. The point, I guess, was that if I were elected the establishment, or the relevant coalition, may not be able to control me. They would have a loose canon on board, and a highly intelligent one at that; and after all, who needs creative, highly intelligent, independent thinkers? Obviously not the Institute of Chartered Accountants !!!! That is how I saw the situation at the time; with this impression being moulded, and in a significant way, by what seemed to me to be an unusual degree of interest in my candidature.

For the record it may be stated that my nomination had no sinister overtones and, in truth, it arose in all innocence and was offered in goodwill. In fact, all that happened was that one day I observed a green piece of paper in my copy of the official magazine of the Institute and on which piece of paper members were informed of the correct date (presumably some other date had been set previously) for the submission of nominations for the State Council election. I decided there and then that I would become more involved with the profession. After all, I said to myself, I had now opted for a long-term career with a leading professional firm. After twenty years (and this statement is far more meaningful than you may ever know) I had come home. Yes, I would offer my services to the profession. Who knows, I thought, I may even get elected.

To cut a long story short, and to be more specific, at the time of these events I was employed in the management consultancy division of one of the Big Six firms. Little did I expect or anticipate the unethical events which were to follow. They started, however, not long after the close of nominations for the election. Shortly after the aforementioned close of nominations I received a telephone call from a person who I did not know, who I had never heard of, and who did not disclose that he was, in fact, both a partner in the Big Six firm for which I worked, as well as a member of the Institute Council. This person, despite the non-disclosure by him of his particular background, proceeded to question me and challenge my nomination for election to the Council. I informed him that it was my democratic right to stand for election and that all that I was doing was exercising that right.

I had actually stood for pre-selection for the Australian Senate on several occasions, as well as for the House of Representatives, and so had been quite active in the party-political process. I failed to be selected on each occasion that I had entered the contest, but I had thoroughly enjoyed the experience; having quite expected the unsuccessful outcome on each occasion. Given this background information, and returning now to the issue at hand, it may be stated that the telephone conversation seemed to continue for some time. Even at that early stage an unfair amount of pressure was, and without doubt, being placed upon me to withdraw my nomination. It was soon to become evident that various parties, at least in the wider firm, did not approve of my nomination.

Several further telephone conversations took place, and with at least one of those conversations being with the aforementioned partner, and with each conversation having the intention of securing the withdrawal of my nomination for the election. Two senior partners of the Big Six firm took a particular interest in the withdrawal of my nomination and with one of those partners making it quite clear that it is the large firms who pay for the Institute and that it is they who will decide who will sit on the Council. I didn't like what I was hearing, after all, and at that time, I still thought that the Big Six firm had integrity. How mistaken I was. Justice, fairness, and equity was, in reality, never a strong point of this firm. In fact, over the ensuing months natural justice itself was well and truly crucified. It died a terrible death. [At that time I also thought the Institute was sacrosanct. But it wasn't. You can't separate a body from the people who control it. The body becomes merely a modified extension of their values. Being a vehicle to act in their best interests.] Given this disregard for ordinary decency, and at the very least towards their colleagues, I now wonder about the meaning of such things as presented fairly . . . . independent opinions . . . . and statements of reasonable assurance . . . . together with a host of other similar sentiments. What do these things mean when it comes to a really critical choice? The fee or the facts . . . . or rather, the probability of securing a potential future fee income, or income stream, versus fairly presenting the correct position. One can only ponder on whether such opinions are, to say the least, worth a row of beans.

It was made very clear to me by one of the partners in the Big Six firm that the other partner involved in endeavouring to secure the withdrawal of my nomination was a very powerful senior partner and that if I did not withdraw my nomination then it could affect my future with the firm. Did this mean that my employment with this leading professional firm was to be terminated if I did not withdraw? I was without doubt, and most unashamedly, being subjected to manipulation, intimidation, duress, and coercion !!!!

I didn't withdraw my nomination and a meeting was arranged with the aforementioned very powerful senior partner. At this stage I could still not understand why it was so important that I should withdraw my nomination for the election, after all, I was a mere 'pleb' amongst thousands. Had anyone considered that I may not even get elected? The meeting with the powerful senior partner was held. The pressure was on. [I sometimes wonder why I am so tolerant of the views of others yet they are not equally as tolerant of my views and opinions. This is, indeed, a puzzlement.] The attitude of this apparently powerful senior partner towards professional staff at his firm, their skills and abilities, his perception of his own self-importance, and his attitude towards the Institute itself was soon revealed when, with scorn, he challenged me, stating how could I consider sitting on the same Council as the Chairman of P&O !!!!! His description of the P&O member was somewhat exaggerated at the time, but close enough to convey the intent of his message. Little did this pompous ass realize that my intelligence level probably left him looking like an intellectual cripple (a decade or so earlier I had been employed by a major consultancy firm which employed one thousand people, the vast majority of whom were professionals, and they in their entire history had apparently never employed anyone with an intelligence level approaching that of my own) whilst my command of my particular area of professional endeavour, being that of strategic management, was the equal of any, and better by far than most of everyone in the accountancy profession. In reality I actually didn't know, and nor did I care, who was on the State Council of the Institute. I was prepared to serve with any of my professional colleagues and I definitely wouldn't have looked upon any of them as first, second, third, or fourth class Chartered Accountants, whatever their station in life; and that included the 'Chairman' of P&O for that matter. As the meeting progressed (it wasn't a short meeting) it was stated that if I withdrew my nomination for the election this powerful senior partner, who was already on the Council, would talk with the appropriate people and see if he could get me co-opted onto one of the sub-committees. 'Which one would I be interested in?' We discussed one or two, to his delight, and the meeting concluded with his empty words ringing in my ears. I never heard from him again. I think this must be a trait at the Institute for I seem to recall that when the 'Chairman' of P&O subsequently became President of that revered body another promise of involvement was made; but nothing happened.

The pressure was now on for my withdrawal. Enquires were made by the less powerful partner with regard to the outcome of the meeting with the more powerful partner. 'Had I withdrawn my nomination?' That question in itself was somewhat of a farce. The less powerful partner was one of my two seconders for nomination !!! [I get so confused with regard to power.] Despite this change of events I knew that the partner for whom I worked in the management consultancy division of the firm, being a person who was not a Chartered Accountant himself, was perfectly willing for me to serve on the Council. I also knew that I was not rich enough to indulge in the luxury of fighting my employer over a point of principle . . . . and this was so despite the fact that the Institute itself would have had to condemn those who were involved in interfering with the due process connected with their elections. The partner for whom I worked also warned me about the attitude of some of the other partners within the management consultancy division. He suggested that I keep a low profile for a while. [These people were amongst the most perverse people that ever walked this earth. They were absolute sods !!!!!] I was not happy with what was becoming the inevitable, but eventually, and most reluctantly, I telephoned the Institute and informed them that I was withdrawing my nomination for the State Council elections. Nobody at the Institute asked me why I was withdrawing, but I remember that it was only after receiving at least three telephone calls from someone down there, asking for my withdrawal in writing, that finally I forwarded what was a brief hand-written note to satisfy their needs. Coercion had won the day.

The Institute elections had been fixed.

There never was an actual election. The annual general meeting was called to, amongst other things, elect six Councillors, five of whom where eligible for re-election. Unknown to me there were only two additional candidates for what was in effect the 'one' vacancy; being the candidate from the in-crowd . . . . and me !!!!! What a dastard stroke of luck. The only Institute election that I nominated for in thirty years and I chose this one !!!!! Had serendipity deserted me ?!!!! If I could be persuaded, and if not persuaded coerced, into the withdrawal of my nomination then there would be no actual election. Everyone would be re-elected (or indeed elected) by default . . . . and life would go on as planned. The Institute would be controlled by the 'correct' people. The marble foyers of prestigious professional offices would continue to portray unquestionable morality and impeccable ethics. Pompous asses would 'pomp' their way from their luxury vehicles to their luxury offices; possibly hoping not to be seen in the same lift as their minions; being the lower life forms that inhabit such firms. And the fees and the profits would continue to roll in unabated. The can of worms, or should that be maggots, would be well hidden. And everyone would be happy.

Well almost everyone !!!!!

One can only ponder on the words of the French poet and critic who once indicated that politics is the art of preventing people from taking part in affairs which properly concern them. The Institute, and its power coalitions, are obviously still in the dark ages. It would seem that it and they haven't yet embraced the changes and the revolution which is taking place at this very time, all around them, and all over the world. When, one may wonder, will the accountancy profession embrace the future ?!!!!

The aforementioned matters are, unfortunately, very sad for our profession and this is so without having even mentioned the case of the senior partner who bragged about the 'bribe' which he and another senior partner of a Big Six firm had paid. [My goodness, Henny Penny, the sky is falling in !!!!!] It was, of course, paid for all the best reasons and, in particular, in order to obtain an advantage to secure the opportunity to secure future, potentially major, fee earning work. It should be noted that upon being told, in a non-trivial way, of this event by one of the senior partners concerned, I immediately told him not to pay the money or he would be dead. I was informed, however, and in a somewhat annoyed manner, that the payment had already been made. It was paid in undue haste the very next day after the demand. The payment was justified on the grounds that the senior partner had built-up the firm to secure the type of work under threat and that he wasn't going to jeopardize that mammoth effort. Another partner who I knew very well subsequently told me that the monies had been paid on the basis of what he described, rather tentatively, as 'business development' expenditure; but a fellow professional, whose status in the firm appeared to be higher than mine, and who was also privy to the discussions, both at the time of the meeting as well as several weeks later when the matter was again raised, indicated that the payment was made in the spirit of, and was neither no more than, nor no less than, a bribe. The whole transaction, as I understood it, had been nothing less than an exercise in 'extortion' on the one part and 'bribery' on the other; and it was based on indirect, but mutually beneficial, motives. For each party it was a suitable reciprocal arrangement.

The existence of the cheque, it is noted, was queried by the young lady who looked after those matters. (The other part of the 'bribe' was paid in another way.) She had written 'where is the cheque' on the letter that later was filed. She had to bank it. Yes, even she was only expecting to received money from that source. She never dreamt that the cheque referred to was actually being paid out !!!!!

[Now what was that about camels, needles, and rich men. It is easier for a camel to pass through the eye of a needle than it is for a rich man to enter the kingdom of God. Well, who knows, maybe they'd opted for leaving paradise to the camels.]

Whether or not this event was tantamount to the payment of a bribe may well be disputed and, not least of all, by the parties concerned. It was definitely presented as a bribe by the relevant senior partner. Irrespective of this, and the specific nature of the event, one can only wonder about the calibre of the people who are at the top of our profession. Given these events, who, one may wonder (and whether it was a bribe, or merely a near-bribe or, in fact, something else) would actually talk in such a way about such a happening? There is indeed one thing for sure, that is, whatever happened this happening fell a long way short of the normatively 'high moral standards' that are expected of our profession and it was not carried out in terms of anything pretending to approach 'good professional ethics' and this is so no matter how effective may be any future efforts at rationalization. This transaction was, unequivocally, a basic act, done by basic people, for basic reasons.

Nor have I mentioned the saga of 'bastards incorporated' being the story, or more correctly the serial, concerning the one hundred and twenty week-long brutalization of a professional, together with the unethical, vindictive, and malicious breach of contract, by those same persons, and several other partners [including the most senior of partners of that Big Six firm and whose direct involvement was tantamount to ignoring the situation (despite two direct and unequivocal written approaches for intervention) and whose indirect involvement was an absolute sham] of what they, no doubt, believed to be a manageable target; and with this being done to achieve their own selfish ends. [The Philistines !!!!] That most senior of partners, it is noted, was also a Past President of the Institute of Chartered Accountants. [It's always reassuring to know that you can count on the in-crowd for justice, fairness, and equity.] Other partners, and not least of all a very senior partner, were as guilty as the perpetrators of this episode because they stood by and just watched. This psychological bastardization of the personal and professional life of a mere employee by what was little more than a mindless and malevolent pack of so-called professionals may, however, form the basis for another book; it being noted here, and merely for the record, that the belief of these people in their own invincibility is only exceeded by their own stupidity.

That reminds me, the very senior partner just referred to above, and who stood by and did nothing that even resembled justice, fairness, or equity was, himself, most sophisticated; at least in his own sort of way. He was the partner-in-charge, nationally, of the division of the firm in which I worked. One evening the partners of that division in Sydney were hosting a dinner for their professional staff. It was held in one of the dining rooms of the firm. There were quite a few partners and staff in attendance, all busily chatting and eating and eating and chatting; and drinking. All of a sudden the doors of the dining room were flung open. In pounded this 'most sophisticated' of partners. 'What the fucking hell are you doing here !!!!!' he bellowed at his fellow partners. I looked up. I was somewhat amazed. But I smiled to myself. [He'd just flown in from some remote place on the planet. Adelaide I think.] He stormed across the room, his face red with anger, yelling out in what was his own cultured style. 'You're suppose to be at a fucking meeting . . . . I've been waiting over there for forty fucking minutes !!!!! What the fucking hell . . . . !!!!!' he raged on as his fist thumped down on one of the tables. The glasses, the dinner, and the dinner plates and, yes, the partners, all seemed to jump ten feet into the air. The dinner came to an abrupt halt. Well at least for the partners. They all filed out in total obedience. Not one of them showed any guts. [I guess the abused abuse !!!!!] As I continued my dinner in a more congenial atmosphere I reflected upon the sophistication of the profession . . . . and its leadership.

The disturbing thing with regard to all of this (for, were it not true, then the farces and fiascos of thirty-odd years as a member of the profession would, no doubt, make good film or television entertainment) lies not only in the specifics of these events but, more importantly, in the fact that these matters provide a window, a sample view, into the mechanicians of the accountancy profession, and which view provides a snapshot of the less tasteful side of professional life; not only at an individual and a client level (for even clients were not immune from treatment with disdain) but also at the firm and the Institute levels.

The preceding matters may, of course, be viewed as individual events. Every event is an individual event. Coles Myer was an individual event. BHP was an individual event. The adoption by the ASX of a the corporate governance listing rule, in such an absolutely abysmal form, was an individual event. The Pioneer, Boral, CSR, TNT, Ansett, Mayne Nicholas, AMP, Multiplex Construction, Leighton Contractors, Holland Stolte, Inghams, Steggles, and Ampol happenings were also individual events. As was the aforementioned and identified behaviour of some of the so-called leading members of the accountancy profession. They are all one-off events. Until those events are viewed as being part of a culture. Being the culture of each of those businesses and bodies. It is, however, even worse than that, for their activities are also part of the very culture in which those bodies and businesses, and institutions, reside. There is, in reality, a whole range of cultures, sub-cultures, and counter-cultures, and along many dimensions, both within and without a business enterprise. These persons who were the perpetrators of this unacceptable behaviour believed, however, that even if their behaviour was simply not acceptable, that it would still be tolerated. And it was. And by those close to those events and who could have changed the course of history. And such events are typically tolerated until sufficient time has past or parties who are sufficiently external to the core culture of those environments object. Then their values are revisited and they are found to be unacceptable to society.

Yes, by their fruits you shall know them . . . .

The counterpart to this glimpse into the interpersonal behaviour of 'respectable' professionals is that which addresses the activities and collective motives of these firms and the willingness, or lack thereof, of this profession to provide their clients with advanced management offerings. These firm-level deficiencies mainly occur, strangely enough, because of the relative impoverishment of these practices in their own field of professional endeavour; being that of business. Both the transitory and the transformational demands of the environment, at least at the cutting-edge, have overtaken their capabilities.

The problems with the accountancy profession are, of course, fundamental and with the most fundamental problem being that of a lack of vision. This doesn't mean that the profession does not have individual members who possess vision. There will be lots of visionaries amongst the ranks of the accountancy profession. And, no doubt, their visions will be of importance in the business world. But the visions which they have are not necessarily visions for the profession.

It should be understood that I do not relate vision to education (for there have been many visionaries who had little education) but, in my opinion, and at the institutionalized level, there is a relationship between that of a relatively low relevant education, and hindrance in the growth, development, and application of vision; for that is a function of culture and power and, thereby, the crushing to death of talent. The accountancy profession, in its totality, has never been highly educated compared with some of the other professions. The requirements for entry have increased over the years, and recent intake profiles reflect this eventuality, but given the increase which has occurred in education standards, and not least of all at the university level, the entry requirements for other jobs, trades, and professions has also risen considerably.

In Australia there are some one hundred thousand (100,000) or more accountants, most of whom belong to the Institute of Chartered Accountants or to the Australian Society of Certified Practising Accountants. The Society has about three times as many members when compared with the Institute and with their respective domains also being somewhat different. The members of the Society are largely engaged in industry and commerce, with some in private practice, whilst private practice is a major occupation area for many Chartered Accountants. [The position, by the way, is different in England where the Institute, with over one hundred and nine thousand (109,000) members, is by far the predominant body, with its membership beginning to approach that of all the other bodies put together; and with the majority of that membership being engaged in industry and commerce or, at least, not in professional practice.] There are, in Australia, at least three tiers of firms, and with those practices being conveniently grouped into the large firms, being the Big Six practices; a dozen or more practices that may be described as being medium-sized; and an absolute myriad of small firms which are composed of sole practitioners and small partnerships. The first tier firms, being the Big Six practices, have about one thousand (1,000) partners in total, and which partners are also members of the Institute, whilst they employ many more professionally qualified staff. These one thousand or so partners, it is noted here, represent only four percent (4%) of the Institute membership and a mere one percent (1%) of the total membership of the accountancy profession in Australia. It is noted that whether or not this one thousand strong body of partners is considered to hold homogeneous views and opinions (which they do not) you can be assured that the views and opinions of the many more professionals who are engaged by these firms are, indeed, heterogeneous; as are the views and opinions of that very large majority of accountants who are engaged in industry or commerce, and other areas of activity, or who are principals or employees of small or medium sized firms.

These introductory comments in relation to the profession need to be expanded on and, in fact, in relation to bankruptcy (being the moral, ethical, and intellectual bankruptcy of the accountancy profession) one would need to appreciate a little with regard to the historical development of the profession. This is particularly so in relation to the Big Six firms for they have controlled the Institute for, what would seem to be, forever. The following potted history does not, however, even pretend to portray a full understanding of developments but, rather, is included in order to facilitate understanding and insight into the matters addressed herein. For the record, there use to be a dozen or so large firms but, over time, not only did they gobble up various medium-sized practices (whether or not, in some cases, such gobbling was, to all intents and purposes, a reverse take-over) they also, themselves, merged. Also, the prestige of the Institute is, it may be noted, somewhat reflected prestige based on the prestige of the Institute of Chartered Accountants in England and Wales and which body was founded in 1880. In order to provide some perspective, in the UK the largest of the Big Six accountancy firms has a fee income which is almost as large as the fee income of all of the members of the Big Six accountancy firms in Australia. The fees earned by the top fifty firms in the UK, in one year, is some eight thousand million dollars ($8,000m) of which the Big Six firms account for some six thousand million dollars ($6,000m) worth of those fees. The fee income of the Big Six firms in Australia is around one thousand five hundred million dollars ($1,500m) in total. This, of course, is not to be sniffed at as it is a substantial fee income for any profession. By way of a note the Big Six firms in the USA have an annual fee income of around twenty thousand million dollars ($20,000m) or more. All of the preceding figures are quoted in Australian dollars and they exclude the income or earnings of the majority of qualified accountants who are engaged in industry, commerce, and other non-professional-practice occupations.

The profession, in reality, has grown and developed based on primary and secondary statutory underpinnings. In the case of its primary underpinnings the requirement for public companies to be subjected to statutory audits, and on an annual basis, provided guaranteed work for the profession; it was only a matter of which accountancy firms would secure that work. The secondary type of underpinning came from the requirement for all of us, including companies, to submit annual tax returns. The profession, or at least its members, established themselves as the authority in that field; being a profession which would act with a reasonable amount of integrity and one which would act as an intermediary between its clients and the taxation authorities. The profession, in aggregate, was thereby secure. In addition to these two basic underpinnings there is also a whole host of other statutory requirements which benefit the profession and not least amongst which is work in relation to prospectuses as well as that relating to receiverships, insolvencies, and bankruptcies; or whatever the correct terminology is these days. In addition to this, and perhaps more fortuitously for the profession, for the twenty years or so from the early 1970s (although it had been building up during the second half of the 1960s) the management information boom occurred. That particular boom had little to do with any statutory requirements which were imposed on businesses enterprises. Business itself needed better ways of managing itself. The boom in management information systems was, therefore, largely driven by business demand itself . . . . although it was, at the time, an up hill battle to convince some of the less progressive business enterprises of the benefits of improved management information.

For the larger firms, and putting aside the serendipity of the management information systems era, audit work was king. The smaller firms typically made a good living from the preparation of accounts and the calculation and settlement of the taxation affairs of clients. The medium-sized firms fell somewhere in between these two profiles, often having a few larger clients and a multitude of smaller clients. [The library at the Institute couldn't supply me with the figures for Australia but now, and in the UK, about thirty-eight percent of total fee income is earned from audit and accountancy work, twenty-eight percent is generated from management consultancy (of which a large part is information technology and systems work) whilst twenty-four percent thereof arises from taxation-based work; and with insolvency and the rest accounting for about ten percent of total fee income. In the US, and today, taxation has already shrunk to twenty percent and consultancy is up to forty percent. The figures for Australia will vary somewhat from these percentages, but not by that much.] Because in the early days, and for the larger accountancy firms, audit was king (with clients tending to retain the same audit firm year after year and with audit and taxation fees accounting for the lion's share of all revenues) audit partners were very powerful. They provided substantial, profitable, repeat business. [Wouldn't we all like a client base with that type of profile.] This, of course, was in the days prior to the appearance of audit tendering, the big squeeze on fee levels, and narrower profit margins. There was, as a consequence, and relative to their clients, little entrepreneurial activity required in order to do very nicely thank you. The culture of these firms was staid. Some audit partners may well have been with the same practice for twenty years or more and still have twenty years or more ahead of them before retirement. I can remember one audit partner in one of the large firms exclaiming to me 'bloody hell, twenty-five more years of this' as he shrank back into his chair and proceeded to eat my lunch !!!!! As more and more working class boys, and some girls I suppose, came through university and entered these firms, they hit the culture problem. Dull, boring, and uninteresting had met bright, alive, and ambitious. I remember once being told by one of these 'brain-dead' partners not to speak with him in the lift as it wasn't appropriate. God, what a bunch of wankers !!!!! Someone once said (I think it was me) that they all belch, grunt, and fart in unison. [I think that's how you spell fart.] But you get the picture. They were, to stretch a point, powerful morons. The large firms often grew and developed because they had successful clients in their client base. As their clients grew (organically and by take-over or merger and with the take-overs or mergers often being overseas-based) then the fees grew; and so did the profits. Success did not require a great deal of entrepreneurial ability. Strategically they were in the land of milk and honey. Just being there was enough. And they succeeded despite themselves. How wonderful is the power of the environment if you are in the right industry.

There's one thing about power . . . . people fight like hell not to lose it. They will even debilitate their own firms or, indeed, their own professions in order to retain power. Power hungry people feast on its intoxicating elixir. Whilst those who crave for, dream of, or merely aspire to have power, enjoy the anticipation of its taste. Power, it may be said, is basically seductive and absolutely enjoyable. As a result thereof, and in accordance therewith, these absolutely average partners, in their absolutely average firms, bequeathed their profession an absolutely average future.

Relatively, and over the years, these once pertinent practices became less germane to their environments until they became almost irrelevant to, and detached from, their own clients. Yes, of course they did the work. And of course they had relationships with their clients. But the work was of less value. Even that most crucial of functions, the external audit itself, became dysfunctional and almost irrelevant. The large firms lost sight of the big picture. They became somewhat remote from reality. As the world of business moved forward the practice of auditing, as practiced by the profession, had been truly superseded. But the profession didn't know. It was too incestuous. The big practices had focused on secondary and tertiary matters and, yes, even on lower levels of relevance (or, dare I say it, irrelevance) yet it was they who controlled the future direction of the profession. The big firms had become mediaeval conglomerates with each of the powerful audit partners having feudal rights to at least their own client base. The profession, over the years, and through the strategic ineptitudes of its somewhat poorly educated, but very powerful, demagogues had become a profession of plumbers, joiners, and bricklayers. More and more the focus was on technical ability and with less and less focus on the essence and substance of business. Their business education and in reality, knowledge, was abysmal. These firms became more and more proficient in audit techniques and at equivocating over accounting standards, and in the enhancement of their skills in such things as company secretarial work, taxation advice and, of course, proverbially speaking, the fifteen different ways to disclose a lease on a balance sheet. But these technical acrobats had lost sight of the world in which they existed. They were remote from business. Soon a set of accounts became a nonsense. The technocrats were with us. And they weren't very good business advisers. They seemed to think that if they could produce a set of figures or, even better, also an alternative set of figures, and from a spreadsheet, then that was reality.

Disaster !!!!!

With regard to the computer age, and going back some years now and to when that period got into full swing, it was these same powerful partners and their staff who didn't know how to audit a computer system. They went round it. Under it. Over it. They even closed their eyes and ignored it. In the end they sat on it.

They put up the 'Out To Lunch' sign for five or ten years and waited for the next generation of well trained accountants to appear who could actually address, in an incisive and penetrating way, the computer.

This is what is happening with corporate governance !!!!!

The joint contribution by the Institute and the Society to the ASX in response to its call for submissions, prior to the determination and subsequent issue of its listing rule on corporate governance, reinforces this view. It was a reasonably lengthy, although sparse, document. Its content, however, was poor and simplistic. It was a run-of-the-mill document which had written all over it 'we don't know what we're talking about' as it proceeded to address, in a basic way, matters which are not vital. The general gist of the joint submission can be conveyed by a quotation which stated 'The company's auditor should ***not*** be required to attest to the accuracy of corporate governance disclosures. The accountancy bodies believe that this question should be reconsidered in three years since corporate practice disclosures are in their formative stages of their development' and which statement contains almost the same messages as those which were sent when the 'Out To Lunch' sign was put up in relation to computers and with the suggested three year period being equivalent to saying five, seven, or ten years, or whatever number of years you want; just think of a number. Yes, the accountancy profession has become remote from the realities of business and this is so even in relation to matter which are, themselves, remote; and, unfortunately, this remoteness is in a direction which itself compounds that remoteness. [It really is disconcerting to realize how far the profession has sunk in the area of intellectual contribution to contemporary business developments. It has no inclination to set the pace. And it is a poor follower. The leadership of our profession, in relation to the fundamental underlying dimensions and in relative terms, really has (either by acts of commission or by acts of omission) achieved a great deal for which it should be ashamed. I alone have spent four years developing material which the Institute, the Society, its research bodies, and the Big Six firms, with all their resources, have failed to satisfactorily address. And yet, due to their arrogance and their conceit, the leadership of the accountancy profession has, time and again, spurned the massive talent-base within its own ranks whilst, at one and the same time, clearly showing, and without doubt, that they overwhelmingly believe in the magnificence of their own mediocrity.] Although the term 'accountant' was, indeed, once synonymous with business (that's one of the main reasons why I wanted to become a Chartered Accountant) the profession was, by default, moving away from business. The partners who controlled these large practices were out of their depth [Heresy !!!!!] but they were well protected by the structures of their own organizations. Both relative and absolute changes had, and were, occurring and these changes were making these powerful partners all but redundant. This was a result of, amongst other things, their inappropriate business education. These were those same powerful partners, it will be recalled, who both implicitly and explicitly determined, and to some extent who still do determine, the future direction of the accountancy profession.

Please do not be fooled by position. The powerful partners in the large professional practices may well advise large corporates on important dimensions (although this is not necessarily at board level or in relation to the most fundamental of business matters) for large businesses tend to deal with large firms. They do not usually seek out specialist knowledge, even highly specialized knowledge, from boutique management consultancy practices such as that of my own. [I cannot, in fact, recall John Prescott of BHP ever contacting my firm.] So who do they consult regarding management? Typically the large professional practices; as well as others. But that doesn't mean that large corporates are getting the best advice or the best assistance. Simply put . . . . They're not !!!!! When the rubber hits the road, doing very well the wrong thing is no good. And doing very well not quite the right thing may be just as bad. I've worked for four of the Big Six firms, five times, in three countries. In my field of professional endeavour I still haven't been impressed by even one partner in one of those large firms. They all seem to be overwhelmingly focused on tactical and operational activity. That is, tactical and operational activity in their own firms. There's few strategic thinkers. They much prefer to trade their futures for the present. They spend little time on the creation, the development, and the packaging of new knowledge. A minimum effort is too much. Immediate returns are required. Chargeable hours is the thing that counts. They're like asset-strippers. They value nothing but today. They crush creativity to death. And therein lies the basic problem with the mediocre and the expedient. The brilliant get murdered by the strategically barren and the operationally powerful; for a while anyway.

The profession reached the pits in the 1980s.

It had gone feral on us !!!!!

This, in fact, was the point in time that reality was revealed. The profession had, in essence, been deficient for some time prior to the 1980s and it has continued to be so since that time; its just that the debilitation isn't as obvious today. And, in any case, the critics of the profession don't get as much media exposure as those who whitewash reality. Had a little more criticism, and a little less whitewashing, gone on previously then the iconoclastic events of the last decade may never have happened, or at least, not in the same devastating way that we had the misfortune to observe.

No better exploration of the state of affairs in the accountancy profession is provided than that which is set out by Trevor Sykes in his book 'The Bold Riders' which is another one of his six hundred page insights into the corporate world. This book is, in my view, an interim account of the debacles of the 1980s. In it he unequivocally castigates the profession. He states that 'if the audit profession cannot function any more usefully than it did in Australia in the 1980s then it might as well be abolished.' His account of the Rothwells rip-off is wonderful. It will be recalled that record audited profits were reported year after year by this merchant bank (having been audited, that is, by a leading firm of accountants) but which profits, when assessed by another of the leading accountancy firms, were determined to be a fiction. Based on that report it was probable that Rothwells had never made a profit from beginning to end. This is quite revealing. Basically, the accounts were bogus. They were out-and-out fraudulent. The auditor, bless his little cotton socks, is still a member of the Institute (according to the latest available copy of the membership handbook) and was a partner in one of the Big Six firms until a couple or so years ago; and this is so even given the auditor's own admissions . . . . not to mention the damning report of the official inspector, Malcolm McCusker QC. The audit, it was indicated in the book, could be viewed more as an act of faith than a statement of fact. Indeed, the auditor himself agreed that the records were scant and unsatisfactory. He had actually written as much in one of his own management letters to the company. And he failed to verify many of the assets. What a shame because had he done so he would have found that they didn't exist !!!!! The auditor, in fact, stated that he had relied more on in-depth discussions with the directors of Rothwells. [How nice. I wonder if that was over a cup of coffee.] Coffee or not, many people (and whether directly or indirectly) lost millions of dollars over this on-going act of gross incompetence; possibly their life's savings. The official inspector, Malcolm McCusker QC, wrote that 'At best, it is difficult to avoid the conclusion that (the auditor) engaged in a course of deliberate blindness to avoid being told what, in fact, was the truth and which would have been readily discovered from reasonable enquiry . . . .' Well, well. My goodness. Just to think. The reason that was given for why the Brisbane office of that leading professional firm were doing the audit in WA was that it was thought that the Perth office was too entrepreneurial !!!

Other amazing accounts of incompetence are also described in the aforementioned book. He also points out that almost every audit firm named therein has since been the subject of a large lawsuit. He then goes on to state that in view of that fact it is unfortunately too risky to say much more. Trevor Sykes does state, however, that greed was the explanation for the readiness of the professions to lower their standards. I think it was worse than that for I believe many of the professionals involved at that time were also incompetent. Or they just lacked competence. Either way, that is a significant problem for our profession, and one which calls out to be rectified now. One story that is related by Trevor Sykes and which, for the record, should be told a thousand times, is that concerning the accounting firm of Mann Judd. That firm, in its wisdom, chose to sacrifice the Westmex account (and, no doubt, the profits which went with that work) rather than endorse what it believed to be unsound accounting policies. Sadly though, he says, this action was not followed by any great rush of clients who were anxious to have their accounts audited by Mann Judd.

The Westmex audits in question were those audits which were carried out in 1988 and 1989, but it took until January, 1996, for the managing partner of the second-tier, but large international accountancy practice, which took over the Westmex audit to be suspended from auditing for five years. No doubt, and just to keep the wolf from the door, he'll be able to undertake some of his non-auditing activities in the meantime. The statement, which was issued by the Australian Securities Commission, stated that the suspension was *agreed to* during discussions with the named auditor before a final hearing on his conduct by the Companies Auditors and Liquidators Disciplinary Board. [They obviously move quickly with regard to these matters.] I wonder how many more audits he's done in the meantime? What his lifestyle has been like in the intervening years? And how much the mums and dads of Australia have lost, both in dollars and in psychological agony, through his lack of competence? For your information, Westmex (and which company was by no means one of the big debacle companies of the 1980s) went into provisional liquidation in February, 1990, only some five months after its 1989 accounts had been given an unqualified audit report by its auditors. Oh yes, and whilst we're talking about these things, did you know, the managing partner referred to above is the managing partner of the same large accountancy practice whose chairman wrote to me ['he had a way with words'] and who castigated me for daring to write what I do. Is it within the bounds of possibility that the chairman of that firm didn't know what his managing partner had done for this major client? It really is nice to know that colleagues are so open and honest in their criticism of me . . . . The hypocrite.

Unfortunately the structure of the accountancy profession almost ensures that the profession will be mediocre. Dante's famous words **'Abandon Hope All You Who Enter Here !!!!!'** are well and truly etched in stone above the entrance to the offices of the Institute of Chartered Accountants; although if you are to see those words you will need to look very closely. The industry is dominated, in reality, by a few firms. Those firms are, in practice, controlled by a few partners. Power in the profession is, therefore, concentrated in the hands of a few people. And those people have, historically, been mediocre; at least, that is, in terms of the leadership of our profession. For those of you who have stopped reading and are now pondering on these profound utterances it may be useful to appreciate that degradation of the accountancy profession has occurred in reality, and that it has occurred along more than one dimension, and that in the end it is the leadership, as with any organization, that must accept responsibility for such matters. Professions, much like the great businesses of history, also falter. They may even fail. Or they may be just superseded. And possibly by their own off-spring. There is nothing sacrosanct about a profession; any profession. Its just that the degradation of a profession is often not as obvious as that of a business. But the erosion of value delivery, whether on an absolute or relative basis, still occurs. Leadership failure has been a real problem in the accountancy profession. One of the great battles which will occur in the profession in the future will be that between mediocrity and meritocracy. There has already been one or two skirmishes in that area. But that battle will not occur unless catalysts crystallize. It is hoped that this book will assist in that crystallization.

The preceding discussion has provided a somewhat useful insight into reality. Useful, that is, because the discussion is hopefully not too cluttered with sophistication and complexities. At this point I will now revisit the accountancy profession and open up a more multidimensional perspective in relation to the matters at hand. The most important point to make is that the large professional practices are, in general terms, successful. They are successful businesses. I agree with professional businesses. But I also agree with businesses being professional. The professionalization of large business enterprises is taking place all round the world. This same statement also refers to the many many more small and medium-sized business enterprises which inhabit the business environment and which are so vital to economies, and to the functioning of societies everywhere. The standard and the quality of management has increased considerably during the past quarter of a century. For those of you who were around and involved in business in the early seventies that fact will not be too difficult to appreciate and this is so whether or not you preferred the way business was conducted in those days. That preference, however, addresses a different dimension. I also remind you that there were just as many rogues in those days as there are today and, indeed, there are just as many rogues today as there will be tomorrow. Nostalgia is nice, but the future is where we must live, and it is the future which we must address as a profession.

A profession of professional businesses is what, to all intents and purposes, is developing in practice. Professionalism, contrary to the views of some, is not determined by whether a business is conducted as a partnership or, indeed, as a partnership where all the personal assets of the partners stand behind their activities; as opposed to operating, say, in terms of a limited liability company and with a board of directors and a top management team. Professionalism relates, amongst other things, to the nature of the products and services that are delivered to clients (professions, of necessity, require non-trivial judgement to be exercised) and to the manner in which those judgements are delivered or provided. You don't need to wear a pin-striped suit, and to speak in such a painfully boring way that you have to keep waking your client up to listen to your drivel, to be professional. Professionals are even allowed to show enthusiasm and to get excited. They are also allowed to hold views and opinions which differ to the views and opinions of other professionals. Without that dimension there couldn't be a profession. Professionals, can you believe it, don't even have to wear a suit. They can be real people or, at least, they can act like real people !!!!! Professional businesses don't even have to have shareholders who are professionals. They can raise their capital from wherever they consider it appropriate. The business itself, however, must be professional.

The large professional firms, whatever may be their structure, are professional businesses. Some may not yet be very good at being businesses. [Some are well and truly making a pigs ear of their new and emerging structures.] Whilst other professional firms may be excellent businesses. These experiences are just the same as in the real world. [My goodness. What a thought. The real world !!!!!] The point at issue is that, in essence, structure is a function of strategy and of technology (whether that technology is hard, soft, or pliable technology) and technology is a function of strategy. As the profession changes, whether by evolution and/or by revolution, the strategies of the different players will differ in substance, and such differences may be observed in at least their technologies, their financing, and their structures. But (other things being equal) they will be no more, nor no less, professional because they are real professional businesses. The era of the professional business has been emerging for the past decade or so and it will continue to emerge during the next decade or so; and on a global scale. The real problem with the professional business, for the accountancy profession, is that it has been too slow in appearing in real form. Of course there have been changes in the management of the Big Six firms (and in other firms) and with a more business-oriented structure now tending to emerge. But this was often within the context of a partnership which had some convenient side structures or companies attached thereto. And typically those partnerships were very localized; and this was so both within countries and within different regions of the world. The professional business has, in reality, and as a vehicle of our profession, lagged environmental demands; and this has been by more than ten years. This virtual absence of real professional businesses (and the psyche which goes with that form of business structure) contributed to the profession revealing it 'pits' status in the late 1980s and the early 1990s. The large professional practices were still encumbered with incompetents (or at least with those partners who lacked competence) and it was not unknown for those parties to be at or near the top of those firms due to their power. No way can the price that was paid, and is still being paid, by our society for the incompetence of our profession be justified, but for the vast majority of the profession it took the glorious technicolour crashes of the late 1980s and thereafter, together with the massive negligence claims which followed, to shake it rigid.

Given, at least in my opinion, this advantageous move towards the era of professional businesses, and on a truly national and international scale, it may well be asked what, of all the available alternatives, is the overwhelming fundamental dysfunctionality that is being, and may well continue to be, experienced by the accountancy profession? The answer is that the profession, in both absolute and relative terms, and along fundamental dimensions, has moved away from business. It continues to move away from business. And, without doubt, this move away from business will be well and truly reinforced if it continues to pursue its present strategic direction. The profession, in practice, now focuses on near business. And it focuses on remote business. But it does not focus on business per se. It does not focus on business itself.

Business Is No Longer Our Business !!!!!

So how can these very successful businesses, the Big Six firms, together with some of the second tier practices, have failed the accountancy profession. How did this oxymoronic situation, being that of successful failure, occur. They have a total fee income in Australia of some one thousand five hundred million dollars ($1,500m) or thereabouts and in an industry which may well have a total revenue (excluding the earnings of accountants in industry, commerce, and elsewhere) of two thousand million dollars ($2,000m) or more. These are large dollar figures for any profession in Australia. How could this outcome have resulted in failure? It was simple. The profession failed to change, and in a fundamental way, and in relation to fundamental changes in the world of business. Whilst, in addition to this fundamental failure to change, in an absolute and a relative way, to changes in the business world, and at an appropriate rate and to an appropriate extent, where fundamental change did in fact occur, such change fundamentally reinforced, in a negative way, the fundamental failure to change in relation to business. The profession has, in effect, been moved both downwards and sideways.

The past, the present, and the future strategic direction of the profession was, and is, wrong; or rather, it is not quite right. The seductresses, however, were very attractive. But what, in reality, is unfolding at this time may be something that future generations of accountants will regret, and for which they may curse this generation, for we may well be relinquishing our very own future.

Basically, had the profession done nothing it would have lost its way, and in a fundamental sense. The world around us changed, as it invariably changes, but it did not change in our favour. What happened in reality was the result of various key variables. These variables included the very name of the profession and which name itself had a tendency to focus attention on figures of one description or another, and not on the big picture. Dollar figures, as could be expected, failed to focus attention on the big sweep of things. Accountancy was seen as Accountancy. Taxation was seen as Taxation. Audits were seen as Audits. And with these areas being predominantly the fee generators and profit providers. This view of the profession was also reinforced due to the fact that the accountancy profession embraces a wide spread of members and whose business activities (with no disrespect, but for want of a better description) were at different stages of development; or were heading along different dimensions. The larger firms were dealing with business enterprises which, in a business sense, they did not really understand. [Some companies went bust . . . . over a period of years . . . . and they didn't even know it was happening.] They had little of a high-value-added nature, relative to the mass of their services offerings, to contribute to their clients, so in essence they kept providing audit, accountancy, and taxation in the same old way. They did the wrong things better. Sometimes they were done worse. The medium and smaller-sized firms had little need to view accountancy, taxation, or auditing in a different way from the way in which they had viewed them for what was ages. For the overwhelming majority of their clients (and they probably had the overwhelming majority of clients by number) the accountancy view of life was normally well within allowable tolerances. Errors, one way or the other and other than at the margins, may not have been significant. The majority of members in practice would probably not have been affected by continuing to view the profession from a narrow perspective. Similarly, and for the vast majority of accountants who are engaged in industry and commerce, the consideration of 'matters fundamental' is probably a remote issue. Often they do other things. Many other things. [In fact, word has it that some accountants do not even prepare accounts.] Whilst for those accountancy professionals at the top in industry and commerce . . . . Who cared?!!!! To rock the boat prior to an 'unexpected' debilitation or disaster was possibly more of a problem than was an absence of action. This situation provided an environment which reinforced inaction in relation to the fundamental changes which should have been actioned by the large professional practices. The leadership of the Big Six firms would have been happy with this situation. That is, they would have been happy not to change had they actually thought about the type of changes which were needed. But as few gave much thought as to what changes should have been made then they were happy anyway (even when they knew that they didn't know what they should have known) for at that time they were quite happy to do nothing worth doing. Everyone was very busy being very busy. And who needs to stop and think under those circumstances? Yes, seeing accountancy in a narrow perspective, and as a financial-based discipline, undermined the profession.

Another critical variable which was, and still is, fundamental is that of education. This issue alone has been the most debilitating factor in the rise of mediocrity in the accountancy profession. I am, of course, addressing relative impoverishment. The education standards of today are far better than they were twenty or thirty years ago. But, on a relative basis, they're not better. And that's what counts. Our level of business education is, in relative terms, absolutely deplorable. Over the years, it is noted, the strategic direction of the profession has been determined by those with mediocre capabilities. Leadership of either the profession or the large professional practices has had little to do with ability, at least in an intellectual sense, and the profession has paid the price. The powerful prevented those with knowledge, understanding, and insight, from making their contribution. Business education includes, but it goes beyond, experience alone. The school of hard knocks is no longer a good enough grounding upon which to base the appropriate performance of a profession in the ever more sophisticated world of business. The profession, as epitomized in its past leadership, is indeed a prime example of 'what you don't know you don't value' and so the accountancy profession failed to progress appropriately. For the National President of the Australian Society of Certified Practising Accountants to claim, in a letter which appeared in the Australian Financial Review in December, 1995, and which stated that the Society sees it as part of its public duty to promote properly qualified and experienced accountants whose quality and integrity is *ensured* by a strict code of professional conduct, compulsory on-going training, quality assurance reviews, and disciplinary processes, is a nonsense. Many of the seventy-eight thousand (78,000) members of that body, as well as Institute members, were and are responsible for preparing the accounts of many of the companies in Australia. What happened when these well trained accountants prepared the accounts of some of the largest Australian companies and, within months, or not much longer, they crashed and their profits, it would appear, seemed to disappear. The Adelaide Steamship Company Limited, I seem to recall, reported record profit after record profit, but shortly after its final 'profit' announcement (prepared, of course, by the well trained professional accountants) it all suddenly evaporated and turned into a consolidated net loss of in excess of one thousand three hundred million dollars ($1,300m) and over the next three or four years the amount of that loss appeared to double in size. How well trained, in truth, were the preparers and the auditors of those accounts. [The moral and ethical integrity of our profession is alluded to elsewhere in this contribution.] With regard to on-going training and quality assurance reviews, well that sounds good, but its no use training accountants not so much in the wrong things (although some things may be wrong) but, more to the point, failing to train them in the right things. When you're looking at a piece of glass and you think its a diamond then there must be something wrong !!!!! It may also be just as bad to know you're looking at a diamond but you don't know whether it's a good or a bad diamond. What the hell. Collect the fee or the salary (and the bonuses) and run. It may never go wrong. Nothing may ever be revealed. To be quite honest, and for those of you who are yourselves accountants, imagine yourself in an apparently sound company which, in reality, is in trouble. I wonder how many of you would, in truth, know that the business was potentially failing months or years ahead (in particular if cash flows seemed to be good and sales were strong) because, it is noted, the crashes of the past decade typically didn't happen over night. Turning to quality assurance reviews. Well, you never know. It may be that no more will we have to tolerate mere ordinary cock-ups. From now on all the cock-ups will be of quality. They will have flair. They will have style. They will have class. They will have panache. My goodness will they have panache !!!!! Whilst with regard to disciplinary action, well let us remember, you don't have to show negligence for the professional bodies to actually take action. Negligence, it is acknowledged, may well be a legal dimension. But displaying incompetence or, alternatively, just a lack of competence, would surely provide sufficient grounds for the profession to take action. So where were all the disciplinary actions against the many many qualified accountants who either incompetently, or with a lack of professional competence, prepared, incorrectly, the financial statements of some of the multitude of companies which went bad in the past five or ten years? And where was the disciplinary action against the dozens of (influential) partners in the Big Six firms who incompetently, or at least with a lack of competence, audited the general purpose financial reports of those companies?

[It would seem that the disciplinary committee is quick enough to initiate serious action against members who may unfortunately go bankrupt (possibly due to *no wrongful behaviour* at all, or even because, hypothetically speaking, their faceless colleagues failed to prepared or perhaps audit the accounts of listed companies in a competent manner, and so they lost their income or their wealth in corporate crashes) imposing, in some cases, a suspension of membership for several years. For the life of me I just don't know what is really so terrible about going bankrupt, except if you lived ages ago when starving people had their hands cut off or were hanged for stealing a loaf of bread, and other people were put in prison for being unable to pay their debts; or worse, and later, they were sent to Australia. Such silly actions hinder unfortunate members in their endeavours to earn a living, professionally, and free from that stigma. Whilst if you can't pay your subscription within three months you can even be excluded from membership. Crimes incurred at an individual level, such as that of bankruptcy and the non-payment of membership fees, always seem to be of far more importance, and seem to be dealt with far more harshly, than are those crimes which are committed on a large scale, such as having a *less than competent* hand in the demise or the crippling of a major corporate and, as a consequence, the debilitation or the ruination of unknown thousands. It's just like war crimes really. If its big enough and you're important enough (perhaps a general or a field marshal or something) then it seems that you can negotiate your way out of almost anything; or at least claim mitigating circumstances and thereby modify the wroth of the establishment. Yes, if you can't pay your four hundred dollar ($400) annual membership fee then you're in real trouble .... but if you have an incompetent hand in a four hundred million dollar ($400m) company collapse which pays ten cents (10c) in the dollar and puts thousands out of work, don't worry about it, you'll be all right in the accountancy profession. Oh !!!!! Sorry about this little aside. I was getting quite carried away there for a moment; putting things into perspective by identifying some of the more anachronistic values of our profession. I must get back to reality.]

And if the response is that those accounts were prepared and audited in accordance with the relevant accounting standards of the time, then isn't that in itself an acknowledgement that the standards themselves were not appropriate or, in essence, were wrong. And doesn't it also indicate that few, if any, of those so-called intellectual giants who lead our profession had actually given any meaningful attention to the appropriateness of those standards. No, they were too busy, off stage left, trying to work out the proverbial *sixteenth* way in which a lease could be presented on a balance sheet. They just hadn't had time to notice that the company was crook. And what about the standards which did not exist and which, had they existed, would at least have mitigated those corporate disasters which inflicted pain and suffering on so many, and which we all read about or witnessed. Bland statements, made by the National President, about strict codes of professional conduct, compulsory on-going training, quality assurance reviews, and disciplinary processes, are a joke. The problems that existed then, and that still exist today, emanate from mediocrity. And mediocrity emanates from, amongst other things, a poor level of business education. And our profession, for sure, suffers from that dimension . . . . and in abundance !!!!!

It may be noted that the aforementioned National President of the Australian Society of Certified Practising Accountants is also a Chartered Accountant. He is also a senior partner in one of the Big Six firms. Masquerading under some other title, he was also on the iniquitous National Joint Limitation of Liability Task Force for the capping of negligence awards. Whilst also, and in his spare time (or is that reserved for his clients) he is Chairman of the Australian Accounting Research Foundation. [It is noted that 'iniquitous' is used here due to the immoral and unethical underpinnings of the capping committee where, amongst other things, immoral relates to the intended and unashamed transfer of damage from our wrongdoers and to their victims, so taking from our victims what truly belongs to them, whilst unethical is used because few of the client's of our profession would voluntarily accept such a relationship with those they retain as professional advisors.] Concentration of power appears to be a very popular concept. It goes on everywhere and not only with the National President. I wonder if they get confused when they carry out their different tasks, duties, and responsibilities. The profession can only benefit. *'One mindset. One message. One voice.'* That could be our next slogan. With a bit of luck (at least for the in-crowd) it could stop discussion dead and, at one and the same time, kill off all their nemeses. Incidentally, the Big Six firms did very well in their securing of representation on the iniquitous Task Force. Can you believe it, out of over one hundred thousand accountants, they chose a Past President of the Institute to be Chairman of the committee. Whilst the National President of the Society (who, as already mentioned, was also on the Task Force) just happened to be a partner in the same Big Six firm as the Chairman. Even when counting the lawyer and the man from the insurance industry, and other cohorts, the Big Six members made up more than half the Task Force. And, oh yes, how silly, I almost forgot to mention it. The Chairman's firm (he's actually the chief executive, or something, of one of the Big Six firms) is currently being sued by one of its previous clients for one thousand million dollars ($1,000m) whilst another of the Big Six firms represented on the committee is also being sued, but for one thousand five hundred million dollars ($1,500m). The word is that the cases are related in some way or another. Now let me stress. Of course these people are objective and independent representatives of the profession. Of course they'll be able to set aside the pressures which are being placed upon their own firms by massive damage claims. And of course they'll be able to make decisions that are in the best interests of the profession in total. If you're not sure, then why not ask them. After all, don't they always behave in a just, a fair, and an equitable manner? .... Or could I be mistaken?

What the large professional practices actioned, as a third critical variable, was the development of their management consultancy divisions; and often in a big way. Some of those efforts were successful in terms of the divisions becoming established in their own right, whilst others were more volatile and fragmented in nature; being less cohesive and less independent operations.

Andersens established itself as the big winner in management consultancy whilst, at one and the same time, having one of the weakest presences of the Big Six firms in the audit domain. It is noted that despite this fact Andersens does have some very prestigious audit clients. The massive growth of the consultancy division of Andersens, which is itself a separate firm, has enabled Andersens in total, and on a world basis, to rocket from number six to number one of the Big Six firms. A senior partner in another Big Six firm once told me that if Andersens were quoting on an assignment, then they may as well not bother. Andersens has been estimated to earn thirty-five cents (35c) in every dollar that is spent on management consultancy (consultancy is a generic term which includes outsourcing services) that are supplied by firms deemed to comprise the accountancy profession. Its income from consultancy dwarfs the income, from that source, of any other single member of the Big Six firms. It also earns more from this source than the three smaller Big Six firms do from consultancy work when the fee income of those three firms, and from that source, is aggregated. The consultancy arm of Andersens, on a world basis, is now set to overtake its accountancy arm in terms of its fee income (it has already done so in the US) this apart from any consultancy fees which the accountancy arm itself earns. [This point in relation to consultancy work will be revisited in the final chapter as it underpins the future of the accountancy profession.] Andersens total worldwide income increased by over twenty percent (20%) in the financial year to the 31st August, 1995. In US dollars it came in at eight point one billion dollars ($8.1b) or, in Australian dollars, it was ten point nine billion dollars ($10.9b) in total; being a figure which is fifty percent greater than the world-wide revenues of Qantas and one which comfortably exceeds the entire income of the accountancy profession in the UK. Andersens has only half the number of partners of its near rivals, being some two thousand five hundred and fifty (2,550) whilst, including partners, it has over eighty-two thousand (82,000) professional personnel; which figure is around twenty-five thousand (25,000) more than either of the next two Big Six businesses. In addition it also has several thousand contractors. Andersens worldwide revenue was split almost equally between that of the accountancy practice and that of the management consultancy business. Given this, although it would appear that Andersens is, to-date, the big winner in management consultancy, it is pointed out, however, that the consultancy approach taken by Andersen Consulting has, both actively and passively, major down-sides. These down-sides include what may be seen as a mass production approach to providing services, with its asset-stripping and burn-out factors; and each of which dimensions must be questioned relative to what is actually in the best interests of clients, consultants, and the profession. The concern which surrounds their production line approach is that many relatively young and inexperienced people (historically their hiring has discriminated against older persons) high on technical knowledge, at best moderate on understanding, and with little insight or wisdom, are put into the field to advise on and install what are tantamount to stencil or blueprint-type solutions. This production based approach may be appropriate for significantly undifferentiated conditions, but it is inappropriate in highly perspicacious or sagacious situations which demand a high level of professional judgement. The mass production approach to consultancy, when combined with ruthless *up or out* employment behaviour, raises important moral and ethical concerns. This approach is questionable, even when benefits are in fact conferred on people, and not least of all where business success undermines professional considerations. Asset-stripping, the suppression of creativity, and burn-out, although common to other situations, would almost for sure be by-products of the mass production line type of consultancy practiced by Andersens. It may even be asked to what extent Andersen Consulting are really consultants. The hiring of young knowledge-based workers for what is tantamount to strip-out and kick-out, the mal-nourishment of professional creativity, and the burn-out factor which treats people as revenue generation machines prior to their trade-in for fresher models, are practices that are, both individually and in aggregate, distasteful.

There are, of course, other concerns of fundamental importance with regard to how this type of consultancy has developed, and how it may develop in the future, not least of all in relation to the future of the accountancy profession and its development.

Having made the aforementioned points in relation to revenues from management consultancy, and not least of all in relation to the growth of such revenues relative to the total revenues of the large accountancy practices, it should also be noted that some ninety percent (90%) of all management consultancy fees paid to accountancy practices are paid to the Big Six firms. It has been estimated that before the turn of the century the top eight firms in the UK will no longer be accountancy practices but would be better described as management consultancy businesses due to the probability that they will earn the most significant part of their total fee income from management consultancy activities. This particular development has had, and will continue to have, a most decided impact upon the nature of the accountancy profession.

These three factors (seeing accountancy in a narrow perspective and as a financial-based discipline; having a membership, but in particular a leadership, with an impoverished business education; and the embracing of management consultancy, in the way in which it has developed, as the future of the profession) are only some of the matters which have helped to bring about the decline of the accountancy profession. Given this particular perspective (and no doubt some people will object thereto, but remember, this is no rigorous evaluation of the situation but, rather, is a glimpse at reality) the accountancy profession, to all intents and purposes, is no longer the accountancy profession, but is something else.

So what is it ?!!!!

By doing nothing the profession would have moved away from business or, more correctly, business would have moved away from the profession. By doing what it did, in reality, it accelerated that situation. Way back in pre-history (let's say in the 1960s and early 1970s) the profession stood shoulder to shoulder in business with its clients. Business was less sophisticated at that time and clients themselves often didn't have the know-how to perform some of the important tasks which they now perform themselves; so they looked to their accountants. Accountancy itself could, in those days, be seen as being synonymous with business. It was entangled therewith and in an almost inextricable way. Over the years the various professional bodies grew in size and their membership (some bodies even targeted the servicing of industry and commerce) were employed by the clients of the professional practices. This trend has never stopped. Eventually clients became at least as competent, if not more competent, in specific areas of professional endeavour than were their colleagues in professional practices. The dichotomous journey had commenced. The multi-faceted shattering of the profession was, in essence, under way. The professional practice had started to deliver highly specialized, highly differentiated, high-value-added, services together with generally generic, and often poorly differentiated, low-value-added, offerings. At first the fees and profit margins appeared to remain high for the generic services. In the end (even though actual changes were masked by high levels of inflation and various periods of economic expansion or boom) relatively lower fee levels and relatively lower profit margins were inevitable for the lower-value-added product and service offerings. Business had devalued the accountancy profession. And it had done this with the help of that profession. There had been a redistribution of value away from the profession and towards business itself. This, however, was not a bad thing for society and nor was it necessarily bad for the accountancy profession in total.

Also from the mid-1970s onwards the business schools started to really pump out MBAs. This flow was slow at first but eventually, in the 1990s, it became an avalanche. This provided yet another source of business professionals. And they were professionals who had a different view of life. Some business school graduates, like myself, were also accountants, but many came from different disciplines. This source of competition increased the threat to the profession but the universities, or at least some of them, made a basic mistake. In their mindless grab for students they introduced the one year MBA program to compete with the two year masters degree. [To disclose my own position and, accordingly, to indicate any inherent bias which I may possess, I personally undertook a four year part-time masters degree and which degree was equivalent to that of a two year full-time degree.] How much, it must be asked, can a person learn in one year? I have tutored at university and I can assure you that the answer is, not that much; and this is so no matter how it is dressed up. The universities, in this one move, reduced the quality of their own competitive advantage. The high expectations of business, when hiring these graduates, were reduced by impoverished results and this was so even when a five or ten year delay factor was built in to allow for the elevation of graduate output into higher executive positions. Worse, however, the universities went on to provide masters degrees which were so airy-fairy in essence that they were hardly worth the effort; for business or the student. Change is of the essence and so changes are required to be made to masters degree offerings over time. But let's get real. Some of the stuff isn't worth studying. The emergence of the MBA, warts and all, did however reduced the predominance of the profession although, relatively, the impact of the MBA on the profession was down-graded from that of a significant threat to being that of merely another threat to the profession; and this was done by the dollar-driven enthusiasm of the universities. The significance of this threat, as it turned out, was further diminished because the profession, in the end, also retained professionals with MBAs. The profession, today, has a relative respite from the external impact of the MBA. But this situation will not continue. Business itself will demand more substance from the universities in relation to the output of MBAs. So this factor, too, being the emergence of the MBA in numbers, if not always in quality, has resulted in a redistribution of value away from the accountancy profession and towards business; but, in this instance, without the assistance of the profession.

By 1980 the accountancy profession was no longer shoulder to shoulder with business. It had, in truth, progressed, but it had not progressed in the same direction or at the same rate as business. The gap between the profession and the business world was widening. The realities of business, although always different to the realities of the profession, had become obviously different. The blurring. The grey areas. The overlays. The compatibility. The mutuality of interest. Each of these were now separating. Whilst today the divergence is very large. This particular situation may well have had something to do with the profession endeavouring to *please* the corporate world in the middle of the 1980s and beyond; and which behaviour contributed to societal devastation.

In relative terms, not only did business itself move away from the overwhelming dollar-figures mentality at a greater rate than did the accountancy profession. [This is not to say that dollars aren't important; they are.] And not only did business embrace business education faster and more broadly than did the accountancy profession. The actual move, by the accountancy profession, into management consultancy ended up accentuating the gap between the profession and business. That move became a significant factor in crystallizing the bankruptcy of the accountancy profession. By the way, before you write this statement off as a non-starter, for intuitively it would seem to be somewhat enigmatic in nature, it may be worthwhile remembering that management consultancy is a generic term. It may also be worthwhile remembering that the products and the services that are offered by management consultants are often dynamic in nature. The name stays the same, management consultancy, but the products and the services change. And therein lies the paradox. With its fundamental focus on dollar figures and its impoverished business education (being the two seductresses which were passive . . . . for choosing to do nothing, or to do very little, was easy) the accountancy profession didn't really know what strategy was, so it blindly sold its soul for thirty pieces of silver; buying into the generic world of management consultancy and, thereby, eventually into areas in which it had little or even no competitive advantage. Management consultancy, the active seductress, was, however, irresistibly attractive.

The large professional firms have become successful management consultancy practices. The large professional firms dominate the accountancy profession. This alignment between accountancy and consultancy appeared, at first, to be a most appropriate one, but unfortunately it lost its way; and the child ate its parents.

Given the aforementioned matters, who then, it may be asked, determines the strategic direction of the accountancy profession? Is it accountants? Is it management consultants? Or is it those business professionals who control those emerging professional businesses? And who will it be in the future? The question with regard to who controls the strategic direction of the accountancy profession is very important for the fundamental objectives of the various parties may well be different. Worse, however, those very objectives may not even be in the best interests of the accountancy profession !!!!!

In the 1960s and early 1970s the large accountancy practices, as management consultants or otherwise, began to carry out all sorts of things in the field of business management. This was the pre-history era. But it was in that era, whilst working for one of the leading accountancy firms in the City of London, that I met a colleague who was higher up the firm and who, unknown to him, was to change my life. He crystallized my general tendencies. In 1967, and because of that brief encounter with that colleague, I decided that I would become a management consultant. Life was very different in pre-history. Those businesses which were automated in the 1960s were still using the old punched card machines. The eighty column card was only replaced by the ninety-six column card as recently as 1969. That's only quarter of a century ago and yet a quarter of a century, particularly to a young person, may seem like an eternity. In those days there were NCR cash registers with more keys to press than you could poke a burnt stick at . . . . and that great monster, the Burroughs E4000 electronic accounting machine, which, as it ate its way through its daily diet of data, used to sound more like the clunkety-clunk of a goods train than like the sound of office equipment efficiently processing its input into output. It was, however, quite a popular machine. There were also key punch machines, verifiers, sorters, collators, and all sorts of other equipment including reproducers; and each item was the size of a large desk. Computers were also around (IBM had reluctantly entered the computer market in the mid-1950s after losing work relating to the Bureau of Census; how lucky for IBM) but they were scarce. Really big companies had computers. I can remember working my way through stacks of computer print-outs as I sat in the head office of Shell in London, in 1967. That was a big company. In 1954 it had been generally agreed by many business people, including various executives of the data processing companies, that some eight or ten computers would satisfy the entire world demand for such devices. This monumental blunder has gone down in history as one of the worst marketing forecasts of all time. By 1956 there were six hundred (600) computers in the United States. It is estimated that by 1960 this figure had grown to three thousand five hundred (3,500) machines. And by 1970 installed sales had reached ninety thousand (90,000) computers. Even then this growth in computer sales had only brought companies to the verge, merely to the threshold, of the events which were to later revolutionize business and, in so doing, make many people very rich and create some of the largest multi-national corporations in the world.

These events are recalled, not for purposes of nostalgia, but to provide a setting for accountancy-based management consultancy in those days whilst, at one and the same time, reinforcing the realization that change is often fast in the business world; and that the nature and the speed of such change did, is, and will continue to impact the accountancy profession, and further, that we, as a profession, need to wake up to ourselves.

Management consultancy, from the mid-1970s onwards, went from strength to strength. The accountancy profession moved on to assist clients with management accounting type offerings such as budgetary control, standard costing, flexible budgeting, and later on, zero-based budgeting, as well as program budgeting; they introduced management by exception and management by objectives; they centralized and then they decentralization various organizations; they undertook economic analyses, long range planning, business and strategic planning, critical path analyses, feasibility studies, pilot projects, and prototyping exercises; they designed both divisional and matrix organization structures, they looked at organizational behaviour, motivation, and leadership, and entered the field of executive search and recruitment, and later, empowerment; they did discounted cash flows, they used portfolio analysis and the capital asset pricing model; they identified and assessed value chains, quality circles, just-in-time methodologies, productivity improvements, excellence programs, customer service standards, and helped to facilitate continuous improvement or total quality management; not to mention the execution of core business analyses, restructuring, management buy-outs, leveraged buy-outs, down-sizing and, of course, right-sizing (or wrong-sizing depending on which way you want to look at it) which then moved on to business process re-engineering, benchmarking, world's best practice, business performance reviews, as well as risk management reviews (not necessarily in that order) and they even facilitated that alleged panacea for all business ills, change management; and now employer-of-choice positioning, the balanced scorecard approach, and the learning organization, to mention but a few activities.

These product and service offerings were, however, middle and lower level management services. Yes, they did major things. And, yes, they did things which were of importance to business enterprises and other public and private sector organizations. But typically, and whether by design or otherwise, they were pitched at supplementing and supporting operational management and at facilitating middle management. Given the aforementioned, and for the large accountancy practices to grow as they wished, then they needed to tap into large-scale markets and fundamental management infrastructure projects. Many of the aforementioned transactional, and often ad hoc, management consultancy assignments generally did not have the large-scale flow-on effects which were desired by these growing practices. They were hungry for dollars and that meant, in reality, they were hungry for growth. The 'sell-in/sell-on' function was, however, too problematic. The utilization of additional personnel on existing consultancy assignments and the securing of additional projects from established clients was, in practice, only partially successful. The management information systems era, which gained pace from the mid-1970s, provided the appropriate opportunity for the large scale growth and development of the big firms.

The accountancy profession, as luck would have it, actually had a distinctive competence in the management information area in the early days. It understood financial management and so it was not too difficult to embrace and master the new and the emerging financial management systems. The profession also had a ready made set of clients and in any case, and apart from that, the image of the profession tended to convey to its potential client base that it understood those type of things. So they helped to introduce computer-based management information, which was followed later by a variety of totally integrate management information systems, which themselves were followed by fourth generation-type database management systems, including query languages, local area networks, wide area networks and, at one and the same time, the personal, or desk-top, and lap-top computer revolutions; and also what seemed like almost everything else.

This boom in management consultancy and, in particular, in computer-based management information and computer-based management information systems, was a distinct benefit to the accountancy profession; at least at that time. The profession was relevant to business. But this, as was indicated previously, was typically at the middle and the lower levels of management. It was not usually at the board of director or top management level per se; and this was so even though they interacted with, or were retained by, those management levels. Put simply, top level management consultancy work, in essence, was not the domain of the accountancy profession. Those type of assignments were more usually undertaken by the prestigious, non-accountancy-based, management consultancy firms.

Today the information revolution has moved on to new fields and the telecommunications age is here; and, in practical terms and to all intents and purposes, it is here to stay. This development presents a real problem for the accountancy profession. Of course there are still new worlds to conquer. The industrial revolution which is occurring in East Asia, both North and South, has only just begun. But to stay on the same spot however, this apart from any ambitions for growth, you need to generate lots of dollars every year; and year after year. With the information technology and telecommunications revolution has come a new and ominous dimension. The existing distinctive competence of the profession in financial know-how is now no longer the linchpin. It is there. But it is not the linchpin. Look around and see who populates the management consultancy arms of the Big Six practices. It's not accountants. At least not in the way it use to be. Once upon a time it was, to stretch a point, almost a requirement to be a qualified accountant. Sure, there are plenty of accountants still working for those firms. And there's lots of left over accountant partners who run the different consultancy businesses within those firms. That justifies their existence. But they could easily, very easily, be replaced tomorrow. Or later today. And not even by accountants. Yes, there are some 'new age' accountants who are undoubtedly very knowledgeable in the new technologies of this age of the information super-highway, with its internet, multi-media, and all that stuff. But the technical and technological knowledge which is underpinning this revolution does not reside in any fundamental way with accountants. Interactive sound, voice, data, image, and video transmission is typically based on computers, telephones, and television. It definitely does not reside with the de-skilled generation of accountants who may still be partners in the large firms. [For the record, this potted, progressive, profile provides a generally accurate, although not precise, view of the accountancy profession. If you want to be picky then please, pick away, but as a background setting the aforementioned information is generally accurate; and it provides a basis for understanding and progress.] So what has happened to the accountancy profession? Where are we ?!!!!

Well we can still prepare accounts, in a fashion. And we can still audit them, in a fashion. And we can still work out the taxation situation based on those fashionable accounts. And we can also use the technology which the non-accountants who are employed in droves by the management consultancy divisions of the large accountancy practices provide to the clients of the accountancy profession. And we can still do other odds and sodds, not least of all in areas where the particular work is somewhat protected by law and which law works (whether partially or totally) to the benefit of the accountancy profession; and this would include areas such as that of insolvency and administration work, and investment advice.

But I think there's been a sort of reverse take-over.

How many partners in the management consultancy divisions of these large firms are non-accountants? What will that figure be by the turn of the century? What will that figure be in twenty years time? What will be the percentage of the total revenues of the large firms that will be derived from management consultancy at each of the aforementioned dates? What will be the profits derived from those revenues at those dates? Who will have the power in those firms at the aforementioned dates? Will that power emanate from, or have anything to do with, the profession? Will that power be exercised in the best interests of all members of the accountancy profession? By that time, will it even matter ?!!!!

To progress along this path, the professional practices will, in the future, be well and truly split into two and with its division being between large firms and non-large firms. The non-large firms will deliver necessary, but relatively low-value-added, professional services into their client base. The large firms, themselves, will be schizophrenic. They will deliver the same type of necessary, low-value-added, services into the same type of client base as that which the army of then non-accountants who are engaged in the management consultancy divisions of those large professional businesses will be eagerly delivering into their client base; except, relatively speaking, their particular offerings will be the very necessary, high-value-added, professional services which clients will be only too pleased to pay for in terms of high-profit-margins high-fees, and high-total-revenues. The accountancy profession as such, having then already been in that state for some considerable time, could, to all intents and purposes, be declared bankrupt.

Yes, to repeat what was stated earlier, the most important point to make is that the large professional practices are successful. They are, indeed, successful businesses. Very successful businesses. But, one must ask, are their activities in the best interests of the accountancy profession? Is the accountancy profession being asset-stripped? Is it being debased? And, if so, is this happening at the cost of its future? And, if this truly is happening, then who is doing it? And how does this affect society in general?

No, I am no Luddite !!!!! In fact, I'm extremely progressive. I am also a management consultant. I do think, however, that we need to seriously, and urgently, re-think the future of the accountancy profession for I do not believe, from observation, that the leaders of our profession have given it much thought at all. Their plans are based on incorrect premises (given, of course, that they wish the accountancy profession to be a high level profession that delivers high-value-added products and services into it's client base) and those plans are hollow. They are little more than words. The leadership of our profession would seem to listen to non-one but itself. They equate their own futures with the future of our profession. And they subsume the interests of the majority of the membership into the interests of their own minority. We, as a profession, are being used, consumed, eroded, and wasted, and with the purpose thereof being to promote one or more other professions, and in the interests of the few; or at least, that is, in the interests of their own professional businesses.

We need a radical change in the profession of accountancy and not a radical change in the accountancy profession. If the large practices wish to pursue their particular interests then that is their choice. But it should not be at the expense of the accountancy profession. And nor should it be at the expense of society. For that is what is happening. The tail is wagging the dog.

Change, however, is of the essence. And the profession needs to be re-invented. But such re-invention should not be for what the profession is not but, rather, it should be for what the profession normatively is in essence. We are not the 'Chartered Institute of Professional Businesses' being the hi-jacked variety of the Institute of Chartered Accountants. Perhaps a change of name, and with it a change of emphasis, may well be appropriate. I got over being a Chartered Accountant ten years after I qualified. It took some effort. But it opened up a whole new world. A different way of thinking. I'm not being derogatory in making this statement. Just factual. The simple description 'accountant' has a tendency to channel thought. I now view myself as a business management professional. This, in itself, is somewhat of a liberating influence and not least of all in relation to the way one thinks, acts, and challenges various matters. Perhaps a change to a different title such as that of 'Chartered Management Advisors' would be a more appropriate term for our profession. It may well move our thinking away from the narrower constraints of accountancy per se and, at one and the same time, be more unifying. Such a move may allow us, within the domain of our profession, to more easily cross multi-dimensional boundaries. The different dimensions of compliance, authentication, and advisory work may supplement and support one another in a more effective way. We may even find ourselves embracing whole new worlds. Yes. Bring on the shakers and the movers. The visionaries. The quantum leaps. The order of magnitude changes. Let's get back to business. Let's get shoulder-to-shoulder with captains of industry and of commerce. And with the responsible entrepreneurs. And with our very own clients .... Well maybe not. Perhaps we shouldn't get *too* excited about our own future. Perhaps, after all, we shouldn't get *too* real.

In October, 1992, I decided to place the following article in the Australian Financial Review. At that time the recession was in full swing and companies had been and still were crashing all around us; whilst damage claims were the order of the day. The article, which is set out below, attracted some degree of interest but made no positive impression on the Institute of Chartered Accountants. They continued, in effect, to do nothing; although one or two people did seem to get upset. The article, to stress a point, is just as pertinent today as it was then. It is reproduced below in slightly altered form. The difference is that it is now fifteen (15) years since the original events and almost nine (9) years since the stock market crash of October, 1987. The accountancy profession, given this passage of time, would still not have any more idea today than it did then with regard to whether a company was in trouble strategically. It may still bleat (in unison of course) that the strategic dimension has nothing to do with the profession and, like Pontius Pilate, continue to indulge in the washing of its collective hands; bobbing and weaving and ducking and diving as it endeavoured to avoid its real and fundamental responsibilities to shareholders, to stakeholders, and to society in general. The article however, and as was indicated, still makes very interesting reading in view of its continued pertinence four (4) years after it was first written. The title was the colloquial shorthand which was used at the time. The case was actually launched against, amongst other people, the particular partner who was responsible for the audit of AWA by Deloittes; as well as a director of AWA. Deloittes, for those of you who are not familiar with that firm, is one of the Big Six accountancy and management consultancy firms. Since this case there have been many out-of-court damage settlements. These settlements were, no doubt, reinforced by the particular ruling in the aforementioned case. The amount claimed in the AWA case was not in itself massive (being in the tens of millions of dollars rather than in the hundreds of millions or in the billions of dollars) but the case proved to be a legal watershed. Important decisions of principle were enunciated, both in the original case and in the decision of the appeal court, and with the rulings made therein being almost certain to affect not only the accountancy profession itself but, in addition thereto, various of the other professions, for many many years to come. The article read as follows:

AWA v Deloittes

Beyond the Obvious

(a note to directors, managers, and auditors
on the costs of strategic myopia)

A 'ghost from the past' visited me recently when I read a summary of Justice Rogers findings in the AWA v Deloittes case. I recall that over a decade ago it was pointed out to one of the largest accountancy firms in Australia that, under the going concern principle, it could insist that a review of the strategy of one of their large corporate clients must be undertaken prior to the conclusion of their next audit. This matter was never addressed by that major firm in those particular terms and the company in question went on to encounter problems far greater than those experienced by AWA.

Although Justice Rogers addressed the legal duty of auditors to assess the adequacy of internal controls and to report deficiencies in the design or operation of the internal control procedures of a business enterprise, ruling that this duty of disclosure is to be carried out irrespective of whether specific irregularities had actually been discovered, it is implied in this judgement that it is also the responsibility of auditors to examine the strategic management systems, procedures, and practices of their client companies, and to report thereon.

Deficiencies in the strategic management systems of companies, whether such deficiencies are systematic, ad hoc, or transactional in nature, can alone have far more devastating consequences for the well-being of a company than impacts which may occur and flow from deficiencies in either the management information systems or operational control systems of a business enterprise.

Had that leading firm of accountants referred to previously actually had the courage to insist upon a review of the strategy of that major quoted public company, under that very under-utilized going concern audit principle, one can only ponder on whether the rape of shareholders which took place during the 1980s would ever have occurred or, on a grander scale, whether the pain and suffering of the recession would ever have been this bad.

Whether viewed from an audit perspective, a consultancy perspective, or from the perspective of accountants engaged in industry or commerce, the going concern criteria is a powerful vehicle by means of which the audit profession in particular, and the accountancy profession in general, can influence the well-being of Corporate Australia. Had this one major firm taken a stand, more than ten years ago, on what, in my opinion, has now been incorporated in the AWA v Deloittes decision with regard to the responsibilities of auditors, the profession today would still have been viewed as the leaders of business.

Alas, this leading accountancy practice shrank from this challenge and returned their focus to the mundane, the moribund, and the fee level.

The audit profession is indeed a profession of middle managers. It feasts on laws and standard accounting practices which, of themselves, aspire to higher levels of professional service, but which appear, in reality, to be applied with something that approaches minimum scope.

The profession itself could have led the way. That one major firm could, some ten or more years ago, not only have established itself as pre-eminent in the quality of its audit work (reaching beyond the obvious and enhancing the knowledge, the understanding, and the insight, of the top management of that leading quoted public company through the application of its own strategic management prowess) but it could also have augmented the positive qualities of what may otherwise be described as a routine audit; raising the level of both strategic awareness and strategic leadership throughout that client company.

Had this major Australian accountancy firm led the way and addressed the strategic management system challenges faced by the top management of that major quoted public company they would, no doubt, have gone on to apply similar rigorous assessments to their other key corporate clients.

Given the high-value-added nature of such services (the benefits from which, if properly conducted, could only have been significant) then other large accountancy firms would also have adopted such practices as part of their own high-value-added audit services and, by now, the profession would have been a profession which is concerned not only with the issues of middle management, such as those of computer systems and internal controls, but a profession concerned with the total well-being of the business enterprise; and not least of all its strategic well-being.

The impact of conducting strategic management reviews as an almost mandatory part of a statutory audit would, I believe, have had a significant impact on Corporate Australia and may have averted the loss, by many innocent and helpless shareholders, of billions of dollars of capital; being a figure that, by now, may have reached an initial amount of twenty billion dollars ($20b) or more.

The use, by companies, of relatively ineffective strategic management practices, which themselves are based on poor quality strategic management systems, has resulted in businesses floundering to an unnecessary extent and, in some cases, has contributed, in a significant way, to the collapse of major companies, together with their vulnerable subsidiaries and their dependent trading entities.

The result of this important audit omission, being the review of the strategic management systems and practices of major quoted public companies, has had almost unparalleled adverse consequences for the Australian economy. Apart from the traumatic impact on shareholders, as mentioned above, thousands upon thousands of people have been left without jobs or have had their careers damaged in some other significant way. The social costs have been tremendous. And the emotional pain and suffering has been beyond belief. Yet the quality of the audit, the mere requirement to assess the strategic management systems of Corporate Australia, could have mitigated this almost unparalleled disaster and changed for the better what is now, unfortunately, the economic profile of our country.

This failure of the top management of Australian companies to come to terms, in an effective way, with the fundamentals of strategic management (a failure caused, one suspects, more because of a myopic eye on costs rather than a visionary view of benefits) was summed up by a top executive of one of our leading banks when he stated 'we don't know where we've been for the past two years' and claimed that the bank probably couldn't even include certain strategic management practices in its procedures, even if it wanted to do so; a damning observation and one which portrayed, in retrospect, the poor quality of strategic management in one of our largest and most prestigious financial institutions.

One can only wonder how much the shareholders of companies such as Hooker, Bond Corporation, Adelaide Steamship, Quintex, Chase, Equiticorp, Estate Mortgage, Rothwells, Girvan, Spedley, ANI, Parry Corporation, Ariadne, Tricontinental, Westpac, the State Banks of Victoria and South Australia, and even AWA itself would, in retrospect, have paid their auditors to pass opinions on the strategic management of their companies. One may also wonder how soon the professional indemnity insurers such as Lloyds, C E Heath, and FAI will come to realize the nature of the beast with which they are dealing and make it a mandatory requirement in their policies that a proper review of the strategic management of public companies is undertaken as part of the normal audit practices of professional firms.

One could perhaps even wonder whether the audit profession could act first and, thereby, pre-empt the corporate debacles which are in the making today and which, when they are revealed in years to come, will once again be met by exclamations of incredulity .... almost as though such disasters had never happened before !!!!!

No-one down at the 'all knowing and all wise' Institute contacted the Australian Consulting Group, my boutique management consultancy practice, in order to discuss the various issues raised therein or to assess how specific improvements could be made for the benefit of the accountancy profession, or for society in general. I did, however, meet with various partners from several of the large and the medium-size firms in relation to providing strategic management services to certain of their clients. Some of those practices, and in particular the medium-sized firms, were quite open about their inability to address matters strategic. We even gave a three or four hour presentation to one of those progressive medium-sized practices with regard to what they should address with their clients in relation to strategic management. That firm recognized their own limitations (they didn't have a large number of public companies as clients) but they suggested that they would be perfectly willing to provide us with an introduction to their firm in the UK.

The large firms, however, were full of their own self-importance and adopted their usual fall-back position of what, in effect, is 'we are large and, therefore, we know everything, so how could you possibly help us' whilst, in one case, two (shall we say) younger partners (who were obviously still wet behind the ears in relation to such matters but full of their own importance) then proceeded to demonstrate, at least to us, how much they didn't know !!!!!

The following year the Australian Consulting Group, which firm specializes in strategic management and strategic management systems, placed its second full page article in the Australian Financial Review. It appeared in October, 1993.

The article indicated how the leading accountancy firms had failed their clients, not least of all through their own attitude towards, and dilatory practices in relation to, the development of leading-edge products and services, and in their own basic area of professional endeavour; being that of business. It also portrayed a profession which, at that time and at least at the first and second tier levels, was very much concerned with the nature its own survival and, given that it would survive, then its own credibility and relevance in the future. It also addressed a profession which, at that time and without the benefit of hindsight, lacked vision, was inward-looking, and was stunned by the unfolding events of those times. It portrayed a profession which was, amongst other things, visiting the cutting-edge of its own incompetent reality and which was in a state of shock. It was, potentially, being sued off the face of the earth. If one major award went against any one of the leading firms then, in its present form, that firm would almost certainly have failed. That very interesting article, together with minor variations, is set out below.

A Profession In Crisis

Graceful Degradation and the Accountancy Profession

(Or How We Failed Corporate Australia)

With at least one of the Big Six accountancy firms staring at its own demise, and possibly in the next few years, and with other first and second tier firms somewhat mortified, or in some cases even transfixed, by their own inadequacies, one can only wonder what radical direction-changing encounters these feudal anachronisms will need to have inflicted upon them before they show real evidence of a dramatic and sustainable shift in their behaviour; and which shift is aimed at recreating their own futures.

Although these firms have diversified into various areas of business expertise over the years, proclaiming themselves to be professional service businesses with competence in many areas, their search for their own relevance continues. Impoverished entrepreneurship, a flawed business-orientation, and a bankrupt research and development component, amongst other things, has left these firms (apart from one) pondering on why they exist.

Where once the expertise embodied in such firms towered above and beyond the comparable knowledge of their clients, today such a strategic advantage has, to all intents and purposes, disappeared. Their main offering, the statutory audit, has become a commodity, with both audit fees and profit margins having been squeezed. This fundamental undermining of the profession has, however, been compounded by other major profit-earners having also been turned into commodities. Taxation, although still a very important source of profits, competes with the highly competent in-house expertise of their clients. Human resource services (given few barriers to entry) competes with an array of alternatives. Whilst the fifteen to twenty year boom in the design, development, and implementation of computerized management information, accounting and control systems, and upon which the computer industry rode to fame and fortune, is over. Corporate Australia has been computerized. The computer market, being in replacement mode, is mature. Compounding these problems are the rapid advances that have been made in the information technology and communications arena and which advances, in reality, have left the accountancy-based firms with little or no distinctive competence upon which to differentiate themselves.

Put simply, the profession has, during this past twelve years or so (for twelve years or so now read fifteen years or so) failed to address, adequately, the future wants and needs of the market place. It failed to change, swiftly enough, with the times. Lost in a forest of technical edicts it did not rise to meet the fundamental challenges of a changing business environment. It did not determine the course of action. It did not set the trend. Its creativity was, to all intents and purposes, bankrupt. As member firms (including some of its leaders) milked the market, the profession became opulent and arrogant; and remote from its own future. As businesses, the larger firms became absolutely average, and blissfully ignorant of their own shortcomings, whilst today they sit out the recession, this hiccup in history, so that they may resume, in a more congenial atmosphere, their contribution to the graceful degradation of our profession; remembering this very traumatic period as though it were only a bad dream, or at worst a nightmare, and so something to be forgotten.

So what of the future ?

Australia today is at one of the most critical cross-roads in its history. Decisions being made now will determine the very nature of our political, social, and economic well-being, both for the rest of this decade and well into the next millennium.

Vital to the securing of a favourable outcome to this challenge is the globalization of the business activities of Corporate Australia.

With massive and emerging markets on our doorstep, a new political, social, and economic order in the old Communist world, a European Economic Community and a North American Free Trade Area each set to claim what each believe to be rightfully theirs, Australia must carve out its own niche.

To be a meaningful part of the Australian success story, to be part of creating the future, a radical redefinition of the profession is needed. These so-called professional service organizations must, themselves, become businesses; and in every sense of the term. They must become trend setters. Their offerings must address fundamental business needs. They must create original contributions for the beneficial use of the business world. In short, their products and services must add significant value to the wants and needs of their clients.

As Corporate Australia expands into overseas markets, and on a global basis, these professional service businesses must get alongside those companies. The profession must carve out a new niche, multidimensional in nature, transforming itself from an accountancy bias (being a fundamental which has served us well for much of this past thirty years and more) into a profession of genuine business mentors; standing, as of right, side-by-side with the business leaders of our times; recognized for our vision, and our capacity to initiate, create, design, develop, and deliver high-value-added offerings that are of significance to clients.

We must rediscover the plot.

Corporate Australia, as it embraces the globalization of its businesses is, itself, deficient. It is clear (as gleaned from meetings held myself with some one hundred or so senior executives in many industries) that one of the weakest management functions is that of 'Strategic Management' itself. This is the function which underpins the very essence of responsible leadership and business decision-making. As though oblivious to the devastating strategic management debacles of the last decade, companies sally forth, gladly courting potential disasters, great and small, as they correctly expand into new world markets (whether with new or revised products and services or through the acquisition of new businesses) and in countries with unfamiliar values and cultures, and where even the quality of management may be questionable; yet the effective strategic management of their new global business enterprises has not been addressed or, at least, it has not been addressed adequately.

Based on the aforementioned meetings, strategic management deficiencies were evident. In the worst cases the dynamic process of strategic management was equated with the static process of strategic planning and which planning process itself is ill-suited to the strategic management of global activities; whilst in virtually all cases it was acknowledged that strategic management is an ad hoc process that was probably driven by events, or crises, using outdated frameworks and methodologies, and that was generated by a process or approach which was definitely not systematized in an appropriate way.

Strategic management is the most fundamental dimension in the total management of a business enterprise. It is all pervading. Its consequences are vital. Strategic management increases the probability of sustainable business success. It deals with matters fundamental. And fundamental matters have significant consequences; both favourable and unfavourable. Best business practice demands sound strategic management. Without sound strategic management (and without the effective systematization of strategic management then strategic management cannot be sound) then boards of directors, top executives, and senior management are, indeed, negligent; and shareholders and lenders alike, should beware.

The action required is simple.

Auditors should redefine their role and demand, in terms of the 'going concern' principle, to examine the strategic management systems of Corporate Australia (or they themselves may be deemed negligent and be able to look forward to being even more prominent participants in the ever growing industry of litigation) and explicitly report thereon. Boards of directors should seek the assurance of such systems (requiring initially a review and then, as deemed appropriate, the design, the development, and the implementation of such systems) or suffer the consequences, themselves, of costly litigation. Insurance companies offering professional indemnity and directors and officers insurance should require, as a condition of negligence cover, frequent reviews of such systems. Lenders should insist upon such systems for the protection of their funds. Whilst shareholders (supposedly the ultimate beneficiaries of corporate wisdom) should require the implementation and the maintenance of fundamentally sound strategic management systems; and which systems should be targeted not only at reducing their risk of loss but, more importantly, at ensuring opportunity-recognition, creation, and development through the systematic day-by-day, week-by-week and month-by-month strategic management of opportunities; thereby helping to ensure the delivery of improved benefits to themselves.

The profession has the power to require the review of strategic management systems (together with their implementation and use) whilst with this power it also has the ability to truly transform itself into a body of professional service businesses; being professional businesses which, once again, can become natural business partners to the corporate world, and thereby providing an essential and fundamental underpinning to the successful globalization of Corporate Australia.

The preceding two articles, it will be appreciated, were written because what is implored therein does not occur. The failure of the accountancy profession to embrace its own responsibilities (for it has done much to avoid those responsibilities) has, today, resulted in that profession being a major contributor to the needless debilitation of our society. Whilst the accountancy profession continues to equivocate in relation to, and concerning, its real responsibilities then debilitation will, without doubt, continue to weave its wretched course (although probably in a somewhat less dramatic, but equally wicked way, as that which occurred during the past decade or more) as those who lead the profession cower from the challenges of our times; preferring to shirk their duties and their responsibilities whilst imposing the penalty for their deceptive behaviour on many and countless others, and whose pain and suffering is not felt by those wrongdoers . . . . for you can be sure that where there is institutionalized incompetence, or merely an institutionalized lack of competence, then there is no personal guilt. There is no feeling of personal responsibility.

Also, much has not been disclosed with regard to the strategic well-being of companies for simply the financial community itself has little knowledge of what the accountancy profession, and not least of all the larger firms, do not do in relation to the going concern principle, for the financial community itself is truly deficient in knowledge, understanding, and insight in that area of audit and accountancy practice. Those preparing accounts and those auditing accounts, in reality, do not know what they are looking at (the cutting-edge of that reality was revealed with the corporate disasters which occurred during the past ten years) and so the profession does not examine the fundamentals in any meaningful way. The profession has failed to become competent to carry out its work, whilst the financial community, including stockbrokers, merchant bankers, commercial bankers, investment advisers, financial institutions, as well as many others, have failed to become competent enough to know that the accountancy profession lacks competence; or, alternatively, they have failed to stand up and declare their knowledge of that fact.

The myth that the knowledge-based service sector, including that of the accountancy profession, is in some way inherently superior to other sectors of the business world has, by now, probably been dispelled. The accountancy profession is neither sophisticated nor is it exemplary. The members of that profession may not wear blue shirts and they may not wear dirty overhauls. Indeed, they may present well and sound knowledgeable. But let me tell you, and based on my own experience, there are more arseholes per square inch in the world than you could possibly imagine, and most of them wear a suit. Having said this, it is pointed out that the behaviour of all members of our profession, and not least of all those who hold the position of partner in the first and second tier firms (and which larger firms are de facto components in the structure of our profession) is not necessarily similar to that which was identified earlier in this chapter, for those people who were referred to previously are the service industry's equivalent of the *basic* production line supervisor in a *basic* mass production factory; and their type of behaviour is well and truly conducive to nothing that is appropriate to the advancement and development of our profession. Their behaviour is a glimpse at the ugly face of de-professionalization. In essence, and as with a pail of milk, there is a lot of good stuff in the bucket (that is, our profession contains many good people who are doing much good work) but, like that pail of milk, there is some scum floating on the top, in both moral and ethical terms; and that is so whether the top is located in the larger firms, in industry or commerce, or elsewhere. Neither the Institute nor the Society will want to read about these things; for they are not good. But with regard to the things that are discussed in this chapter [for it is emphasized that we are not addressing moral, ethical, and intellectual matters in a trivial way (for we all fail at that level no matter how good may be our intentions) but, rather, we are addressing those dimensions in a fundamental sense] the profession must change, and it must change swiftly; for its culture has been corrupted, and by their type of behaviour.

Generally, it may be stated that slowly but surely, and not least of all through apathy, arrogance, and intellectual impoverishment, the profession has become bankrupt. Reactive expediency has been a real problem in the accountancy profession. The leadership would probably not see it that way. They may well not see relative degradation at all. The profession, however, is well and truly hooked into the follower mentality. Virtually all of its so-called 'breakthroughs' have already been broken through elsewhere in the world, and often some years previously. My own leading-edge work which has produced an absolute abundance of opportunities for application in fields ranging from corporate governance, through the strategic management of companies in their entirety, onto the forecasting of the probability of excellent, sound, or poor business performance and success, not to mention the debilitation or even the ultimate demise of companies, would seem to be too difficult for our profession to embrace; even for purposes of going concern evaluations. Until the profession in Australia finds its own identity, and until it embraces the future with confidence, it will continue to be blighted by that most odorous of mentalities which dictates that all things worth doing must emanate from overseas. That attitude of mind, epitomized by the 'anywhere but here' philosophy, can only be self-defeating.

Despite what was stated previously, and with regard to the fact that not all partners in the large firms behave in the non-professional way in which certain partners of high standing in those firms actually do behave (and hopefully those delinquents and others are, in reality, a small percentage of the total) it is, nonetheless, the powerful partners in the large firms who are on trial for their 'crimes' against society; for, indeed, it is they who have created a bankrupt profession. It is their values, and it is the values and cultures which they have allowed to develop and to flourish in their firms, which have facilitated the dysfunctionality which the profession faces today; for it is they who have had, and still have, the power to change the profession; and for the better.

I personally may be condemned for daring to raise these issues in the public arena; and this despite the fact that these matters are very much in the public interest. I may well be told that I could have addressed such matters in a different way. Those platitudes are, however, a fiction. Constructive criticism and invigorating discussion, as was indicated previously, are not exactly traits of the accountancy profession. Negotiation in environments with the characteristics and the attributes that are portrayed by this profession is achieved through confrontation. For only then is worthwhile action taken. Only then is real attention given to the fundamental issues and challenges of our times. Confrontation may not be an emotively acceptable term. Consensus. Discussion. Reasonable interaction. And all that stuff is more congenial and more easily accepted. But reality is different. Only when those in power are grabbed by the short and curlies, and those short and curlies are given a tug, and a good hard tug at that, will their hearts and their minds follow. No, the leaders of the accountancy profession should not be looked up to, and adored and glorified, for they have failed our society, and in a fundamental way; and they continue to fail our society. They have gladly embraced collapsing worlds. Simultaneously they have embraced superficial success and fundamental failure. The massive fee incomes of the large firms do not, in themselves, equate with the strategic well-being of the accountancy profession. The large accountancy firms are moving towards becoming (and, from their perspective, correctly so) multi-disciplinary professional businesses. As their areas of activity become more concerned with management consultancy, computers, technology, and the provision of various outsourcing services, and anything else that is somewhat remote from professional accountancy (and whilst they also continue to embrace other disciplines, including not least of all that of legal work, and even real estate) then you have got to wonder where the accountancy profession, and business advising, reside.

The profession must play its cards. And it must let the dice roll. But it must, and it must most positively, play its cards, and in a way in which we can all see and appreciate. The accountancy profession can no longer sit on the fence and, by default, be taken over by, and be subsumed into, the emerging professional service businesses (and without our agreement) and this is so no matter how successful and valuable may be those emerging businesses. Despite any rules or regulations of the accountancy profession with regard to who is qualified and who is not qualified to do what, sheer influence and reality itself (and the good intentions of others . . . . but which intentions may be remote from the best interests of the profession) are far more powerful in determining our future. Merely because the President of the Institute or the President of the Society is an appropriately qualified accountant, or that those who serve the profession in an official capacity, on one committee or another, are suitably qualified, does not mean that the best interests of the accountancy profession (when it is viewed from the perspective of the accountancy profession) are being correctly developed, or are being appropriately addressed, or served. The President of the Institute of Chartered Accountants in Australia at this time was previously a most senior partner in Andersen Consulting. He is now head of EDS in Australia. That company, internationally, is a multi-billion dollar provider of outsourcing services. Whilst it is also a company that has recently merged with a non-accountancy-based management consultancy business. There is, at least on the face of it, nothing wrong with this situation. The President of the Institute has every right to hold that position. Who knows. Perhaps it was his turn to be President. [I wonder when it will be my turn to be President. I guess there must be several thousand members ahead of me, so by that time I think I will be very old.] This apart, one may well ask where is the accountancy profession heading? The answer may be, at least symbolically, in the same direction as has already been taken, and on a personal basis, by the (as I write) current President of the Institute of Chartered Accountants in Australia !!!

Much has been said . . . . and much remains unsaid.

Strategically, however, the profession has got it wrong. Let's not mince words. I am looking here at the underlying degradation of the accountancy profession. I am addressing the broad sweep of things. I am focusing on the big picture. I am considering the fundamental level and thereabouts. I am making powerful statements with regard to blame for the strategic stuff-ups in the basic strategy of our profession. And I am stating that those basic stuff-ups reside fairly and squarely with the leadership of our profession and not least of all with those leaders who have been in residence during the past fifteen years and more. These are the people who, during that period, have been at or near the top of the large professional practices in this country; as well as others. These are those professionals who present themselves as being the highest calibre Chartered Accountants. Its a laugh. They have made one basic mistake after another. Their leadership has reduced the profession to one of mediocrity. Yes, the plumbers, the joiners, and the bricklayers of our profession, being those who have led our profession during this period have, indeed, created a profession of plumbers, joiners, and bricklayers !!!!!

Although the image and reputation of the Institute of Chartered Accountants would seem to have generally remained in tact [it still has the appearance, albeit somewhat soiled and tarnished, of a professional body which is, if not in command, then one which is still abreast of the situation in the business world] the reality is different. The very reason for the existence of the profession, its basic purpose, has been eroded. It has been eaten away, as though by white ants. It has been gobbled up from the inside by its own professional termites. Through their actions, and their inaction, they have failed to maintain and to enhance the very substance of the profession. They have failed to meet the challenges of the business world. They have failed to be leaders. And they have failed society. And society itself has paid the price. And that price continues to be paid to this very day. The agony, the pain, and the suffering of many was a direct or an indirect consequence of professional incompetence or, at best, a lack of competence. But it was also worse than that for that level of incompetence, or lack of competence, was not only transactional in form, but it was also institutionalized. It was, and by implication, condoned by the profession through basic deficiencies in its own written standards. The accountancy profession to this very day (and even under the new standards which were recently issued) continues to support an underlying philosophy which reinforces the failure by our profession to come to terms with business realities and a relevant reporting thereof. It has failed to embrace new philosophies and new paradigms. It has, and in an overwhelming sense, failed to address the fundamental wants and needs of our society. And this is so because the profession has failed to address fundamental matters of accountancy in order to, and in a relevant way, meet the challenges of our times.

Paradoxically, and at the cutting-edge of reality, the accountancy profession today, is form with little substance !!!!!

Much is done . . . . High perceived value is delivered . . . . But low real value is obtained . . . . for when the profession does not know the state of the strategic well-being of a business enterprise then the very foundations on which it builds its edifice are rotten. That on which the accountancy profession relies for the credibility and integrity of general purpose financial reports is basically flawed.

The institutionalized damage which has been inflicted by the profession on individuals, families, and our society in total (and not least of all due to the fundamentally flawed credibility and integrity of its reporting philosophy and the intellectual impoverishment of the accountancy profession in the area of their own field of professional endeavour) has been, and continues to be, tremendous. And it is unforgivable. But it is even worse than that, for in their hypocrisy and by their very own actions, the leadership of the accountancy profession has endeavoured to deny this damage, or at least they have endeavoured to deny their responsibility for such damage whilst, in addition, the profession has failed to embrace the future in any meaningful way.

As for those who argue that Australia is a-ethical, and that these matters, by implication, should not be viewed too harshly, I can assure them that they are wrong. Australia, in this respect, is like many other countries in the world. Decent people want to be treated with decency. In the end most people want a reasonably secure income and a relatively happy life (however happiness may be defined) and the accountancy profession, through its basic failure to be ahead of the game, or at least on top of its own field of professional endeavour, has failed society.

Various people within the accountancy profession may feel some concern in relation to the matters which are raised in this chapter and, undoubtedly, in this book. Some of those people may feel concern, but support the raising of these matters . . . . whilst other people may feel concern, and oppose the raising of such matters. There will, of course, be all sorts of other combinations of feelings; and with the outward expression of those feelings ranging from that of genuine comment, one way or the other, through to a variety of contributions which will amount to nothing less than fence sitting; whilst other people will make seemingly profound statements but which statements will be no more than, nor no less than, disingenuous pronouncements concerning its content.

What should be remembered, as a basic premise and having consulted the Institute Handbook in relation to this particular matter, is that ethical considerations require members to conduct themselves in a manner which is consistent with the good reputation of their profession and to refrain from any conduct which might bring discredit to their profession.

This, in itself, is quite an interesting annunciation.

What, it may be asked, is conduct 'consistent with the good reputation' of the accountancy profession and what, in truth, is conduct 'which might bring discredit' to that profession?

I for one, given this expression of ethics, will continue to focus on matters of fundamental importance and of great magnitude and consequence; being matters which themselves may not be obvious but which may include aspects which are gross or debilitating. It should be noted that by not raising fundamental deficiencies such as those concerning the moral, the ethical, and the intellectual impoverishment of the accountancy profession (in effect, by being 'ethically muzzled' or, on reflection, should that be 'unethically muzzled') who is doing who a favour. Surely supporting the views of the in-crowd is *not* what the ethical annunciation clause requires. If it does, then it's a bit like the type of revelations we've heard from the Royal Commission into the Police Force in New South Wales. Those who knew, by keeping quiet, allowed the innocent to become victims (like shareholders, stakeholders, and society in general became the victims of the accountancy profession) and those who spoke up were victimized. Sure, by keeping quiet the honest cop didn't rock the boat; they kept their jobs; and they were paid. Although some did resign from the force. But is that ethical? There again, whilst the various problems weren't crystallized then people didn't have explicit concerns with regard to their police force, and they seemed to be fairly happy. But many people 'knew' that things weren't right. Well that's the same in the accountancy profession. We are not doing what society expects of us and nor are we doing what we know society should expect of us (and that is so in relation to fundamental matters even after the application of the latest pronouncements of the profession with regard to what is required to be done in relation to the preparation and the audit of accounts) so unless those who do understand the big picture matters, and the broad sweep of things, are themselves prepared to put professional embarrassment aside at a profession-wide level (being a matter which, it would seem, is an insurmountable hurdle for some) and to demand a more morally responsible profession, then many more innocent victims will suffer at the hands of the accountancy profession; and we as a profession will continue our degradation.

The aforementioned ethical annunciation is, itself, a double-edged sword; being one which is open to ambiguous interpretation with regard to who is upholding the good reputation of the profession (those who speak out or those who don't) and who is bringing discredit to the profession (those who seek fundamental change for the better or those who apply impoverished practices) whilst political activity in relation thereto (given an outbreak of war between those who wish to muzzle freedom of speech and those who support open discussion) could also run amok. Let us hope that the ethical enunciation clause is not intended to choke-off the discussion of important, significant, or fundamental matters no matter how awkward may be discussion of those issues. Given this, it is noted, at least from a benevolent perspective, that it is not that there is a wilful desire by the accountancy profession not to do what we should do (the intellectual capability resides within the profession to properly address the fundamentals . . . . I know, I have spent much of the last five years or so working on one or two fundamental matters myself . . . . and I have written in excess of four hundred pages of commercial property rights exploring various of the dimensions which relate to such matters) it is just that the leadership don't seem to understand what is required, so they don't do anything. After all, they talk to each other (and to other members of the in-crowd) and they seem to have assured themselves that when the profession did, indeed, visit the reality of its own incompetence (or should that be its lack of competence) during the past ten years or more, it wasn't the profession (being the preparers and auditors of accounts) who lacked competence (or, alternatively, who were incompetent) it was just the extraordinary circumstances of those times. The profession, it was agreed, was a victim. And this despite it being gutless, spineless, and useless when faced with the cutting-edge of its own reality. A lack of competence, or indeed the presence of incompetence, it would seem, has nothing to do with our moral, our ethical, or our intellectual impoverishment. In fact, within the profession (and what better authority can there be for such a view) the belief is well established that as we were not incompetent, and as we did not lack competence then, after all, we are not professionally bankrupt. How wonderful is this news, and not least of all for all those who have been devastated or destroyed by our abilities and our capabilities. How wonderful is psychological rationalization.

As the 'all singing, all dancing, humming like a bee' neo-classical establishment, and in particular the 'I couldn't agree more with myself' dull, boring, and uninteresting accountancy profession, grapples, in both a personal and a corporate way, with the psychological dimensions of the aforementioned matters I would point out that John Cleese, in quasi training mode, once made an address to an upper crust audience in the United States. Perhaps the audience was part of their establishment. Whatever it was, this videod speech made the somewhat profound point that you can't say **'Well we got that right . . . . Now let's fix it !!!!!'** because life doesn't work like that. You first have to admit that you got it wrong. Only then can you really begin to fix it. Only then is the mind sufficiently receptive to embrace reality. How many of the chairmen, the chief executives, or the managing partners of those large accountancy firms, upon hearing about or, perhaps, upon reading this book will react along the lines that 'He will never be retained by our firm !!!!!' rather than in the more appropriate and positive way that 'His comments are cutting, but they are true, even if we don't wish to acknowledge that fact . . . . Let's talk !!!!!' Whilst also, and in addition thereto, what will be the reaction of those with power and with authority, and who lead Corporate

Australia . . . . for this book affects them equally; and its substance may have a fundamental impact on the future of their companies.

The accountancy profession is much in need of a transformation, but transformational leadership is not exactly what has, in reality, been delivered by its leaders. Whilst many businesses, and even whole industries such as that of telecommunications, have been busy transforming themselves during the past five, seven, and even ten years, the accountancy profession itself has continued to remain all but dormant in fundamental areas of importance to its own future. Some Presidents, it would seem, came into office to achieve nothing, and they were very successful at it. They would appear, and then they would disappear, only to be distinguished by being undistinguished. You would hardly have known that they had ever existed. The status of President was enough. The leadership, both inside and outside the official bodies, seemed to have no real perception of the profession as a crucial, underlying, societal force, and one which, both for its own benefit and for the benefit of our society, needed to transform, and so embrace the challenges of our times. The focus was on problem avoidance (and preferably at the expense of others, and by the erosion of our own moral and ethical standards) rather than on opportunity search and crystallization. The profession, in all this time since the events of 1987 and thereafter, and whilst others all around us were in a state of transformation, failed to move swiftly enough to transform itself. The accountancy profession, by its own actions and its inaction, has now perhaps earned the right for outside forces to institute that transformation.

Yes, the accountancy profession, in relative terms, is a bankrupt profession, and this is so not least of all on moral, on ethical, and on intellectual grounds.

This must change.

Having read what you have read, your own reactions to this book (being both your initial reactions and your subsequent reactions) will tell you a lot about yourself. This is a point which is worth noting. But whatever you may think of what I have written so far.

Please . . . . Be my guest . . . . Read on . . . .

Chapter Three

The Visionaries & The Visions

Once upon a time I and about three or four hundred other people attended a Liberal Party State Council meeting. A group of us were stood around chatting in a sort of foyer area just off the main auditorium. We could see through the large double doors into the meeting room and, if one cared to glance that way, you could actually see, hurling forth from the podium, and into the well positioned microphone, no lesser person than Bronwyn Bishop. I guess someone in our group must have looked up to see what was going on and happened to remark that hardly anyone was listening to her. At that point, and from a well seasoned member, came the unforgettable response 'Not to worry . . . . She'll be in the Senate soon . . . . And then nobody will be listening to her !!!!!'

I can't help recalling those words when I think of the Institute of Chartered Accountants and, in reality, the profession in general. Having shown our incompetence, or at least a lack of competence, in assessing the well-being of business enterprises (remember we couldn't spot a corporate disaster when it was staring us in the face) one can only wonder whether business will ever again listen to us with regard to the fundamentals. Is it possible, one may ask, that the profession has, in effect, also moved itself into a place (in this case in the business world) where no-one will listen to it; for in that place what we have to offer or address counts for little, for our offerings are not at the cutting-edge of business. Put simply, what we deal with is not first order fundamental reality.

What then is the profession trying to achieve? What is it trying to deliver? What essential concept, or indeed what group of essential concepts, are encapsulated in a set of financial statements? Could it be truth? Well not really . . . in fact . . . not at all !!!! Or maybe its fairness? But fairness with regard to what? If the foundations upon which accounts are presented have more in common with a chocolate 'aero' bar (being essentially porous and likely to melt in the heat) than with the realities of business, then how, in the end, can anything be presented fairly? Perhaps its trying to deliver confidence? But is that confidence in relation to the past or is that confidence in relation to the future; or is it both? Indeed, what reliance can, in practice, be placed on a set of accounts and what does an audit report which is based on accounts that are prepared by other professional accountants really mean? [Oh, by the way, I can't remember when I stopped voting Liberal (I vote Democrat now) but some time after that I also dropped out of the Party. I hope that one day Bronwyn will cease that silly monarchy stuff and become a republican. Perhaps Prime Minister Howard will take up the cause. Oh yes, and just for the record, Bronwyn (as you know) now has a safe seat in the House of Representatives. But I've also begun to wonder whether anyone in there is listening to her either ?!!!!] It seems to me that the nearer you get to the top the more remote you become from reality and from the things that ordinary people want. The trouble at the top is that half your life is spent in incestuous activity. You come to believe that what you think is important, actually is important, and anyway, the usual dysfunctional in-fighting that occurs in the upper echelons tends to divert energy towards the vile and away from the vision.

The point being made, and in relation to the Bronwyn anecdote, is that strategic mistakes occur. What may be good initiatives (some are bad or mediocre to start with, and are just presented as good, whilst others are composed of a whole kaleidoscope of qualities; with yet others degenerating into adverse circumstances) do not always come to fruition in the timescale which is anticipated or, alternatively or in addition thereto, they do not come to fruition in the way in which they were originally envisaged. Some initiatives never come to fruition at all. The difference in the two dimensions is that Bronwyn may be a public figure, but whether or not she, personally, is a success is not a matter of public interest, for she can easily be replaced. For the profession not to be successful or to fail society is, however, unquestionably a matter of public interest; for there are no easy alternatives thereto and the cost to society of mediocrity and spasmodic failure will be, is now, and has been in the past, colossal. [The age of our golden success, for that term is relative to the challenges of the times, was in the past (it is not now) whilst our next golden age is still located some time into the future.] It is important that society listens to the profession, but it is also the onerous responsibility of the profession to ensure that its messages, and its deeds, are of value to our society; being of fundamental value and, at the least, relevant. It is, consequently, in the public interest that the profession is successful whilst, at one and the same time, it is in the interests of the accountancy profession that we do not lack societal relevance, or become irrelevant to society. It is important then, as a corollary, that we as a profession are focused in our role, and are at the leading-edge of relevance; even if that transformation hurts the powerful. And this is so whether or not the powerful are inside our profession.

Isn't it interesting that invariably it is those very institutions that are so unquestionably accepted by society as being the vehicles for advancement which are so often the bodies which, in reality, constrain progress and cripple vision. [Universities exhibit this particular trait on some dimensions.] The profession, to all intents and purposes, is an out and out follower. I shouldn't be saying this for, no doubt, someone somewhere will be getting their knickers in a knot, or their Y-fronts twisted, but you know, sometimes what they offer as leading-edge stuff may be nowhere near that status, but because pronouncements are made by a respected establishment body, or perhaps by some well known or high status professional person, their proclamations are accepted as being advanced; and few people even bother to question the implied assumptions. Often the profession just follows the UK. But normally there is some variation on their recommendations and practices just to show the world that the profession here has a mind of its own. Creativity to the profession is, unfortunately, an anathema. It is merely an incremental move along some obscure or remote dimension and which move, to many in the world of business, would be virtually irrelevant; and with such moves often being non-fundamental in nature. [Incidentally, and talking of virtual irrelevance and non-fundamental in the same breath, do you think that next time you technocrats pick up a bottle of beer and get that *'I think I feel a techo coming on'* urge, that you could do us a favour and don't devise the *seventeenth* way in which to present a lease on a balance sheet but, rather, perhaps you could try to address the underlying basis upon which general purpose financial reports are prepared; it would be more relevant and far more useful to society.] Quantum leaps and order of magnitude changes have well and truly been foreign to many past leaders of our profession [they much preferred their zones of comfort] being concepts which, in themselves, strike fear into the hearts and the minds of people everywhere and, based on my observations, not least of all into the hearts and the minds of the leaders of our profession. We, as a profession, I feel, have somehow been willing to sacrifice society for our self-interest, and to hide behind 'a need for' international agreement, or 'the need to apply' best practice; and this has been so even when best practice wasn't best at all !!!!!

[To be fair, some of the leaders of the accountancy profession did make an effort, years after the stock market crash of 1987 and years after the years of incompetent preparation and auditing of the accounts of so many of the major companies in Australia. The Institute and the Society supported a small working party to produce what became known as the 'Expectation Gap' report. Its actual title was 'A Research Study On Financial Reporting And Auditing - Bridging The Expectation Gap' and which study was first published in early 1994. The document, which ran to some two hundred (200) pages in length, was very good. I personally spent about three (3) weeks reading and analyzing the document. I had thought {how deluded can you be} that at last those in power in the profession were going to do something worthwhile, so I prepared and then submitted a twenty (20) page contribution, including a covering letter, which addressed various matters that were of particular interest to me. I shouldn't have bothered.]

In my professional lifetime I can only recall two real visions in the accountancy profession. These visions were, of course, driven by visionaries. Given this, it is evident that visionary occurrences in the profession are about as scarce as chicken's teeth. The first visionary event has already been referred to in my 'Black Hole' article on corporate governance which article was included earlier in this book. This major happening occurred in the UK in late 1976; or, at least, that is when it was revealed in all its glory for public and professional consumption. This first vision was the current cost accounting revolution. The guidance manual ran to four hundred (400) pages. It included the exposure draft and the valuation guidance notes which were prepared by The Royal Institute of Chartered Surveyors. The current cost accounting initiative was prepared for the Accounting Standards Committee (the governing body of which was composed of the then six major accountancy bodies in the UK) and by the Inflation Accounting Steering Group. The whole thing had, in fact, been prepared at the behest of the Inflation Accounting Committee which was set up by the British Government under the chairmanship of Sir Francis

Sandilands. The current cost accounting proposal had been developed in an attempt to correct the deficiencies of historical cost accounting and which latter system failed to provide much of the information which was primarily required by the users of accounts. [Has anything changed?] At that time the challenges of inflation were rampant and worldwide. The point was made that for current cost accounting to become the generally accepted system of accounting it must have the ability to form the basis of a comprehensive accounting system which would embrace all forms of financial reporting; including those reporting systems which were designed for use by management. This leading-edge and path-breaking proposal, as was indicated previously in this book, was rejected by the membership of the aforementioned bodies in 1977. It was, indeed, all too difficult. The battle for an order of magnitude change in the management practices of listed companies was lost. Mediocrity had won the day. Some of the more easily understood aspects of inflation accounting were introduced later, and they flowed through to Australia, both at that time and after, but in reality the substance of the particular initiatives amounted to little more than a shadow of the original vision. It may be noted that today, in 1996, the accountancy profession recommends, and indeed strongly recommends, that all entities present *supplementary* financial reports which are based on current cost accounting in addition to their conventional financial reports; whilst stating that current cost accounting statements may, and as an alternative, be presented as the prime financial statements. It has taken over twenty (20) years for the profession to still only be at the stage of strongly recommending supplementary statements based on current cost accounting. Yes, a real visionary opportunity had, without doubt, been foregone.

The second visionary event, in the Australian context, was that which was referred to above, being the 'Expectation Gap' report and which report showed much promise. [Isn't it interesting how visions come out of crises?] I personally thought that the report showed so much promise that, as already mentioned, I set aside a fair amount of time to devote to this initiative. My submission in response to the report, which was dated the 17th February, 1994, was limited to one fundamental underlying theme, being that of the strategic well-being of business enterprises. My contribution considered the report in relation to that one theme both in total and with regard to each of its specific recommendations. An assessment concerning the contribution (positive, negative, or neutral) which each report recommendation made to bridging the expectation gap, was set out in my submission. Many other matters which were also important were not addressed by myself.

It should be noted that the expectation gap had been divided, in the expectation gap report, into two broad parts; being that part of the gap which was caused by 'unreasonable expectations' and that part of the gap which was caused by 'inadequate performance' by the profession. Unreasonableness may, however, be in the eye of the beholder and may appear to arise due to, amongst other reasons, the impoverished knowledge of the profession in the area of strategic management. Whilst inadequacy will depend on where the standards are pitched. The report divided 'inadequacy' into two sub-components with that division being determined relative to the existing standards as laid down by the profession and legislation. The first sub-component related to deficiencies which could reasonably be expected should not occur relative to the standards. The second sub-component related to deficiencies which reasonably should not occur but for which requirements in relation thereto were not particularly addressed in the standards.

The expectation gap report itself states that 'the area most seriously being questioned by parties outside the profession is the component described as *inadequate* performance' and upon which aspect the working party placed significant emphasis. It is noted that the easiest areas in which to elicit comment are those that are evident and this is so because to question something which does not exist often requires much deeper knowledge, understanding, and insight in relation to one or more matters. The working party also recommended that the focus of the profession should be on pro-active matters and not least of all in relation to corporate governance. The greatest failure of the report, however, and when taking these two aspects together, is its failure to pro-actively address non-existent matters in the area of corporate governance.

The authors of the expectation gap report should, however, be congratulated for recommending that the profession should take an aggressive position with regard to its initiatives and to fundamentally reject any posture which admits a dependency upon regulators or other parties. The report stated specifically that *'the accounting bodies must take a leading role on corporate governance and be prepared to exert overt pressure on entities which do not meet corporate governance standards'* and which view is very different and, indeed, is the antithesis of the submission which was made by the profession to the ASX in relation to this topic, and which submission was made almost exactly one year later. Recommendation 13 of the submission to the ASX stated that *'the disclosure benchmarks should **not** require the company's auditor to be involved in attesting to the accuracy of the corporate governance disclosures'* and which statement was presented as the considered opinion of the accountancy profession in Australia. How pathetic.

The juxtaposition of these vastly different views (being the view expressed in the expectation gap report and the view expressed in the corporate governance submission) is quite interesting. The former document, which was obviously authored by progressives (irrespective of whether or not you agree with all of its contents) implored the profession, in a fundamental way, to take the lead whilst, one year later, the anathema of the accountancy profession towards vision, creativity, and leadership was overwhelmingly evident in the latter enunciation issued by the retards of progress. Given the expression of these very different views then one is left to wonder whether or not the leadership has any worthwhile philosophical underpinnings with regard to the modus operandi of the accountancy profession.

Now let me be quite clear. Because one agrees with, or does not agree with, the particular findings or recommendations that are put forward by a working party which has examined a particular situation does not, in itself, determine whether or not that person is a promoter or retarder of progress. It may mean that, given due consideration, one may not agree with the particular findings or course of action which is being recommended. If that person, in fact, believes that there are other positive approaches which would more beneficially achieve the targeted objectives (or, indeed, any enhanced objectives) then that is a positive situation. My view in relation to the expectation gap report is that the underlying philosophy can be encapsulated in the statement (my words, not theirs) things are not right, they can be improved, and we, as the accountancy profession, should take a pro-active stance in relation thereto in addition to assuming active control of the improvement process. I agree with the aforementioned, albeit partially implied, philosophy of the expectation gap report and this is so despite my specific criticisms of that report. In addition I also believe that the authors of the expectation gap report did, in all reality, anticipate an inclusive process, and one of genuine discussion and debate, prior to the finalization of that document in, what was intended to be, a published report and action plan.

Reality, however, was different.

My opening point stated that in general terms the expectation gap report represented an important development in re-establishing our profession in its rightful position as an important and integral member of the business world. It went on to state that during the previous decade the profession, whilst progressing, had declined in relative importance; having been 'side-lined' due, not only to our own actions, but also to our failure to change, at least at the same rate and in the same direction, as society in general, the business community in total, the financial community as a sub-set thereof and, more specifically, in accordance with the actual and implied wants and needs of both shareholders and stakeholders.

These are points that are still being made in this book today.

The submission went on to point out that we have become little more than a 'bits and pieces' profession; being riddled with niche products and services but with few, if any, substantial new and emerging product and service offerings. The expectation gap report, it was stated, represented an opportunity and important step towards the redefinition of our profession. My submission contended that the report may even be the vehicle which has the potential to trigger the attention of the many visionaries amongst our ranks, being visionaries who may have all but given up the accountancy profession as a lost cause. The last sentence of the first point of my contribution in response to the expectation gap report read 'Let us hope that it (the expectation gap report) is a vehicle propelling an opportunity without bounds for, sadly, we need such a vehicle'. These were stirring words.

But would they stir the dead ?!!!!

In my written submission I addressed various of the matters which were raised in the expectation gap report including those which addressed the simplification of accounts, the adoption of a management responsibility statement, and the inclusion in the general purpose financial reports of a management discussion and analysis document.

I was most surprised that the working party could find no merit in pursuing a requirement to introduce simplified financial reporting as, after all, simplified reporting was not intended to replace conventional reporting but, rather, it was intended to be in addition thereto. If only a small percentage of those parties who are confused by non-simplified financial reports were to obtain a genuine understanding of the 'big picture' by being provided with simplified financial reports (the 1995 Financial Statements of BHP exceed fifty pages and with an additional forty-five pages being needed for its Report to Shareholders) then some progress would have been made with regard to the bridging of the expectation gap. The management responsibility statement was good but it was minimal in content. In my own opinion the management discussion and analysis document, as a concept, could have been advantageous in enhancing the user-friendliness of financial reports. However, I rejected the document in total on the basis that the recommended content would probably not reduce the expectation gap and that it may very well increase that gap.

What on earth were these visionaries thinking about?

Part of my submission in relation to this point was that comments with regard to risks and uncertainties which could affect the future activities of a business enterprise (other than those risks and uncertainties which are already common knowledge or are of such a general nature that comment thereon adds little or nothing to understanding such matters) may, in practice, add to the provision of misleading information. The management discussion and analysis document may well be a good internal document but as a document for external use it could end up being dynamite. It may, in principle, be admirable to be open and frank with regard to current perceptions concerning future risks and uncertainties but we, as a profession, would be entering a proverbial minefield and may, in practice, run the risk of being naive in relation to such matters. [One can only wonder how many decades ago it was since the 1980s.] The realities of business are such that various reportable, but inconsequential, risks and uncertainties would be discussed and analyzed for public consumption in general purpose financial reports (as though such risks and uncertainties were important) whilst yet other risks and uncertainties (and which other risks and uncertainties were 'unfortunately' not foreseen at the time) may never be discussed. The real issues that are not already public knowledge, or tantamount thereto, would therefore probably not emerge in this type of report, whilst their crystallization (when some of those matters did occur and also reached the light of day) would be greeted with amazement and utter surprise. With regard to the audit responsibilities of the accountancy profession in relation to risks and uncertainties (for presumably we, as a profession, would not be leaving those shareholders and stakeholders who already have an expectation gap problem to the whims and the fancies of the politically astute) due caution would need to be exercised.

The fundamental principle underlying this matter is that which is concerned with the role of shareholders, as owners of a company, and the role of management as managers acting on behalf of the shareholders. Shareholders, who have delegated responsibility to the board of directors of a company to manage on their behalf, must acknowledge the location of that boundary whilst, likewise, the directors of a business enterprise must themselves reciprocate and recognize that such a boundary does, in fact, exist. Wisdom, therefore, is required in this relationship, and not a requirement to present in writing, and to the world at large, a catalogue of uncertainties and risks which may or may not occur (and in the particular manner in which the events are cognitively anticipated) but which, by their very revelation, may cause either unnecessary aggravation or, worse, the loss of opportunity, debilitation of the business enterprise, or the undoing of the company.

Whether or not risks and uncertainties are ever reported in the form recommended in the report, such an exercise (when viewed from the perspective of the expectation gap debate) would be self-defeating. It is evident that, for those risks and uncertainties which were honestly reported, the actual variation in outcome (even with all the goodwill in the world) could be tremendous.

The reportable risks and uncertainties may fizzle to nothingness or, alternatively, explode into monsters. Whilst unreported risks and uncertainties that crystallize and become public knowledge, or which are reported in hindsight, would undermine the credibility of such a report. Given this unfortunate situation, yet another category of risks and uncertainties, being those which are created by fast moving events, and which circumstances genuinely did not exist at the date of the relevant report, may appear and, in truth, become the most significant uncertain or risky events to impact the business enterprise in the reporting period. In my opinion the whole gambit of risks and uncertainties, and the formal reporting of those risks and uncertainties in the context of the preparation and audit of general purpose financial reports, would be fraught with difficulties, and would probably aggravate the expectation gap; and in a significantly adverse way.

Had the visionaries, in this case, left reality behind?

It was also suggested that comment be made with regard to the objectives and strategic plans of a business enterprise. This, at any meaningful level of revelation, was an even more inappropriate suggestion than was that which was referred to previously and in relation to risks and uncertainties. Not only do objectives and strategic plans contain all the conceptual problems commented upon above (for risks and uncertainties are themselves an integral part of objectives and strategic plans) but it is in those very areas of revelation that the identification of the potential for business success may be revealed, and to one's competitors. Motherhood statements in relation to objectives and strategic plans could only aggravate the existing expectation gap as such statements would fail to convey sufficient detail and insight with regard to known and unknown future fundamental initiatives of a business enterprise; adding further confusion as more and more detailed levels of information emerged over time and with regard to the specific actions and initiatives which were actually taken by a company. One can only ponder on whether Australasian business leaders such as Alan Bond, John Elliott, Christopher Skase, Kerry Packer, Robert Holmes a Court, Sir Ron Brierley, and Rupert Murdoch, as well as overseas business entrepreneurs such as Conrad Black, Tiny Rowland, or Robert Maxwell, all being past or present heads of major national and international business enterprises in which shareholders and stakeholders invested large amounts of capital and other resources, would genuinely have committed themselves to the revelation of their real strategic intentions and their strategic consequences; given, of course, that they actually knew of, cared about, or identified with the goals, the objectives, and the strategic plans which were postulated by their different levels of management.

[Parenthetically speaking, just imagine Kerry Packer and Rupert Murdoch reporting (whether continuously, quarterly, half-yearly, or annually) to their shareholders, stakeholders, and to the world at large, and in terms of their general purpose financial reports, with regard to their multi-hundred-million-dollar expenditures, costs, and investments in the areas of the Telecommunications Information Superhighway revolution, their Free-To-Air/Pay-TV activities, and their Australian Rugby League versus Super League visions (an important chunk of which expenditures, costs, and investments are in intangible benefits) and trying to assess in order to report to shareholders (and with a meaningful degree of accuracy) the known, unknown, and unknowable uncertainties and risks which their empires have embraced as a result of those initiatives (including the multi-million dollar cost of legal battles and potential damage awards) and all dimensions of which are to be assessed in 'crystal-ball-gazing' mode and, in addition thereto, divulge meaningfully, and to those same parties, their (non-motherhood) corporate and business enterprise strategies and which strategies are forever changing as reality itself unfolds, in often surprising form, and which strategy disclosures are severely hindered due to the fact that they themselves, being Kerry and Rupert, and even with their talents, simply don't know (although they may well have created many scenarios whether pleasant or otherwise) their own non-trivial strategies much below that of the big picture level and the broad sweep of things when operating in such awesomely dynamic and highly complex environments where not only are products, competitors, and markets appearing or disappearing, but are also changing in important, significant, and fundamental ways and at designated, ad hoc, and random points in time. {That sentence, if you happen to be interested, was two hundred and sixty-eight words in length . . . . but boy, does it convey the message.} What rubbish it is to even start to believe that meaningful statements, in the form proposed, and with regard to specific objectives, goals, strategies, tactics, risks, and uncertainties, can be set out in general purpose financial reports in such environmental conditions and, even worse, with the belief that a high degree of confidence can, in fact, be attached to those statements. (Forrest Gump wasn't quite right when he said that 'Life is like a box of chocolates; you never know what you're going to get' for that message is too static in nature. John Lennon probably captured it better when he wrote in one of his songs that 'Life is what happens to you while your busy making other plans' for those words have more dynamic connotations. Yes, life is turbulent, so why try to report it as though it isn't !!!!) Given the recommended actions, and under turbulent conditions, credibility would be absolutely crucified. The expectation gap would become massive. The accountancy profession, rather than playing games with these fugacious and ephemeral concepts, should get real about business. It needs to appreciate that there are other, more appropriate ways, in which to address this situation, and with a higher degree of confidence, than by the use of the recommended approaches in the expectation gap report. Whilst further, and to compound the situation, it is noted that those other ways are applicable to all environments (for turbulence is the order of the day and, of necessity, it needs to be embraced) and this is so for all business enterprises, whether they are large, medium, or small, and whether they are local, national, regional, multi-national, or transnational in nature. However, the praise which should go to the authors of the expectation gap report, and rightly so, and with regard to both of the aforementioned matters, as well as in relation to other matters, emanates from the fact that they, as people, wished to tackle the challenges of our times and, thereby, help to transport the accountancy profession into a new era of increased relevance to the world of business. This, at the very least, is their vision and, as such, they are indeed visionaries !!!!!]

Underlying the recommendation of the expectation gap report to include objectives and strategic plans in financial reports is a fundamental failure to appreciate reality and which reality is, in practice, located firmly in both the present and the unknown future environments of a business enterprise. Strategic planning, which was never a very effective tool in the arena of applied management, is a static rather than a dynamic management aid. Their most beneficial uses may be expected to be observed either in stable environments, when the critical factors for business success are indeed changing slowly and in small increments and, therefore, strategic plans (when anyone actually bothered to refer to them) remained relevant for some extended period of time or, alternatively, in turbulent environments, being the environmental type which may be expected to dominate during the next decade or more and when strategic plans, as a tool, are developed in order to 'stop the world' and take a snapshot of the then current and expected conditions with a view to assisting with the next short iteration of strategic decision-making; and which plans, on preparation, are accepted as having early redundancy and a very short life expectancy. These two environmental types in which the same tool, strategic planning, is used are dramatically different; whilst the purpose for which the strategic plans are developed are well and truly light-years apart. In the former case the plan is created with every intention to be used as 'the plan' for the future, whilst in the latter case it is a mere, and sometimes instantaneous, disposable that may have few enduring characteristics. The basic flaw with strategic plans is the implied belief that they can be achieved. That the myriad of variables can be controlled. That is the very essence of poor strategic management; for the philosophy of control, rather than that of management, predominates.

The statement which was made by the board of Coles Myer that it was considering moving away from its strategy of 'co-ordination and integration' to that of a 'disaggregation strategy' and which statement was followed by a statement that the 'disaggregation strategy' had, forthwith, been dumped and that the previous strategy had been reinstated, illustrates (and irrespective of this behavioural stupidity) not only the potential fragility of strategies in turbulent environments, but also the remoteness from reality of motherhood-type strategic statements. [Either strategy could, in concept, be developed in 'one hundred' different ways whilst each development could also be actioned in 'one hundred' different ways.] This vacillation is a glorious technicolour example of the frailty of strategies (at any organizational level) and is an example which just happened to be played out in the public arena. Many debates with regard to strategy would never surface for public consumption. Whilst other events of that nature may not even be recognized, by boards of directors or top management, as even having occurred where those parties are blase to such, albeit less dramatic, happenings. Sometimes the board, due to the rule of managerial bureaucracy and which bureaucracies tend to usurp board power, may not even know at all about such happenings. This situation was rumoured to have occurred, at least in the early stages of a recent strategy development, down at the NRMA.

I indicated in my written submission that, given the above, it would not be responsible for the accountancy profession to adopt the requirement for the inclusion of comments, in general purpose financial reports, with regard to the objectives and strategic plans of a business enterprise and, in particular, where such an initiative was, in fact, intended to bridge the expectation gap for, in non-stable environments, matters which could be perceived by many shareholders and stakeholders as being stable in nature (if they were to be reported at any level of practical relevance) would not materialize as such in reality, but would be very different.

Recommendations which, at first glance, seemed admirable were, on closer examination, riddled with cancers and of many different types. A similar statement could be made in relation to the report recommendation concerned with including management forecasts and budgets in general purpose financial reports. The expectation gap report recommended the investigation of the appropriateness of requiring the inclusion, in general purpose financial reports, of summarized twelve month cash flows and profit forecasts, along with the disclosure of the bases and major assumptions on which those budgets and forecasts were prepared and, further, that such an investigation should also examine whether or not it would be appropriate to express an audit opinion in relation thereto.

It is, without doubt, essential, as is mentioned in the expectation gap report, that there be a culture shift within our profession and, in particular, with regard to financial reporting and auditing. It was my view that such a shift in culture could be achieved in several different ways and that, in consequence, the accountancy profession should be careful that the public evidencing of such a shift did not, in itself, aggravate the expectation gap. It is evident that, in concept, the most obvious manner in which a shift in culture may be evidenced is by the incorporation of prospective, as well as historic, information in the general purpose financial reports of companies. Such information may include, as is implied in the report, budgets and forecasts, the credibility of which may then be reinforced by being subjected to the scrutiny of an audit. It is my view, however, that the inclusion of budgets and forecasts in financial reports would be fraught with difficulties (given the present strategically deficient state-of-the-art in the preparation and auditing of general purpose financial statements) and that such an initiative would almost certainly create a wider gap in expectations. This would occur because the vehicle for the delivery of the culture shift, being that of specific forecasts and budgets, would not be sufficiently accurate from one period to another and would, as a consequence thereof, undermine the integrity of the information. It must be appreciated that whether or not any particular budget or forecast will, in reality, turn out to be sufficiently accurate (and thereby provide integrity and credibility with regard to bridging the expectation gap) will not only depend on the technical skills and abilities of those involved in the preparation of those budgets or forecasts but, more importantly, that accuracy will be a direct derivative of the level of turbulence, and in particular in the external environment or multiple external environments, in which a business enterprise operates or, in reality, intends to operate. Given these two major dimensions (being skills and abilities as well as the level of environmental turbulence) a company, when reporting internally, may be able to tolerate resulting variability in actual outcomes; and may well re-forecast on a continual basis. When reporting in the public domain, however, relatively high degrees of accuracy, from one period to another, will probably be required by shareholders and stakeholders otherwise confusion may reign; whilst continual re-forecasting would, no doubt, undermine the credibility of any information so provided.

Knowledge of a client's business was also raised as being a very important dimension. A sound knowledge of the business should, of course, be fundamental to both those who prepare accounts and those who audit those accounts. This view is expressed in the report. The expectation gap report further states that an auditor needs to have a level of knowledge of the client, and of the client's industry, which will enable the auditor to identify the events, transactions, and practices that may have a significant impact on the financial information. The report indicates that knowledge of specialized industries is required. It is also indicated in the report that the level of knowledge required to undertake an effective audit engagement should include a general knowledge of the economy and industry within which the entity operates as well as a more particular knowledge of how the business entity operates. These matters would seem to address two broad dimensions of knowledge being those of general environmental knowledge and enterprise specific knowledge; whilst with regard to enterprise specific knowledge such knowledge may be viewed as being, on the one part, what may be termed 'component' knowledge and, on the other part, what may be termed 'transactional' knowledge. The purpose of the aforementioned knowledge is intended to allow those who prepare accounts as well as those who audit them to consider how such knowledge affects the financial reports when that knowledge is taken as a whole.

The expectation gap report states that professional requirements regarding the obligation of auditors to have knowledge of the business of a client is adequate and appropriate. This assertion with regard to adequacy and appropriateness is simply wrong and is one of the reasons why, as a profession, we failed to meet the challenges of our times. The recommended level of knowledge may be considered to be adequate and appropriate as a first iteration in obtaining knowledge of 'the business' of a client (in fact it is not) but there exists a significant *chasm* between the aforementioned type of knowledge and the ability to prepare or audit a set of accounts based on relevant knowledge; and this apart from other dimensions including those of understanding, insight, and wisdom. The chasm is both wide and deep. And the knowledge which is located in the chasm is that appertaining to the strategic realities of the business enterprise; and it was that particular lack of knowledge, understand, insight, and wisdom which facilitated the excesses of the 1980s and which lack thereof aggravated the disasters which emanated from that period. Although we may, as professionals, gain knowledge concerning, amongst other things, the corporate structure of a business, its markets, products, and services, the location of its production facilities, special legislation which may affect the entity, and an understanding of its information technologies (all of which may be termed profile knowledge) we know little about the specifics of the management of strategies. We, therefore, know little about the fundamental sustainability of what we are observing, or about the volatility of such sustainability or, for that matter, about its artificiality and, further, we make little or no attempt to find out about such things. Yet it is the strategic realities, and our lack of appreciation of those realities, which has contributed so greatly to the expectation gap for, because few of us can grasp 'strategy' in our hands (so as to say) and recognize its reality, we ignore the management of strategy and, along with it, its potentially devastating impacts, consequences, and outcomes for as indicated elsewhere in this book : 'what we don't know we don't value'. If it is so fundamental to the preparation and the audit of general purpose financial reports that a sound knowledge of the business of a company is obtained (as, without doubt, it is) then it is imperative that we also understand the strategic management processes of our clients, and evaluate them; and properly. The statement which is included in the expectation gap report that the situation is adequate and appropriate is, in essence, farcical.

In addition to this it is stated in the expectation gap report that preparers of financial reports and auditors are undergoing a re-education process with the development of the financial reporting conceptual framework. The education section in the report, in consequence, tends to address parties external to the accountancy profession. Supporting discussion under the two headings of education and communication (where they, in fact, focus on the accountancy profession) tend to address the age old matters of fraudulent financial reporting, the prevention and the detection of fraud, and associated ethics. It is postulated that the position of a company can very rapidly deteriorate in a way that could not be foreseen at the time when the accounts were published (which can occur but which, in my opinion, is a very much over-rated contention) whilst the age old view that we, as a profession, are misunderstood (based on the obvious truism that auditors can only provide a reasonable assurance and not a guarantee) once again takes the report back to rediscovering the wheel.

The cutting-edge, in relation to our profession, is that we must unequivocally accept the evolving and somewhat crystallized views held by society with regard to the purpose for which we exist. Our failure to adapt, and to be one of the leaders in relation to that adaptation, has been one of our critical failures. It may well be true that it is the responsibility of the directors of a business enterprise to manage a company and present its general purpose financial reports, but it is the unequivocal responsibility of the accountancy profession to prepare and to audit those reports. The decay, or even disintegration, of what the profession incestuously believed to be the frame of reference for its output and opinions was inevitable, for remoteness from reality eventually occurs in introspective, inhibited, non-visionary, organizations; and this is so no matter how well rationalized are arguments to the contrary.

As is stated in the report in relation to audit scope changes (and let us be quite clear that the audit function and the preparation function, although each having their own specific responsibilities, processes, pressures, and politics are unequivocally two sides of the same coin and not some abstraction, unrelated, and remote from one another) the purpose of an audit, amongst other things, may be defined as being to provide an independent opinion compared with the opinion of those who may have an interest in a company (be they shareholders, directors, employees, financiers, suppliers, government, society, or some other stakeholder) that they, the auditors, have received (at least from those responsible for its management and strategic direction) an adequate account of the proper conduct of the affairs of the business enterprise.

Fraud and its detection (which can usually be crystallized in explicit form and quantified to an acceptable level of assurance) may be a high profile and obvious concern of various parties, and correctly so, but the wastage and loss which accompanies the inappropriate strategic management of a business enterprise (and whether or not accompanied by fraud) can relegate fraud, as well as other unlawful activities, to a significantly less important level.

Given the aforementioned matters, and in the context of my focus on the strategic well-being of business enterprises, attention will now turn to the 'going concern' principle, being a concept that is described in the expectation gap report as being so generally adopted in the preparation and audit of financial statements that its use can be assumed in the absence of any specific statement to the contrary. This unwarranted familiarity can (and, at least on the balance of probabilities, no doubt did, during the last decade) result in little thought and little relevant professional work being undertaken in that area in order to support the acceptance of that concept as a basis for the preparation and audit of accounts. The gap in expectations which emanated from that source alone was, almost for sure, extremely large, and very costly to society.

The use of the going concern basis relies fundamentally, and almost exclusively, on the appropriate strategic management of a business enterprise and yet it is not a necessary requirement of the accountancy profession (whether in relation to the preparation of financial statements or in relation to their audit) to undertake a specific, rigorous, and structured examination of that dimension. The accountancy profession places significant emphasis on the effectiveness of the internal controls that a business enterprise has put in place in order to protect itself from serious fraud, whilst it also emphasises the need to report any serious and uncorrected deficiencies in that area but, overwhelmingly, it continues to ignore fundamental strategic management ineptitudes and this is so because, in reality, it has little knowledge, and does not know what it is looking at, in that area of business management.

It is the fundamentals of a business enterprise which determine the quality of the going concern opinion and not the apparent availability of financial resources for, in the end, if the strategic fundamentals do not exist, or do not exist in sufficient substance, then the financial resources will, in the overwhelming majority of cases, also evaporate; or at least trigger significant or fundamental problems. Should there be little or no relevant work undertaken in relation to the strategic management of a business enterprise in order to support any professional opinion which may be formed with regard to the use, or otherwise, of the going concern basis (and this is so whether in relation to the preparation of those accounts or in their audit) then it is clear that any opinion which is so formed in relation to the use, or otherwise, of such a basis can, itself, only be based on poor professional standards and with such an opinion (whether or not causing actual damage or harm to shareholders or to stakeholders and society) having possibly been formed recklessly, careless of the consequences. This inept type of work is not appropriate to the high standards to which the profession is suppose to aspire and, in truth, it is this type of work which may once again (and through the direct and the indirect ineptitudes of the Big Six firms and other large accountancy practices . . . . for they in effect control our profession) bring the accountancy profession into disrepute; and with such poor work possibly forming the basis of yet even more damage claims.

The financial viability of a business enterprise is, in the end and on a sustainable basis, overwhelmingly derived from the strategic management of that business enterprise. The ability of a business enterprise to obtain, or secure continuance of, major borrowings and credit facilities (other than by chance or connivance or such similar activity) is a function of the strategic management of that company. The securing of borrowings or credit facilities does not necessarily and of itself provide fundamental strategic well-being but, rather, it may only create an illusion of such well-being; with funding being no more than a vehicle for the buying of time to create fundamental strategic well-being, or to delay acceptance of the fact that the business enterprise is not, fundamentally, a going concern. Financial funding is, in the normal course of events, only a derived indicator of the continuance of a business enterprise as a going concern (conveying little or nothing with regard to the quality of that continuance) whilst in some cases it may well be absolutely misleading. Statements concerning major borrowings and credit facilities, as is recommended in the expectation gap report may, in consequence, only fuel future rounds of negligence claims where such statements are not themselves underwritten by an appropriate and thorough examination of the fundamental strategic well-being of a company. Going concern statements with regard to financial funding must, accordingly, be unequivocally underwritten by appropriate strategic management reviews; being fundamental multi-dimensional reviews which are well and truly far beyond those implied in the Handbook of the Institute.

In addition to the aforementioned matters the expectation gap report refers to the assessment of risk exposure in relation to the going concern principle. The dangers attached to risk assessment exercises which are not also an integral part of a comprehensive strategic management review targeted at assessing the strategic management of a business enterprise, can be enormous and could well expose a professional firm to a major claim for professional negligence. It is essential, therefore, that a holistic approach be adopted with regard to the assessment of whether or not the use of the going concern basis is appropriate in any particular case. Inappropriate, or incorrect, risk evaluations (in particular when such assessments are carried out in a fragmented manner and separate from appropriate strategic management reviews) may, in themselves, cause much damage to a business enterprise and, in the extreme, with inappropriate risk evaluations resulting in the debilitation or perhaps, ultimately, the demise of a company. Unfortunately for the profession the large accountancy practices have jumped on the bandwagon (which is not surprising as it is a trait of the larger firms to hold themselves out to do, what would seem to be, almost anything) so they are now busily offering risk management (assessment, evaluation, and reduction) projects as though there's no tomorrow, yet these assignments are carried out by people who have what may be a superficial understanding of strategic management. [This bandwagon effect is quite a common event, and so as the train passes by (others typically kick-start the product or service offering) we, as a profession, and led by the larger professional practices, almost compulsively it would seem, have to get on board the train.] A somewhat similar situation occurred with regard to a different product offering of one of the larger firms, and at an earlier point in time, and which product offering was hot property for a while. They even gave it a name which belied its own reality. [For the record, bandwagon products and services have been quite popular over the years.] I suspect that in the case in question (for I doubt whether they, themselves, realized reality) a client, whether past, present, or prospective, pointed out that although the offering seemed to be intuitively appealing, the basic conceptual underpinnings of the product were flawed. [I wonder how often members of our profession actually set down, even for their own benefit, the basic conceptual underpinnings and the pros and cons of their product and service offerings, and from the perspective of what they are, in essence, delivering to their clients.] Whatever may have been the trigger for concern, mutterings were heard along the lines that basic problems did indeed exist, and unofficial acknowledgement of the truth of the position did occur. The product offering wasn't withdrawn. It may well have continued to be sold and so ran out its course. But it was realized that, with all the goodwill in the world, damage may well have been inflicted. And this was possibly so in relation to almost all previous clients. No-one was sued or anything. There was, to the best of my knowledge, never any question of clients claiming damages. There is often little desire by a client to actually take that course of action and not least of all because of its unpredictable ramifications. No-one, it may be stated, went bust. There were definitely no insolvency people involved. And, in any case, if damage inflicted can be blurred or even dissipated (which is often quite easy) clients don't really stand much of a chance of proving anything in court. After all, it could very well be more embarrassing to them than it may be to their advisors. It's just that we as a profession (for ultimately the accountancy-based and the non-accountancy-based offerings form mere components in what are all-encompassing professional service businesses) seem to be so receptive, so easily prepared, to peddle products and services which will earn large profits, but without really understanding what, as professionals, we are really doing. That is, what the impacts, the consequences, and the outcomes may be in reality. But that's the way the professional service businesses have gone. They offer products and services as though they're MacDonald outlets that are selling Big Macs, Quarter Pounders, McFeasts, French Fries, and all the rest of the low-value-added, high-dollar-turnover, offerings. That is, at least in part, how the larger professional service businesses have managed to rock-up worldwide annual total fee incomes that are in the billions of dollars as they de-professionalize and asset-strip the accountancy profession. And that, without doubt, is an ominous development. Yes, let us be quite clear that once, as professionals, we enter the field of management proper then the level of professional expertise which is incorporated in product and service offerings increases substantially when compared with the professional expertise of the products and services which are delivered by the plumbers, the joiners, and the bricklayers of the profession. Risk assessment assignments of whatever nature, including facilitation only projects, consequently have significant ethical dimensions which should be carefully considered by our profession. Risk assignments can be embraced, but that should generally be in the context of, say, a strategic management review; whilst such reviews should definitely not be undertaken by those with an impoverished knowledge of strategic management itself.

By way of clarification it is noted that two practices are now becoming more common in the profession. The first is that work which sits outside an actual audit, but which may affect an audit, is now more prevalent. An example of this type of work, as was mentioned above, would be risk management assignments and which assignments are commissioned by management. This work, whether carried out by the firm that undertakes the audit or by some other firm, is potentially available for use by the external auditor. The second point is that the work-type boundaries in the large professional service firms are, in broad terms, somewhat blurred, and so almost any type of work could be carried out by any part of one of those businesses. To illustrate this, Andersens is split into two separate firms, being those of Arthur Andersen and Andersen Consulting. Whether or not any particular assignment is classified as advisory or consultancy work by that business, in reality, both arms of Andersens carry out consultancy/advisory assignments. The blurring which may occur in large firms which are not so clearly differentiated as Andersens could be even more pronounced. Given this, then the rigour which was referred to previously, and in relation to the *basic conceptual underpinnings* of product and service offerings, becomes critical. Further, and in addition to the preceding comments, the latest fad is for the large professional practices to become quality approved, and thereby to get a big tick for their efforts. That approval, despite perceptions to the contrary, does not refer to the substance of the products and services of the firm but, rather, it refers to the processes which those products and services go through from beginning to end. If you wish to deliver rubbishy products or services into your target market, then that is your choice. The quality dimension referred to is that the rubbish was produced in accordance with processes the quality of which processes have been certified. Taking these two developments together (being, in essence, assignments which are undertaken which are outside the work actually executed during an audit *and* the blurring of advisory and consultancy work) the point to note is that 'bandwagon' products and services may well be relied upon by the preparers and the auditors of accounts and, as a consequence thereof, the expectation gap may actually *open* or *close* as a result of important work which was undertaken as an indirect part of the preparation and the audit of accounts but which work, in reality, has a direct bearing on the preparation and the audit of those accounts. Those who prepare accounts and those who audit accounts must and in relation to both direct and indirect work upon which reliance is to be placed (and whether that work was undertaken by those preparing the accounts, or by another section of the firm conducting the audit, or by some unrelated party) ensure that they are well aware of the basic conceptual underpinnings of such work. They cannot just accept the work because an apparently respectable firm, including another section of that same firm, undertook the assignment. We must endeavour to avoid the modern equivalent of the days when the profession would accept a letter from the directors as evidence of the value of inventory for by accepting indirect but important work that was carried out by other parties, but without examining the basic conceptual underpinnings of that work, then we are accepting the contemporary equivalent of those past times when outside representations were sufficient evidence of reality. If those examining indirect work do not really understand the basic conceptual underpinnings, as may well be the case in the area of strategic management (and not least of all in relation to risk management reviews) then our profession, being the preparers and the auditors of accounts, may well be behaving negligently. In view of this let me say now, by way of a note with regard to risk management reviews, that although there are circumstances when risk management reviews may be carried out with a relatively low risk of inflicting damage on a client (as with passive and quasi-passive risk management reviews, when knowledge transfer and the heightening of awareness are the main outcomes and/or when risk-driven action-initiating-projects trigger action which only breaches non-critical boundaries; and which passive risk management reviews are, at least in static form although not necessarily in dynamic form, essentially non-strategic) generally non-passive risk management reviews (including those which impact areas which, from a risk perspective, may appear to be strategically indifferent {as epitomized by the indifference curve of the economist} but which may have strategic ramifications) should be part of a strategic management review; and this is so due to the potential for risk management reviews to alter the strategic impacts, consequences, and outcomes of a company.

Strategy-impoverished risk management reviews are, and without doubt, a risk in themselves, and this is so not least of all when those reviews are facilitated by advisors who, in truth, have an impoverished knowledge of strategic management.

Having said this, it is again stated that the basic conceptual underpinnings which come to bear in the preparation and the audit of general purpose financial reports are flawed. This is revealed by the porous nature of the work that is required to be undertaken in relation to the going concern basis and the fact that the basis itself has widespread use but, paradoxically, very restricted relevance.

The various matters that have been addressed above include the simplification of the financial accounts of public companies, the adoption of a management responsibility statement, the inclusion in the financial reports of a management discussion and analysis document, the presentation of the objectives and strategic plans of a reporting company, and the reporting of management forecasts and budgets to shareholders, stakeholders, and society (including the competitors of a business enterprise) as well as the need for adequate knowledge of the business of a client, education and communication, and the most fundamental of areas, being that of the use of the going concern principle. Various other matters were also addressed in my original submission in response to the expectation gap report. It is stressed that many of the matters that I did not address, and which matters appeared in the expectation gap report, were also of importance to our profession. Given this, then I wish it to be known that I agree whole-heartedly with the adoption of a positive, pro-active, and decisive approach to the bridging of the very real expectation gap which exists between the accountancy profession and business enterprise shareholders, stakeholders, and society in total. I would further state, however, that in parts of the expectation gap report it would seem that we, as a profession, are endeavouring to avoid the necessary and sufficient action to attain the bridging of that gap whilst, in other parts thereof, the report recommendations would appear to be exacerbating the expectation gap by failing to view or examine our actions from the perspective of both shareholders and stakeholders; and on a dynamic basis over a number of years. What is clear (and what strives to emerge from the expectation gap report) is that we, as a profession, are indeed searching for solutions and resolutions to our current challenges. The provision of yet even more information will, however, not necessarily bridge the gap and it may, in some instances, even aggravate that gap. An important point to note, however, is the quotation which I provided early in the preceding discussion and which read 'Let us hope that it (the expectation gap report) is a vehicle propelling an opportunity without bounds for, sadly, we need such a vehicle' for that quotation was spot on, despite my criticism of the various matters which I have addressed (many other matters raised in the report, it is noted, were perfectly valid recommendations) for the visionaries of the profession who prepared the expectation gap report actually did provide a vehicle upon which the accountancy profession could base vibrant and invigorating discussion and from which invigorating and vibrant discussion could emerge quantum leaps, as well as order of magnitude changes, which would allow our profession to truly embrace its own future.

Submitting anything was, in reality, a waste of time and effort !!!!!

I should have read the foreword more carefully. That is, I should have read in between the lines. Included in the foreword to the expectation gap report were the words ' . . . . we commissioned this research study to provide a basis for discussion within the professional and business community.' [In my submission I had offered to meet with whoever was deemed appropriate in order to clarify, or expand upon, any of the matters that I had raised in my submission.] The foreword continued, 'The working party has been supported to go beyond the area of audit and into the areas of financial reporting and corporate governance in order to comprehensively cover all expectations' and then went on to state that 'The two professional bodies believe that the debate on this research study should initially centre around those issues which can be practically adopted in Australia and are consistent with international best practice. Those recommendations which require modification of international best practice should sensibly be first debated internationally before being adopted in Australia.'

Preceding these quotations it was stated that the expectation gap issue 'goes to the very heart of financial reporting in this country. It is vital that this important issue is given a frank and open airing to clear any misconceptions and ensure that both preparers and users of financial reports fully understand the reporting and auditing process. We believe it is only through vigorous and open discussion that such an understanding can be reached.'

What a laugh. The preceding quotations had already set the scene. The ground rules. The boundaries. The follower mentality. It was clearly spelt out for us all to see. Debate, it said . . . *'should initially centre around those issues* (which) *are consistent with international best practice'*. But why? Aren't we capable of coming up with our own creative insights which weren't first dreamt up in the UK or in the USA? And who said that international best practice was best anyway ?!!!! That's one of the biggest cop-outs that was ever imposed on our society. [It's like that economic rationalists farce a few years back when almost every man and his dog thought that it was good to play on a level playing field . . . . until it was realized that everybody else had the field tilting their way (even when they changed ends) and that the only country that intended to play on such a field was Australia.] I actually wrote a letter to several dozen leaders of the profession at the time and which was entitled 'When Best Practice Isn't Good Enough' pointing out that international best practice is simply *not* good enough. That is, right now, and at this very moment, it simply isn't good enough; and, further, that it's not necessarily getting any better. Just because some so-called 'best practice' comes from overseas. And just because it's produced and backed by one or other (or even more) members of the international establishment . . . . That, in itself, doesn't make it best. Such practices may well be what are practiced internationally. But please don't elevate their particular practices to the position of our goals . . . . and then declare them to be *the best* available. And please don't ask us to wait a bit (maybe a year or two, or longer, or for ever) whilst all the other dead-heads (who are themselves also waiting to grunt, belch, and fart in unison) are dragged, kicking and screaming, into taking new and relevant actions whilst Australian shareholders, stakeholders, and society in total, is crucified on the accountancy profession's bureaucratic procedures. What on earth is *best* about applying going concern practices which don't tell you when a company is on its knees, or is about to fold ?!!!! Let's get real for once. The problem with our neo-classical establishment is that they seem to think that just because a particular set of procedures are practiced internationally, then they must be good. So we in Australia, and under the 'anywhere but here' philosophy, throw common sense aside, and hail them as being best. In reality the reason we don't introduce things forthwith is simply because it might upset other members of the establishment; here or overseas. We would rather shareholders, stakeholders, and society in total, suffer, than allow Australia to even appear to be progressive . . . . It's all crap !!!!!

The turn of phrase . . . . *'It is vital that this important issue is given a frank and open airing to clear any misconceptions and ensure both preparers and users of financial reports fully understand the reporting and auditing process'* .... is, of course, only establishment-talk for 'we've got to make that lot see it our way otherwise they'll know we've screwed it up'. Not to mention that wonderfully democratic assertion that .... *'We believe it is only through vigorous and open discussion that such an understanding can be reached'* and which sentiment, when applied in practice, was pathetic.

The Institute (and presumably the Society because they tend to make joint accountancy statements) held an expectation gap road show. The purpose was for members to put their points of view for consideration by the powers that be. My goodness. At last we were to be heard. Participation was to be limited to one hundred people only. I enroled with eagerness. At last progress was to be made. I spent the whole day prior to the Sydney meeting preparing my contribution. For one reason or another I arrived late for the meeting and had to sit on the front row. The actual meeting itself, however, had not commenced. I don't know, but I guess I'd missed morning coffee or something. When the President of the Institute of Chartered Accountants (it was actually the aforementioned 'Chairman' of P&O) declared the meeting open, it was evident that there was, in reality, little intention of securing any major contribution from the ordinary members who were present. There was nothing explicit. It was just built into the structure of the meeting. This all important event was to last only half a day and members were to be allowed five minutes each to speak on those most fundamental of matters which were included or, as the case may be, were not included, in their two hundred (200) page report. Meanwhile there, and before our very eyes, was a panel of 'experts' from the in-crowd. What a surprise. They had each come complete with their particular talk, oration, sermon, lecture, chat, address, or what have you and, in at least one case, an all-singing all-dancing presentation; and obviously for *our* edification. Were they really interested in what the 'plebs' had to say? I doubt it. Eventually, and throughout the course of the meeting (that is, not so much all at once, but more, so as to say, in an intermittent way) half the morning went on their presentations. I say, eventually, as in the history of the Institute it had probably never experienced such a bun-fight as that which was experienced that day; or should I say morning.

I had prepared a well-honed ten minute contribution. It was all typed in large characters so that I could read it easily. The powers that be, who were seated on the stage, looked up; or should that be, looked down. The President spoke. 'Would anyone like to ask the first question?' No-one seemed willing to be the first to speak. I had not intended to raise my issues so early but, under the circumstances, I thought that I may as well take the opportunity; but first of all I queried the use of the term 'question'. Why is it always 'questions' that must be asked. I didn't want to ask a question. I wanted to make some points. I wanted to say what I wanted to say. I didn't want to receive their wisdom. We always hear their views. We read about them all the time in the media and in *Charter* the Institute's 'propaganda' magazine. And, in any case, they'd written a whole report on the matter. This was an opportunity (being the only opportunity) for the 'plebs' to put their views. What did they say, a *'vigorous and open discussion'* of the many fundamental matters of concern to ordinary members. This was the one and only opportunity to actually speak, as real people, face-to-face, about real issues, and to supposed leaders of our profession. No, I didn't want to ask them anything. I wanted to convey, for what it was worth, my views, my opinions, and my observations and, if the truth be known, to my colleagues and fellow members; virtually every one of whom I did not know. I didn't really care whether the leadership agreed or disagreed with my particular views and opinions. They, in any case, only seem to listen to themselves. All that I had expected, and anticipated, was a frank and open exchange of views, opinions, and ideas. No, I had things to say . . . . and I wanted to say them !!!!!

'Excuse me Mr President but I've prepared my contribution and it takes ten minutes to read.' I was allowed five minutes. 'Others will want to talk.' I mumbled something about it should have been an all day meeting (to which there were various mumblings of agreement) as I walked the few paces to the lectern positioned on the stage. 'No. Down there.' He pointed. 'Use one of the microphones on the floor.' I looked at the microphone perched on top of its tubular erection. 'Mr President, sir, there's nowhere for me to rest my papers whilst I'm reading. You're sat at a table with your own microphone. My papers may fall all over as I endeavour to turn the pages. And apart from that, I came hear to talk with my colleagues. Not to address you lot up there. I'd like to see them . . . . and I'm sure that they would like to see me.' On went the banter. I still only got five minutes. I opened up with an advert for my services. And I announced my name. The President seemed to heave a heavy and, what seemed to be, an audible sigh whilst, at one and the same time (so as to say) and proverbially speaking, collapsing over the table in a heap. He'd never actually met me before. And he didn't know what I looked like. But he had received some of my writings.

I began my contribution at page four. Or was it page five? My colleagues had missed out on some wonderful words. I just hoped it would make the five minute deadline. What usually happens at this type of meeting is that not many people get up and give their views and opinions, or whatever . . . . and definitely not when it's a meeting of Chartered Accountants; even when there are one hundred in attendance. It was no different on this occasion. So I seized the chance to speak again . . . . and again . . . . and again !!!!! [My political activities, as President of a Liberal Party Branch in Western Sydney, had really honed my skills in this area . . . . and, in addition, having also come from the wrong side of the tracks, and proud of it (working class boy, red-brick university, and all that stuff) what did I care about the establishment; they aren't exactly the sort of people I admire.] I seem to recall the President saying, later in the meeting, that he'd seen me making some more notes on one of the topics (he was actually referring to me by my Christian name by that time) so he asked, in a kindly enough way, if anyone else would like to speak before he once again gave me the floor. He was, in all truth, quite nice for a President. And he seemed to have a good sense of humour.

At some point I stated to the assembled platform of speakers, including the President of the Institute, that the Big Six firms had been an absolute disgrace to our profession, and that it was they who had brought the accountancy profession into disrepute during the past decade. The Big Six firms, with all their might, and all their power, and all their resources, still couldn't get it right. They still managed to screw it up. And not just once. But year after year after year. It would appear that some of the leadership of the profession must reside in 'cuckoo-land' as my sentiments seemed, at least to me, to come as quite a surprise to one of the Big Six partners perched up there on the stage. Perhaps he thought that it was the *sole practitioner* in your local suburb, or the *two person partnership* in some outback town, who had grabbed the head-lines in the financial press (and every other national newspaper for that matter) as well as virtually all the other media outlets, as they reported the absolutely abysmal failure of the accountancy profession to identify, or to even just forewarn, of the corporate disasters of the last decade or so. Yes, upon reflection it must have been our very own, very friendly, kick-about country practitioner who did it. It was he who had brought our profession into disrepute. How could I have been so blind as not to see something that obvious !!!! I can hear it now. 'This is the World News . . . . a Mr Ned Kelly, a partner with his brother Dan in Kelly & Kelly, Chartered Accountants of Woop Woop, has been identified as the villain who contributed to the downfall of one of Australia's most respected multi-nationals. The company, which continued to report record profits until late last week, is thought to have debts of several hundred million dollars, and a hopeless deficiency of assets. A senior partner from one of the Big Six accountancy firms (believed to be a Mr Aaron Sherritt) who is getting paid a fat fee for providing information with regard to the matter, but who wished to remain anonymous, informed us that the string of record profits had, for several years, been based on fictitious financial reports. He went on to state that many of the company's assets had never even existed but that Mr Kelly had not actually noticed that particular fact. Mr Kelly, who appeared to be in a deep state of shock, was heard to mumble something about a scapegoat, as he was driven away in Mr Sherritt's recently acquired luxury motor vehicle. A spokesperson for Mr Sherritt, in a later statement, indicated that the 'scapegoat' comment was believed to refer to a farmer friend and client of Mr Kelly's who, it was thought, had recently expanded into animal husbandry. In a brief press release The Institute of Chartered Accountants said that it had no intention of taking action against the unfortunate practitioner for at least one or two years, if ever, as it is believed that he was, in fact, a victim of circumstances. An angry crowd of mums and dads who had lost their entire life's savings in the company crash, and who had gathered outside the Woop Woop offices of Mr Kelly, were dispersed by police. Four people were taken to hospital. Police reported that there were no arrests as enough damage had already been done by that most despicable of professionals, Mr Kelly. It was also reported that many mums and dads who had confidently invested in the company, based on a prospectus prepared by Mr Kelly's mate, a Mr John Byrne of the firm Hart Byrne & Co, who had a practice just down the road from Mr Kelly, were later seen leaving the scene distraught and weeping; their lives having been shattered through professional incompetence. It is believed that there is no truth in the rumour that Byrne, Hart, and the Kelly brothers are, in fact, the famous bushrangers, or that they often met in the local pub to discuss ethical issues, to play their didgeridoos, and to sing endless rounds of our national anthem, Advance Australia Fair; given, of course, that we can use the term 'fair' at a meeting of accountants and auditors. In other news . . . .'

Perhaps the real partner from the real Big Six firm didn't, in all truth, believe that the profession had been brought into disrepute. That is, perhaps he just didn't believe that the profession had been brought into disrepute at all.

Another speaker, much later in the meeting, and whom I did not know, went to the microphone and stated that some of the things that I had said, needed saying. He confirmed his opinion later, in the lift, when, after a lively meeting, all attendees who were still left standing, dispersed. Most people would, no doubt, have gone back to their perhaps dull, boring, and uninteresting professional existences but, who knows, maybe one day they will recall that meeting and remember it as being *even more exciting* than a budget speech. It may even be remembered as the most invigorating event that they had ever experienced in their entire life; at least as a Chartered Accountant.

Even I would admit that it was a rag-bag of a meeting and that I contributed to that outcome. But the purpose of the meeting was for 'them' to hear from 'us' and not the other way round. They seemed to have forgotten that crucial point. At the coffee break the President came over to me and, quite voluntarily, offered to include me in the next road show event; wherever that was to be. I guess he must have been a bit sea-sick at the time [perhaps he'd been on one of his own boat trips] because, at least on that point, I never heard from him again. And just for the record, some time later I decided to write to one of the authors of the expectation gap report to enquire with regard to developments. I didn't hear from him either. I guess they'd now had a chance to meet with some real Chartered Accountants (being members who weren't their own employees) and who had real views, and real opinions; and they'd had enough. Reality, it would seem, was too hard for them . . . . So they all went back into their cocoons !!!!

Never mind. Who knows. Perhaps in another thirty years or so I'll get another chance to express my views and opinions to the all powerful down at the Institute. But, there again . . . . Perhaps not.

It is noted that early in 1994 the Institute published a white paper entitled 'Chartered Accountants in the 21st Century' and which document showed much promise. Amongst some of the attributes and characteristics which were identified therein as being of particular importance to future accountants were those which follow. [Incidentally, I sometimes wonder who the people who come up with these reports mix with for it seems to me that I've been utilizing the various identified dimensions, and to a high level, from my first day as an articled clerk; and so, no doubt, have many of my colleagues.] They included 'intellectual abilities conducive to logical, deductive, and abstract thinking; the identification and solving of problems; the handling of ethical dilemmas; and forward thinking' as well as 'well developed interpersonal skills, enabling the accountant to motivate and develop others, delegate tasks, resolve conflicts, demonstrate leadership, manage people, and to interact with diverse groups of clients' plus 'personal attributes, including morality, integrity, energy, motivation, persistence, compassion, judgement, and a commitment to life-long learning' to name but a few. Admittedly the preceding points are statements of motherhood. [It's as though we start at the base line every time, assume that nobody has any idea about anything, and that we haven't been doing whatever it is, and for years, and then, surprisingly, we once again rediscover the wheel.] However, despite motherhood, I can't help but think that somewhere along the line the leadership of the profession has lost sight of its own espoused aspirations; some of which were spelt out in the aforementioned document. Using my own case by way of example, and in relation to the expectation gap report, someone like myself can make a major submission in relation to the report (being, that is, major to me, in time and effort, whether or not it was major to those who handled those matters) yet that person (in this case me) is not subsequently involved, not even by telephone or fax, in a simple exploratory, or perhaps explanatory, discussion with a view to enhancing their contribution to the (according to the Institute's library, non-existent) final action plan and report which had been referred to in the foreword to the 'gap' report. I actually did get a letter of acknowledgment for my submission and in which it stated, amongst other things, that the author had 'particularly enjoyed the three opening pages and the conclusion' although there were a few issues in between with which the author did not entirely agree. The sincerity of the letter was obvious enough but, bearing the aforementioned comments in mind, one can only wonder why discussions were not held with regard to exploring further my twenty page submission. Given this, some of the above points (which points had been identified in the Institute's own '21st Century' document as being part of a 'daunting' skills base) had been virtually ignored by the leadership who were so sincerely espousing those values; and not least of all the important values of intellectual contribution, and communication. I guess these comments speak for themselves. Even though they tell us that they genuinely want members to get involved and participate, I wonder if they do. Perhaps it's just that the powers that be don't believe that other members have valid views and opinions. It would appear that the most fundamental matters which were addressed in my submission were never expanded upon, and by anyone, as far as I can see (at least not in the context of the 'gap' report itself) and they definitely weren't included in any new professional edicts. It may be interesting to know what contributions other people (both members and non-members) made to the report, and who those other people were, and what their particular roles are in life; and what was the motivation for their contributions. And I wonder who, if anyone, was involved (other than the working party itself) in progressing the final report; individual members, that is, and others : not just representatives of this, that, or some other establishment body.

I suppose some members of our profession may feel threatened by other members expressing views and opinions which differ from those of their own, and this may be so not least of all when those other views and opinions are expressed in a forthright manner, and when the recipients of those views are outside the protection of their own comfort zones (as with the protection that is afforded by their status within their own organizations) and this may be more so if the very act of being challenged by lower status persons is not one of their common experiences. Funnily enough, those very same people may feel safer reading this book. They perhaps wouldn't feel so intimidated. And they could pencil in their own little notes in the margins. Then, if they wanted, they could give me a call. I'm quite happy to discuss things. [Other people can also feel free to contact me for I'm not restricting myself to the 'timids' of the world.] If you don't agree with what I've had to say, then that's all right. I'm quite willing to agree to disagree. No hard feelings. In any case, you never know, I may begin to appreciate your particular perspective. Perhaps at some point in time and as a result of sound argument [now I could be mistaken but I seem to recall that this sort of thing happened in 1953, or was it 1957, or perhaps it was twice, but in 1962] you may even cause me to reconsider, or even to change my mind. Worse, we may even end up agreeing with one another. How terrible.

To be . . . . Or not to be . . . . That is the question ?!!!!

Was the expectation gap report truly visionary? Were those who prepared that report true visionaries? Are their recommendations (as well as some of those contributions which were submitted in response thereto) to be, or not to be, some time in the future? Or is it nobler for our profession to suffer the slings and arrows of outrageous fortune (as well as even more damage claims) than to take up arms against a sea of troubles? What, one may ask, did Hamlet mean by these particular words? Could he have foreseen the sea of troubles upon which the accountancy profession itself would be tossed? Being first raised up, and to a great height, only then to be smashed down, and to even greater depths. Will we, as a profession, bear our ills, the nature of which we are familiar, and so fail to act appropriately (preferring, rather, to protect our delinquents under a most iniquitous capping regime and which regime, much like a cancer, may spread throughout Australia) or, as leaders, will we dare to embrace new professional knowledge and understanding, and so new opportunities, and thereby reach out to our new horizons; being horizons with which we are not now necessarily familiar, but beyond which new horizons lies the future of our profession? Yes, that truly searching question as posed by Hamlet is, indeed, extremely challenging !!!!!

Chapter Four

Hope For The Future

I wonder how many of the many thousands upon thousands of my fellow professionals in Australia and the United Kingdom have actually taken time out (and I mean a significant amount of good quality time) to think about what we, as professionals and as a profession, are doing, what we are achieving, and what are the impacts, the consequences, and the outcomes of those actions and achievements both for themselves and for their organizations; as well as for shareholders, stakeholders, and society in general. As a newly qualified Chartered Accountant aged twenty-three, and with the world at my feet, and an exciting future ahead of me, I moved from the status of, in terms of one description, local yokel in a provincial practice, to being employed by one of the leading accountancy firms in the City of London. During my sojourn in that vast metropolis I would occasionally visit St Paul's Cathedral. It was in that most beautiful of constructs that I first read the words of the poet William Blake, a man who had tramped those same streets, but two centuries earlier. His words, at least for me, create inalienable beauty whilst, at one and the same time, inspiring vision. Simultaneously, they capture the galactic and the microscopic; nature and the soul; and the abstract, the conceptual, and reality itself. Attention is, thereby, purposely focused on the magnificent. From his 'Auguries of Innocence' come the words . . .

To see a world in a grain of sand
And heaven in a wild flower
To hold infinity in the palm of your hand
And eternity in an hour

These thought-provoking words have remained with me for some thirty years. I guess I was predisposed towards matters visionary, as well as those creative, constructive, and philosophical, and from an early age. Business, to me, was also a natural. My father had his own somewhat challenging business for much of my early and teenage years. As I grew older I came to love art and the theatre and, in particular, musical productions. At the age of fourteen, however, I had to choose between attending art school or sitting the exams to study at the school of commerce. Although my art teacher had implored me to utilize my creative abilities in that particular sphere I had already set my sights on becoming a Chartered Accountant. I wonder sometimes whether or not that decision, at that tender age, was the first major mistake of my life.

Before you decide to set in concrete any misconceptions (whether favourable or unfavourable) with regard to me or my disposition, let me assure you that I am not idealistic, I am not quixotic, and I am no dreamer. Although I do have a propensity to indulge in each of those dimensions both separately and in combination. I have worked in conjunction with, and along side, my share, and possibly some of your share, of absolute bastards. Whilst I am also pragmatic enough to know that little is fair in life (whatever that may mean) for anyone, and that it never will be fair; and that this is so for everyone. But I do believe that we can improve the lives of others (as well as that of our own) by endeavouring to change both what is targeted and the way that things are achieved. As a business management professional I know that I can deliver real benefits to people who I know as well as to people who I do not know, by promoting justice, fairness, and equity in the world of business. With regard to that challenge I can also confirm that I am not misty-eyed, for by altering anything of consequence in the world of business, damage is done to at least the images, the reputations, and the egos (and also, sooner or later, to the bank accounts) of powerful people. By embracing change, and by adopting the suggestions which are indicated herein, there would be a more just, a more fair, and a more equitable distribution of income, wealth, and power in the business world, and throughout society. However, the fundamental strategic question which will need to be considered by the powerful in both the public and the private sectors, in order that change and innovation will occur, is:

'Who will win . . . . And who will lose ?!!!!'

[and what will happen in the transition]

It may be noted that the predispositional qualities that I have attributed to myself, and which I identified above, are amongst the most critical of the qualities that I have used as a management consultant. Those qualities are probably just as important, if not more important, than is my innate intelligence, my indispensable knowledge, and my technical skills and abilities. William Blake, by the way, was once considered mad by those who did not understand his work. In more recent times, although not totally fathomed, he has been determined by those who know, to be brilliant, although formidably obscure, in a completely rational and explicable framework. I am not mad either. I hope, however, that my work will be accepted more readily than was his and by those who do not comprehend, but who intuitively realize, that it will have tremendous value to the business world, and to the totality of society. Let us hope that the powerful also have vision.

One of the greatest impediments to the introduction of a quantum leap or order of magnitude change in the applied practices of the accountancy profession is most likely an unidentified sub-set of powerful partners in the large accountancy firms, for innovative action of that nature would reveal that their applied practices in the past and, in particular, throughout the past ten years, were fundamentally flawed and, further, that had more appropriate practices actually been applied previously then, indeed, many of the corporate debacles of recent history would either not have occurred, or they would not have occurred to the extent to which they actually did occur. In fact, and in my opinion, not one of the major corporate crashes or debilitations of the aforementioned period would have eventuated as they did had the accountancy profession wholeheartedly embraced strategic management and, not least of all, strategic management systems. This is so due to the fact that the day-to-day, week-to-week, and month-to-month management of strategy itself would have provided the basic conceptual underpinning for the management of those business enterprises as well as for the preparation of their general purpose financial reports. The eventual disasters which we observed, both unfolding and in finality, would have been intercepted earlier and corrective action would have been taken; or those businesses would have been wound-up and with a much smaller shortfall or loss. It is noted, however, that with many outstanding damage claims (and with some of those claims in the hundreds of millions of dollars and with others of one billion dollars or more) an inferred admission of a mistake, and of this nature, may not be politically acceptable to the powerful partners of the large firms who either influence, or control, the strategic direction of the accountancy profession. They would prefer to let society continue to bear the costs. [Their obnoxious moral and ethical position was revealed in glorious technicolour when certain 'leaders' of our profession pursued the capping of negligence awards, *even under a regime of proportional (as opposed to joint and several) liability*, rather than accepting responsibility for the full amount of any damage (as determined by a judge) that *our* delinquent members actually inflicted on *their* victims.] In addition to this, the insurers who, during the past decade or more, have provided professional indemnity and directors and officers insurance cover, may also show reluctance for the introduction of leading-edge practices, at least at this point in time, due to any adverse implications with regard to their settlement figures. The changes alluded to would also affect companies of all sizes, types, and natures, and not least of all large publicly listed companies, for they would be evaluated along fundamental and inalienable dimensions which will cause the standing of those major corporates, as well as their subsidiary companies and associated business enterprises, to be viewed by their shareholders, their stakeholders, and society in general, very differently. Some would be winners. And some would be losers. Yes, some would be very big winners indeed. But the biggest winner of all would be society in total. For the winning and the losing would not be a 'one off' event but, rather, it would be an on-going experience which would, of necessity, redistribute resources, both tangible and intangible, into more appropriate uses. Whilst profits, generally, would increase, or at least be of a better quality when compared with what would otherwise have been the case. And incomes, and the standard of living of our population, in total, would also improve. Fundamentally, and in general terms, there would be a significant improvement in the strategic well-being and strategic direction of Corporate Australia.

You may wonder why, preceding the above comments, I spoke about my personal disposition, in particular in a book like this which addresses corporate governance, strategic management, and the need for institutional bodies and major corporates to embrace the challenges of our times; and in a truly genuine way. It is, however, important to realize that the accountancy profession is fundamentally concerned with adding to and/or detracting from the basic well-being of our society. It is also important to recognize that society is composed of real people, and real families, and that each of those real people have real personalities, emotions, hopes, and aspirations; as does each and every member of our profession. We, as a profession, impact real people. People like me. And people like you. And wouldn't you be somewhat annoyed (or feel cheated or deceived) if, because the accountancy profession couldn't or, indeed, *wouldn't* tell you that a company was not a going concern, or that it was likely to suffer debilitation, and it went out of business within months of the preparation and audit of its accounts, or debilitation was suffered in that time, and you lost your wealth, or your superannuation, or your job, or your business, or your family. [Some people lost everything as a result of the company debacles of recent years.] Wouldn't you, to say the least, be angry. When we therefore, and as a profession, fail to add to the well-being of our society or, on an optimal basis, we fail to add to the well-being of society to the extent to which we could, then it is unequivocally individuals who suffer, and perhaps their families; not some cardboard cut-out of a human being, devoid of feelings, and who is suspended in cyberspace complete with an economic rationalist's model of the universe, and a calculator, in order to ensure that the best monetary deal is always obtained. In the end, one way or another, the costs and the benefits, the pluses and the minuses, the profits and the losses, the surpluses and the shortfalls, end up, directly or indirectly, with individuals; as does all the emotion. The point is so easy to forget when, as a high flying professional, you work for, or are dealing with, major corporates. Accordingly, and as a profession, we must be cognitively alert to our responsibilities to our neighbours [to love your neighbour as yourself is, I believe, the particular message] and, in accordance therewith, we should endeavour to optimize our contribution to society. And to achieve that, we cannot ignore our *potential* as a profession. To do so, in social terms, is criminal. The anticipations and the expectations which we experienced as newly qualified accountants (with high ideals, good morals, sound ethics, and opportunities in absolute abundance set out before us) should, therefore, be recalled, and then reinvigorated. For in those days everything was achievable.

To embrace quantum leaps and order of magnitude changes we must be committed and we must be strong. For strength is an internal fortitude and a characteristic which is often observed more clearly in those in adverse circumstances. The accountancy profession has its share of bullies, as well as its share of thugs, psychologically speaking that is (for with psychological brutality, which is a common practice in managerial relationships of all types, there is no blood, and there are no broken bones; and often the damage is not easy to see) but thankfully the profession also has its share of strong professionals; being members, despite the bullies and the psychological thugs (and the implicit and the explicit pressures for conformity which are forever present in our profession) who are prepared to express their views and opinions, and who, thereby, are prepared to overcome those formidable obstacles to achieving our future. These are the members who are no longer prepared to stand by and, without objection, watch our profession mutate into superficiality as it fails to grasp the very essence of its own future.

This book, and in that context, is a strong book.

Nothing, as most of us will know, is for ever [except, of course, eternal life] and so, as the accountancy profession travels, almost passively, towards the end of this century and into the next millenium, I will restate what I am addressing. What I am looking at specifically. It is the future of the accountancy profession. It is its future as a distinct and a separately identifiable profession. But I am looking at an accountancy profession which exists and is incorporated (albeit partially . . . . but very powerfully) within the vast and emerging professional service businesses; for they (and due not least of all to the presence of weak countervailing power in the profession) are, implicitly or explicitly, overtly or covertly, actively or inactively, significantly determining the future of the accountancy profession. I am, therefore, unashamedly addressing, and without doubt, power and control. Being power in relation to the profession. And control of that profession. And this is distinct from, but is significantly related to, the power and control, and influence, which is exerted by the large multi-profession service businesses; and this is so whether the genesis of those businesses was accountancy-based or otherwise. I am, and without doubt, considering, and in concept, the problems, the opportunities, and the challenges that call out to be addressed by, and which are relate to, the strategic well-being of the accountancy profession. And this is in the context of the forces, and the contemporary developments, which are crystallizing on a worldwide basis and which affect many individual professions, both on a national and on a global scale. I am, therefore, and without doubt, well and truly addressing the very future of the accountancy profession.

So what has the profession endeavoured to do in order to address its problems, its opportunities, and its challenges? Well, in what has now become its quasi-traditional style, it began by tackling the superficial rather than the substantial !!!!! The trouble is, we're still waiting for it to get round to the substance. This statement may come as a surprise to many and indeed cause some degree of confusion due to the public image of the relevant bodies, and not least of all the image of the Institute of Chartered Accountants. The profession, after all, is seen as being solid, competent, and capable. The myth, of course, lies in the structured bureaucracy of the profession where a whole set of processes and procedures convey the impression of knowledge, understanding, and insight (which thereby imply that profound consideration has been give to all matters of relevance) whilst constructive criticism is either muzzled, or it managed out of existence; or it is ignored. So much for communication.

[Now what was that statement. And in their very own report. I think it said that communication will be one of the critical success factors for professional accountants next century? I presume it means communicating amongst themselves. Communication, that is, amongst the leadership. Sorry. Hold it. Things are happening. I've just had a 'telepathic' from the President himself. He says that the requirement to communicate which I am referring to is not just amongst themselves, being the in-crowd, but that it is also intended to be between the Institute and the membership and between the membership and the Institute; as well as with clients. But he says that the ruling isn't effective yet. He said there's a few years to go till the new millenium. Hang on. He's still sending. He says he's sorry things have gone the way they have with the profession this last ten or twenty years. Oh yes, and that he's sure that one or other of his successors will be willing to talk about things with me early next century . . . . Yes, indeed, it is nice to see that things are now moving much faster in the profession !!!!]

In passing, and just for the record, if you think the Institute in the UK is any better than this lot here then I draw your attention to three letters which appeared in the February, 1996, International

Edition of 'Accountancy' which effectively indicate (at least in the opinion of their authors) that remoteness is perhaps alive and well in the profession. The three letters came from the US, Hong Kong, and the UK. The specific issue was the then current merger initiative, but the general message is, in fact, more basic. The first letter castigates the Institute leadership for its tendency to dilute the value of membership. The second, in effect, questions the value of the Institute to society, stating 'I think it is time for our Institute to come out of the stone age . . . . our qualification is the best start, but after we have this qualification our Institute is of little use' to us, thereby indicating that post-qualification training and education may not be appropriate. The third of these letters states that 'the Institute has great difficulty communicating with its members' and that it's a pity that it doesn't spend more money and effort representing its members instead of (presumably) the ambitions of the leadership. These letters may or may not be representative of the views and opinions of members. In any case, even the majority view may not be an informed view as little effort is made by the profession to provide substantial on-going support for constructive debate and discussion on fundamental issues; and definitely not in relation to opposing, or alternative, opinions. In the previously mentioned letter from Hong Kong the author stated that 'the only dissenting opinion was an inserted letter' in an official mail-out on the issue whilst he also queries the last minute 'token gesture' with regard to the provision of contrary argument; and which contrary argument itself also got plenty of condemnation in the official pronouncements. [I didn't think much of the contrary argument personally but, then, that isn't the point . . . . what about other contrary arguments which exist or may be developed . . . . and what about next time that we have another major issue which, by right, we should all be asked to address . . . . like taking action to protect the Big Six firms from themselves ?!!!!] Overwhelmingly, and at least in Australia, the views and the opinions of the in-crowd are promoted, and with underwhelming exposure, and on an on-going basis, for that of dissenting argument and which argument, if such argument were properly presented, may actually become the overwhelming view of the profession. And please don't feign indignation, and claim that we have democratic elections, for elections alone do not equate with democracy (look at the old Soviet Union if you want proof of that and where mock democracy was an important factor in eventually killing-off the second most powerful regime on earth) for information, ease of communication, and free and open debate and discussion (of both existing and of new ideas) are each also necessary for effective democracy. The point to note, and irrespective of whether or not the merger in the UK goes ahead, is that in many countries, and worldwide, the profession has real problems; being fundamental problems. Relatively the profession is less relevant to society today than it was in previous times. In fact, it may, today, be absolutely less relevant. After all, when in passive background decline, the contribution of our profession to problems was less obvious. But when, and in recent times, the profession failed in both active and foreground mode, and at the cutting-edge of reality, and in glorious technicolour, then its failure was obvious; and the damage that we inflicted on society was seen to be obscene. Whatever the case may be (and some may well object to what I have written) instead of rising up to meet the real challenges of our times, the incestuous leadership of the accountancy profession continued their mindless endeavours to transform us into even better plumbers, joiners, and bricklayers, in their vain attempt to rectify *their* ineptitudes and to overcome what were now *our* problems. The power coalition within the leadership of the accountancy profession (and which power coalition is not fixed in form but, rather, is fluid in nature, for it groups and re-groups around specific issues, but which coalition emanates from what typically amount to the same sources) are, as a consequence, looking in the wrong place for *our* future !!!!!

So, to repeat what was asked earlier, what did the profession do?

Well for one thing it endeavoured to convey the impression that it had little or nothing to do with the corporate debacles of the past decade. The farcical statement by a Past President of the Institute and chairman, chief executive, managing partner, or whatever, of one of the Big Six firms, that it is the management and directors who make the primary decisions and that auditors only report about those results, tried to avoid the primary responsibility of both preparers and auditors of accounts to report appropriately in relation thereto. The going concern assumption means just what it says and that is that the preparers and the auditors of accounts have assumed that a company is, in reality, a going concern. This assumption with regard to the going concern basis does not mean hide behind some artificial twelve month liquidity test. Some companies, where the preparers and auditors of accounts had assumed the going concern basis, didn't even last out a year before collapsing. Favourable test outcomes, even when those test outcomes are based on the best tests available (current twelve month tests are simply not the best tests available at all) provide no excuse for not recognizing reality. Not to look for reality is a disgrace. To recognize reality, and not to take action in relation thereto, is fraudulent. But to hide behind some technicality, and because you don't know what to look for, is negligent; for help could always have been sought from other professionals.

In addition to endeavouring to distance itself from the corporate debacles of the past decade the profession also endeavoured to protect its deviant members from damage awards made, after a court case, and by a judge (as opposed to voluntary out-of-court settlements) by trying to persuade State and Federal Governments to pass laws (and which vile law was passed by the New South Wales coalition government of John Fahey) and which laws were intended to be structured in a way which grossly favours the accountancy profession and, in particular, with a view to capping the amount which could be awarded by a judge as damages. This cowardly behaviour was based on the immoral and unethical view that if the accountancy profession could, in fact, get the law changed in its favour, then its members would not be punished to the full extent of their wrongdoing. Their actions were justified, by various parties, on the grounds of avoiding frivolous and vexatious litigation and by the use of other flimsy and fallacious arguments. But there were other more effective ways to address such litigation. And, in any case, the legislative agenda was not aimed primarily at that aspect. The issue of frivolous and vexatious litigation merely travelled with the change in the law. The basic agenda was aimed at avoiding being instructed to pay out large dollar amounts to victims for genuine damage that had been inflicted by members of our profession on their victims and, thereby, avoiding (as best could be) the myriad of consequences of not being able to pay the full amount of those damages. [The equivalent task force of the Institute of Chartered Accountants of Scotland, and whose findings were published in late 1994, even rejected a change in the law away from joint and several liability on the grounds that it would merely replace one inequity with another inequity; whilst a report co-authored by Austin Mitchell, a British Labour MP, Tony Puxty of the University of Strathclyde, and others, and which report is entitled 'The Auditors Liability Charade', condemns the profession for its behaviour and suggests, amongst other things, that more consideration should be given to the fundamental expansion of audit work and to the unethical practices of accountants.] Yes, it would seem that the underlying motives of these people, these so-called 'leaders' of our profession who champion the capping of damage awards, even under the philosophy of proportional liability, really do need to be carefully examined; for, given their selfish ambition, they truly are remote from what are the moral and the ethical expectations of our times.

Both of the aforementioned categories of behaviour were basically damage control initiatives and were aimed at, and as a profession, avoiding our responsibility for our own shortcomings. In reality it amounted to the power coalition endeavouring to protect the in-crowd and who, in broad terms, were the same people. Only the actors change roles. Not only were the aforementioned initiatives immoral and unethical, they were also undemocratic, for they were pushed through without any real opportunity for the one hundred thousand (100,000) or more members of the profession to understand what was happening and to express a view in relation thereto. There were to be no arguments to the contrary to be placed before the membership. That was too risky. Simply, it was the one percent (1%) of the membership of our profession (who are concentrated in the large professional practices as partners and colleagues of one another) who were looking after themselves at the expense of the (extremely highly dispersed) ninety-nine percent (99%) of members who were once again being treated with utter disdain by, what is tantamount to, the arrogant leadership of the large firms. Incidentally, and just so we don't lose sight of perspective, these words may well be cutting, but what we are dealing with are fundamental matters which affect the very future of the profession (its image, its reputation, its credibility, its integrity, etc, etc, and so forth) so when, in fact, democracy (based on appropriate information, discussion, and debate) is abused, and the President of the Institute, who is suppose to represent all members (one must wonder about applied corporate governance in the context of professional bodies) fails to intervene and point out the essential nature of the unfolding actions, then someone, even if it's only an ordinary member such as myself, needs to speak out. The preceding comments themselves may seem harsh to some people but I think it should be remembered that, although most of these people (but not all of them) are probably pleasant enough folk, they have no qualms whatsoever about inflicting their actions on other people; being members and non-members of the profession alike. As long as they achieve what they want to achieve then of course they're happy. [You'll notice that they don't have people like me on their committees. They may well have plenty of *ring-ins* so as to say. But not too many independent thinkers; with guts.] They couldn't care two damns about society or, for that matter, their fellow professionals, as long as *they* can reap the benefits for *themselves*.

This, however, is my profession too. And just as much as it is their profession. And I am alarmed at the lack of competence and with the degradation that has occurred over the years, year-after-year, and from what appears to be the same sources. The absolutely average, having messed it up, now want to hide behind the image and reputation of our profession, as well as their own images of respectability, whilst they proclaim their innocence. And I for one don't buy that misrepresentation, no matter how powerful they may be, what their status is in life, or what wealth such people may possess. These people (whether being sued or not) failed our profession, for they failed to address, and in an appropriate way, fundamental matters; and they now wish to manage public perceptions and, not least of all, to their own advantage.

The profession also undertook the expectation gap initiative and which initiative has been addressed elsewhere in this book. That, in itself, was a positive action and from which, hopefully, some worthwhile benefits will flow. The report itself, however, failed miserably in coming to terms with the fundamental dimension on which all other work is based. *It failed to come to terms with the strategic well-being of the business enterprise.* Nonetheless, the expectation gap report was a very important contribution to the future of the profession in Australia. It was prepared after similar initiatives in other parts of the world. It took into account various of the findings in those other reports. And it built upon those other findings. It is hoped that the benefits of the expectation gap report will not be wasted or disintegrate.

The preceding three points is generally what the accountancy profession did and which amounted to two negative initiatives and one very good positive initiative. There is, of course, more detail. Other reports were produced. There was the one that I have already mentioned on education and the one which I shall be referring to later on corporate collapses. But, in essence, the above is what they did.

But what are they now doing?

Well the profession has now issued a whole host of new edicts and other information some of which may well be based on the aforementioned expectation gap report. These edicts include the March, 1995, policy statement entitled The Nature and Purpose of Statements of Accounting Concepts; the June, 1995, practice edict on The Audit Report on a General Purpose Financial Report; the October, 1995, guidance statement on the Expression of an Opinion on Internal Control and the auditing standard entitled Quality Control for Audit Work, as well as Risk Assessments and Internal Controls, Knowledge of the Business, Performance Auditing, and the edict on the Going Concern, to identify just a few of what is a myriad of pronouncements. [In passing, and by way of a note, the profession can write what it likes in its different pronouncements (they can use all the correct words and they can use all the correct phraseology) but that doesn't mean that the work indicated is being carried out or, as is more probable, that the substance of what is delivered is, in truth, appropriate. At this stage, and for the record, I will also note that some people may consider that what I have written in this book is somewhat cynical or perhaps negative, or even both, but I think that at some point in time each one of us must be prepared to differentiate between cynicism and negativity, on the one part, and, on the other part, recognize and acknowledge reality (the attributes applicable to cynicism and to reality can sometimes be confused) and thereby embrace positivity in order to meet the future with new ideas, creativity, enthusiasm and, not least of all, appropriate initiatives.] The aforementioned pronouncements which are referred to above have, no doubt, helped to clean up some of the outstanding matters which may well have needed attention but, and in no uncertain way, they failed to address the change of mindset or, rather, mindscape which is so urgently required throughout the accountancy profession. You see, what the profession needs to do, *and it is within its power to do it,* is to grab hold of the corporate governance debate and set the strategic direction in relation to corporate governance. In that way the accountancy profession could make a real contribution to the world of business. We would then, and once again, be at the cutting-edge of reality and with fundamentally sound leading-edge contributions. We would determined the state-of-the-art in that field. Whilst the profession would, if we dare use the term, be the creators of international best practice; at least in the anglo-saxon world. The profession itself would be of the essence in relation to corporate governance.

So let us start by looking at the terms strategy, strategist, and strategic management. Business is strategy in action. Strategy is crystallized vision. And crystallized vision is the configuration of resources and the mobilization of energy to achieve purposes. Strategy itself, however, is both ethereal in concept and concrete in reality. It is the present and it is the future. It is implicit and it is explicit. It is global in one state and it is constrained in another state. It is relative in its position and it is absolute in its application. It is critical in its implementation and it is vital in its utilization. Strategy is a process and it is dynamic. But above all, strategy is a vehicle, and its purpose is to deliver relative business success, on a sustainable basis, through the continual matching of a business enterprise with its forever-changing environments.

!!!!! Strategy is Vision in Action !!!!!

Strategy, however, is also a paradox, for it has an unavoidable state. Strategy, even at the very moment of its conception, also experiences its own degradation. The environments in which it functions change, either for the better or for the worse; the vision degenerates into action; and the integrity of its utility is eroded. Strategy, however, is also multi-dimensional. It is a living thing. It is regenerative. And it is exciting.

Strategy is concerned with how to achieve objectives. It relates the business enterprise to its environments; it defines the catchment area within which it will employ its resources; and it determines the corporate enterprise or business entity risk profile. Action is the embodiment of strategy. And there are many alternative, and viable, strategies that a business enterprise may action to achieve its objectives.

Strategy emanates from within every component and every element of a business enterprise. It is inalienable. It is an agent of change. It threatens the status quo. It addresses the future. It crystallizes opportunities. Whilst ultimately, it secures internal benefits from external sources.

Strategy, and amongst other things, deals with domains, task environments, markets, products, risk, power and countervailing power, entrepreneurship, culture, business politics, stakeholders, technology, resource deployment, cash flows, the substance of a business, the quality of the business substance, the futurity of actions, profits, and losses, the sustainability of profits, the quality of earnings, the acquisition and the utilization of strategic value, and the propensity of a business enterprise to create shareholder value and, as a consequence thereof, shareholder wealth.

Strategy may be viewed, for purposes of simplicity, as corporate strategy or as business strategy; the two interacting inexorably, and with the concepts which are utilized in their development, and their management, overlapping significantly whilst, at their finite source, the single-business entity, their differences become translucent. Corporate strategy may be seen as that component which addresses the total business enterprise. It determines the portfolio of businesses and investments which the total enterprise includes within the scope of its activities, together with its major financing decisions; in particular in relation to the level and mix of shareholder capital and debt, and its longevity. Conversely, business strategy may be viewed as addressing the real business activities of a total business enterprise; being the activities which together constitute the basic substance of a corporate enterprise. Investment and financing decisions may well cascade down, feed up, or even permeate through, the structure of a total business enterprise, and these dimensions, in themselves, may very well interact with and constrain business strategy, but in the end it is business strategy that addresses the essence and, thereby, delivers the purpose of the corporate enterprise.

These two concepts, being the concepts of corporate strategy and of business strategy, may in themselves be clearly definable, but in practice their definitions will blur, and this is so whether or not blurring occurs in a simple single business entity organization or it is in an organization with a highly complex and interlocking corporate enterprise structure; for that blurring occurs through the dynamic dimensions of applied strategy.

Strategy resides in, and emanates from, all parts of a business enterprise; and it is totally interactive. Relationships are all-pervasive in nature and organizational boundaries are somewhat irrelevant in form. Its time horizons are multifarious, whilst its impacts, its consequences, and its outcomes are discriminatory. Strategy is reality; and the management of that reality, whether in its compelling and imperative mode or as the management of future expectations, is essential. Management of this nature is what both corporate enterprises and business entities have come to know as strategic management.

The management of strategy is, without doubt, both necessary and vital, and it is effected throughout the entirety of a business enterprise. Its characteristics are that, normatively, it should be carried out in continuous mode, on-line, and with real-time and virtual real-time components; and it should be management of abnormal, if not extra-ordinary, quality. Strategic management, in its applied form, requires positive action which is conceptualized in a kaleidoscope of perspectives. Problems, opportunities, and challenges should be defined in multi-modal form, being both static and dynamic in nature; addressing executive, managerial, and operational perspectives both in the internal and the external environments, as is relevant. Flexibility of action and highly sensitive discrimination are essential. And with an appreciation of heterogeneity being at least as important for sound strategic management as is an appreciation of homogeneity.

Strategists, and strategic managers of quality, are scarce. A person is no more a strategist because that person actions strategies than a person is a businessman because that person is in business. Both strategists, and strategic managers of quality, can abstract and conceptualize with ease. They see things that others see, but they also see things that others do not see. They understand things that others do not understand. And they utilize things that others do not utilize. Strategists, and strategic managers of quality, possess vision, knowledge, understanding, insight, and not least of all wisdom. And it is the presence and the use of those qualities which imbues a business enterprise with its source of effective strategic management.

The tools, techniques, practices, procedures, models, guidelines, frameworks, methodologies, and systems, being the essential strategic management infrastructure of strategic management, are many and varied; whilst, in practice, their employment is often haphazard. Their utilization goes beyond that of common sense; demanding application both in art form, and as a science. They are, by their very nature, both abstract and conceptual. But their utility is valuable, their impacts are real, and their consequences are diverse, as they underwrite the actions of strategic decision-makers; the drivers of strategy.

Strategy has a sovereign and an inalienable existence within a business enterprise. It is not remote from but, rather, is an integral part of, a business enterprise. For strategy is created from power, it resides within resources, it has a cognitive and an incognitive presence, it is absolutely comprehensive, even when it is totally flawed, and it emanates from decisions, and from indecision. It embraces risk, whether known, unknown, or unknowable. It is changeable in form. And it is ever-changing in substance. Whilst it is actioned by people. And this is so whether or not those people are acting with authority. And it is mercilessly at the mercy of the external environment. Strategy, in its applied form, has paramount authority within and over a business enterprise. It is unavoidable, it is sovereign, and it is inalienable.

The inalienable sovereignty of strategy in a business enterprise does not, however, imply that strategic decision-makers, being those with legitimate power and those with illegitimate power, are preordained with omniscience and omnipotence. Power does not imbue decision-makers, the generators of applied strategy, with infinite knowledge and perfect execution. Strategy is subject to the paramount power of the environment. It resides in the realms of judgemental and inspirational action. And in the world of imperfect knowledge, of uncertainty, probability, randomness, and chaos. Strategy calls out for decision-makers with talent, skill, ability, judgement, and wisdom, being decision-makers who focus on the many dimensions of ever-changing reality; avoiding matters superficial and trivial whilst, at one and the same time, embracing matters fundamental and of substance.

Business enterprises are living bodies; encouraging, demanding, and extracting strategic decisions, and which decisions need to be equal to, and more ingenious than, the problems, opportunities, and challenges which are thrust upon them by the vagaries of the environment. To survive in a world of major contingent events, significant unexpected happenings, and fundamental direction-changing encounters, change is of the essence : strategic change. And essential to sound strategic change is appropriate strategic management of the business enterprise.

Yes, strategist are real people. They contribute to the creation of strategy. And that may be through decisions, advice, or actions. Strategists may be identified by a variety of titles, being high status titles such as that of chief executive, managing director, entrepreneur, or business strategist. Or they may be lower status people with low status titles; or they may be people with no title at all. Given this, strategists may be analysed into decision-based, advisor-based, and action-based strategists, with these groups being epitomized by the board of directors, strategic specialists, and operational executives; and with advisor-based strategists being conceptually divided into strategic initiative specialists and strategic management specialists.

Both decision-based and action-based strategists, such as chief executives and production managers respectively, may seek advice from specialists who have an intellectual underpinning in the field of strategic management (whether in, for example, market development or strategic management systems) whilst those same strategists may or may not interact with one another in relation to business enterprise strategy. Whatever the reality may be, however, a necessary dimension that is integral to the achievement of purposes is the execution of action. Action delivers purposes, and this is so whether that action is deemed by parties, either internal or external to a business enterprise, to be favourable or unfavourable in nature. It is action that reveals the real strategies of a business enterprise for, in the end, it is what is actioned (and not what is hoped for) which crystallizes strategy. Accordingly, it is strategic action which the corporate plans and the business strategies of a business enterprise endeavours to encapsulate, and for the benefit of the business enterprise; and with corporate planning and business strategy 'creation, design, and development' being just three of the strategic management processes which provide knowledge, understanding, and insight with regard to applied action; be it past, present, or future action.

Strategy, then, is not a fixed phenomenon by which a business enterprise is to excel or be crucified; although either outcome is quite possible. It is a vehicle, a transmutation, which twists, curls, floats, tumbles, and contorts as it relentlessly strives to match a business enterprise with its forever-changing environments and, thereby, create reality. Vision must be related to action, whilst action must be related to benefits; and vision, action, and benefits must, themselves, be exploded and imploded into strategic impacts, consequences, and outcomes. At the corporate enterprise level and at each and every level and dimension of strategy thereafter (and for strategies within strategies) strategy strives to achieve order within disorder; and this is so no matter how unsustainable or how fleeting is that state. There is, in fact, no one solution to be searched for and found, and which revelation would elicit the ultimate in eurekas, for strategy is the matching of internal turmoil with the turbulence and the volatility of external vagaries; being vagaries of cosmological complexity. For it is strategic management and, within strategic management, strategic management systems, which addresses that challenge. *But alas, there are no accountancy standards which relate to either of those dimensions, worldwide.* And in relation to this point, and for purposes of clarification, the management of the vast majority of business enterprises is not based on the utilization of strategic management systems but, rather, it overwhelmingly relies on the output which is obtained from management information systems. Of course directors and boards of directors, in their deliberations, consider strategic information. That is absolutely essential. But, on the one part, strategic information is typically not systematized to any great extent whilst, on the other part, and due not least of all to the use of impoverished strategic management systems, neither directors nor management can even rely on output which is obtained from those latter systems; at least, that is, not to the same extent to which they can rely on the output that is obtained from management information systems.

In fact, just for the record, and so that you don't doubt this assertion with regard to the relative reliance of management and boards of directors on management information systems, then just ask yourself if your company or a company that you know (perhaps BHP, Email, Burns Philp, TNT, Ansett, News, ANI, Southcorp, FAI, Coles Myer, Goodman Fielder, or Westpac) could significantly downgrade its management information systems. The answer, of course, is typically No !!!! Any company, whether large, medium, or small which did away with an appropriate form of management information systems would immediately lose tremendous value. If it were a listed company its shares would immediately plummet in price. Yet, twenty-five years ago it was a struggle to get many companies to invest in such systems; and this was so even though the management information systems boom was itself business driven. Since then there have been tremendous advances in computer technology, software products, and management knowledge. Today, those systems are even more advanced. In fact, they are almost advanced beyond belief. Whilst, at one and the same time, they are now even more indispensable to business. These systems, without doubt, add tremendous value to a business enterprise. And this is so because they allow companies to do what they could not do otherwise.

They facilitate profits.

But management itself, including boards of directors and not least of all boards of directors of large public listed companies, have distorted their focus on management to the point to which today there is an extreme over-reliance on management information systems, and their output, whilst, at one and the same time, there is an impoverished focus on strategic management systems, and the output from such systems.

There are, in fact, three general types of systems upon which a company depends. The first group are the operational control systems. These are those systems which every business have, from the smallest to the largest, otherwise they would not be in business. A manufacturer of widgets has a system to manufacture its widgets. An insurance company has a system to process its policies. And an airline has a system to produce its tickets. These systems are, in the normal course of events, fairly good due to the imperative nature of those systems. If they don't work then you're out of business; and possibly in the shorter term.

The second group are the management information systems. Those who have any exposure to business at a managerial level are very familiar with at least one of the tremendous variety of this type of system. They provide both feedback and feedforward information. These systems include enterprise, or executive, information systems which systems are often merely an advanced form of management information system, but with their basic conceptual underpinnings being highly correlated with common form management information systems. These systems, amongst other things, produce both financial and management accounting information; as well as a whole host of other information.

The third group are strategic management systems. These systems today, even in major corporates, are typically abysmal. They are in their infancy; being at a stage much akin to where management information systems were twenty years or more ago. Even those large companies which consider themselves to have advanced systems of this type are merely in their embryonic stage. In only five or ten year's time, when these systems are commonplace, those companies which are adept at utilizing such systems will have gained a tremendous strategic advantage in relation to their competitors (not just then, in five or ten year's time, but now, even whilst they are developing and using such systems) and this is so whether those competitors are local, national, or international competitors. Strategic management systems, and I cannot stress this point sufficiently, are absolutely imperative for globalizing companies, and this is so not least of all in their on-line and their real-time forms; for the purpose of these systems is to manage strategy itself. They facilitate the adding of significant value to a company and that value-adding should not be delayed, but should be happening now. For given that strategic management systems are, in themselves, at least as valuable to a company as are its operational control systems and management information systems, then to fail to embrace strategic management systems at an early date is, indeed and in all truth, reckless.

Today it is also a struggle (as it was in those earlier times with management information systems) to encourage companies to invest in strategic management systems, for the problem is that directors themselves are practitioners of strategic management but, like many practitioners, they do not necessarily know a great deal about strategic management itself; and they probably know even less with regard to strategic management systems. But this situation will evolve in due course. And overwhelming benefits will be obtained by those companies which adopt these systems. For those benefits will be located throughout a company; with the board of directors utilizing such systems in one way, whilst top management will utilize those systems in another way, and other dimensions of management will utilize them in yet other ways.

Incidentally, when I stated previously that the profession could prepare accounts, in a fashion; and that it could audit them, in a fashion; and that it could also still work out the taxation situation based on those fashionable accounts; please don't misunderstand me, the profession itself does much good work. Thousands upon thousands of professional accountants spend their whole time undertaking those very activities. Just imagine the massive effort which is involved in producing the monthly, quarterly, half-yearly, and annual financial and management accounts for each and every division, subsidiary, joint venture, business unit, market, product, and whatever else you may think of, in order to provide information for the management, the stakeholders, and the shareholders of BHP. Now add to that effort both the internal and external audit and taxation functions; and advisory inputs. Now multiply that effort by some unspecified figure to account for the top one hundred companies in Australia. Now add some fraction to that lot to account for the rest of the top one thousand companies in Australia; whether they be listed or unlisted and whether public or private companies. Now add on the rest of the effort to account for the remainder of the businesses in our economy (including not least of all that of the proverbial corner shop) and which is composed of approaching a million businesses and other public and private sector entities. Yes, the accountancy profession itself provides a massive input to Australia. And its added value will, without doubt, be tremendous. And positive. What I am addressing, and more so for the 'top' one thousand companies, and other large organizations, is that the assessment of the very foundations, the basic underpinnings, of those entities, by those who prepare accounts and by those who audit them, is not appropriate. Even today the profession, both as preparers and as auditors of accounts, probably wouldn't have much idea with regard to assessing the strategic well-being of a company; and, historically, they probably didn't care. In addition thereto, and for year-after-year-after-year, nobody else seemed to care either, as the directors of those 'invulnerable' companies, their financiers, institutional investors, stockbrokers, merchant bankers, corporate advisors, business journalists, and everybody else opted out of reality [the accountancy profession probably even forgot to carry out their own absolutely inadequate and very misleading going concern tests . . . . or they just saved on the work . . . . basically to keep the fees down to what they thought were client-acceptable levels . . . . and what a saving that was . . . . bearing in mind the subsequent demolition] until, that is, the debacles of the past decade woke them all up again, being the shareholders, the stakeholders (including not least of all the boards of directors and the accountancy profession) as well as society in general; and with a massive jolt. No, it wasn't the large-scale loss of jobs, or the unbearable social devastation that occurred, which delivered that most unpleasant of jolts. And nor was it a new-found moral or ethical enlightenment. [Some of them would have wondered what those words actually meant.] It was simple. It was the 'D' word that did it. 'D' is for Damages !!!!! And damage claims arrived like snowflakes from heaven in a blizzard. Heaven? Yes, heaven for the profession. For hopefully some fundamental good, in the end, will emerge from this period of trauma; although, no doubt, the snowflakes came from hell for the recipients of the damage claims. In fact, damage claims came thick and fast. And like what seemed from everywhere. And before long we had a damages snowdrift of in excess of some eight billion dollars ($8b) in total. Damages, damages, and even more damages. It was, without doubt, damage claims, and the threat thereof, which focused their minds and their attentions. *At last their massive propensity to make money was suddenly being matched by an equally massive propensity for them to lose everything.* The two-pronged debilitation of the accountancy profession by its so-called leadership (being the de-professionalizing of our profession and their abject failure to enhance the substance of our very own professionalism) had at last paid dividends : the chickens had come home to roost !!!!!

Previous to the 'jolt' everyone sailed along on calm waters, so as to say, consciously or sub-consciously teaming and lading their 'concerns' and hoping, or even just taking it for granted, that a company, or a business enterprise, or a business entity, would be there next year; and with any problems being lost in the wash as going concerns continued going on. And in any case nobody did much even if a company wasn't there next year but had, in the meantime, folded. In pre-debacle days hardly anybody got sued in Australia; although one auditor did go to prison. But that was in 1969. Occasionally they may have had to make a pay-out of some description or other. But definitely not for some huge amount of damages. So when the year was up, that is the arbitrary going concern test period had expired, they didn't so much think about having survived, and being off the hook. They just didn't think of the 'hook' at all. At least, that is, not until there was a real threat of danger. Even then many accountants and auditors wouldn't have done much; apart from perhaps worry. Although the more cunning of their numbers may well have revisited their own working papers. Just to (so as to say) check their workings. For others, however, there would be little, or nothing, to check !!!!!

It may then be asked, rhetorically of course, that given that from an historic perspective the vast majority of companies seemed to survive the one year going concern test period as recommended by the accountancy profession (whether those tests were carried out totally, partially, or not at all) then does it really matter, on a prospective basis, whether those who prepare accounts and those who audit those accounts, actually know, or have an opinion with regard to, the state of the strategic well-being of a company when they report to shareholders; and, thereby, to stakeholders and to society in general?

Well I guess that, at least as a first approximation, we could use the disaster which beset the 'Titanic' to exemplify the situation. In the case of the Titanic (being, let us assume, the company in its totality) did it really matter whether the deck-chairs were neatly ordered (that is, the finances looked good) or whether the brass hand-rails were well polished (stand-by credit facilities were in place) because, and unknown to the owners of the shipping company, the ship itself was going to sink and virtually all of everything was going to end up on the seabed, or somewhere;

and eventually disappear. The argument proffered would have been that they would never have known, in prospective mode, that the Titanic was going to collide with an iceberg or that, alternatively, an iceberg was going to collide with the Titanic; or perhaps that some synthesis thereof would occur on the voyage.

But is this 'sinking' assumption correct ?!!!!

The superficial answer, of course, is 'yes' given that we keep on doing things the way that we do them at the present time. But what if we adopt mind-boggling innovations and, thereby, change the way we look at businesses. For just one fleeting moment let us believe that those who prepare accounts, and those who audit them, can look at a company strategically. Given that particular event, then in that fleeting moment the answer to our question may well beçome 'no' and the above assumption is not necessarily correct. In that very moment, in that very instant, the accountancy profession has embraced new challenges, and a relevant future.

There are two fundamental questions which may spring to mind in relation to the Titanic and which questions should have been addressed; for not only were massive losses incurred, in human, emotional, and material form, but there was also a massive waste of potential, and in many forms, as a result of that disaster. In fact, would you believe it, although it is presumed that this most magnificent of ships was sea-worthy when it set sail on its maiden voyage, there are, today, those specialists who even question the very substance of its structure. Other specialists however, and at the time, considered that the ship was so magnificent that it is believed that they actually lost sight of what this vessel was in reality, and the very challenges that it may willingly embrace and unavoidably encounter, so they focused on its impressive superstructure, its brass hand-rails, and its deck chairs; as they failed to consider some of the most basic, albeit extremely challenging and massively multi-dimensional, matters which, had they been considered and then determined in wisdom, would have brought so much on-going benefit to so many people (whether they were directly or indirectly involved therewith) at that time, and later.

The questions which should have been asked, at least from the perspective of the owners of the shipping company, are both general and specific in nature. The specific question addresses whether or not the ship would successfully complete a particular voyage. Whilst the general question addresses whether or not the ship would successfully complete subsequent voyages. Travelling with both of these questions are the implications which concern the quality of the specific voyage, as well as voyages in general, and the interim and final condition of the vessel.

Actually there were two immediate assumptions which were made previously, and not just one, and with these assumptions being the aforementioned 'sinking' assumption, as identified, and the other being the 'collision' assumption; and each of which assumptions are closely inter-related with the matter of voyages, both generally and specifically, as well as the matter of the quality of those voyages; whilst, at one and the same time (but in addition thereto) the condition or well-being of the vessel, and at any time, is also vitally important.

Neither of the assumptions, by the way, were necessarily correct.

Our profession, when preparing and auditing accounts, could not and did not answer any of the aformentioned questions (other than by coincidence) properly. And I also believe that, in reality, the profession, at least at first, was not concerned that it had not adequately addressed these matters. The profession, after all, hadn't really been confronted with substantial penalties at that point in time whilst, in effect, they also answered to themselves for their own ethical behaviour; not least of all in relation to the fundamental strategic well-being of a business enterprise. For one large firm of accountants to raise questions of competence, even at a general level, and in relation to an industry or industry segment, never mind in relation to a specific company, may well have provoked retribution by another large firm of accountants. [I'm raising questions of competence now, and only at a general level, and no doubt somebody somewhere will be getting hot under the collar; for, like incest itself, such fundamental topics may well be taboo.] And for the Institute of Chartered Accountants to raise these matters, and with conviction, and on a sustainable basis, and in relation to both those who prepare accounts and those who audited those accounts, was equally unlikely; for the Institute was controlled by the same people who controlled the Big Six firms. So you see, the accountancy profession was well and truly structured for nobody to do anything very much at all; and this would have been so even had there been an Urgent Issues Group in existence, for they may well have placed any concerns on the back burner whilst perhaps hoping that these burning issues would, sooner or later, be extinguished. As entrepreneurial lunacy got out of hand, that icon of business respectability, the Institute of Chartered Accountants, was found to be 'missing in action' so as to say, whilst losses were stored up behind the dam wall as companies continued to report record profit after record profit. Did nobody stop and ask the salient question . . . . Is this for real ?!!!! The accountancy profession, in any case, probably didn't know that the strategic management of these companies was, in many cases, absolutely basic; for the profession itself didn't know much about strategic management. For its own knowledge, too, was basic. [Please, keep any protestations for later, and just look back at our dismal record. Take a hard look at all those companies which so 'surprisingly' went under, together with all those companies which were merely debilitated, and then ask yourself : Would the profession, in concept, act differently today? What, if anything, has changed? Are we asking the salient questions, even now, and with regard to various industries, industry segments, and specific companies or parts thereof? I don't think so . . . . Do you ?!!!] If the preceding questions with regard to voyages are now revisited, but in a much more significant context, we may begin to appreciate that there are, indeed, tremendous business, financial, economic, and social benefits to be obtained from the profession being able to answer, and actually answering, those questions; and in active, and not passive, mode. No ducking. No diving. No mindlessly vague language. Just give us the answer. How healthy, how well, in terms of its strategic management, is our company?

Bearing these matters in mind, then the basic rhetorical question which may be asked is concerned with whether or not it is good enough that the accountancy profession is only required to carry out what amounts to the most simple and superficial of tests (as is currently recommended by the profession) in order to establish the fundamental validity of the underpinnings of general purpose financial reports (and upon which tests their 'fairly presented' opinions unequivocally rest) or whether, indeed, society in total, stakeholders generally, and shareholders in particular, can and should reasonably expect and require, in the ordinary course of events, a much more meaningful opinion from those who prepare accounts and from those who audit those accounts?

Oh yes, and just so we don't lose sight of that almost innocuous comment that I made earlier, being the 'as a first approximation' statement, let me stress now that multi-dimensional everything is what is available to be considered in strategic management. This would include examining the obvious and the superficial aspects of something (or everything) cascading down through the subtle and the sophisticated levels, and outwardly, in a quaquaversal-type way, both generally and specifically, and in a dichotomous manner, as well as along one or more continuums, and in terms of continuities and discontinuities, and in static and dynamic mode. As well as, of course, much much more. And with the art being to, amongst other things, constrain the boundaries for consideration and to examine the relevant in order to obtain, and in terms of the particular purpose, an appropriate strategic result.

In order to address appropriately the aforementioned matters we should endeavour to consider various dimensions concurrently so, for now, let's switch back into (quasi) corporate governance.

Henry Bosch, a well known figure in Australia, and possibly not only the minds-eye but also the auditory personification of the archetype member of the neo-classical establishment, recently wrote a book which is entitled 'The Director At Risk' and which book is, as may be expected, a most conventional approach to corporate governance. [It is noted in passing that Henry was, in a previous life, Chairman of the NCSC, being the now defunct National Companies and Securities Commission.] The approach in Henry's book, which is overwhelmingly characterized by the compliance-based 'accountability' syndrome, and which book, in accordance therewith, includes only a hint of the much more active 'management' strain of corporate governance, reveals the state-of-the-art as practiced by establishment-appointed boards of directors. It is not exactly the type of leading-edge approach to corporate governance which is required in order to embrace the realities of turbulent times. Henry even refers to 'a strategic plan which will probably be revised annually' and which reference presumably came straight out of his worldview paradigm. [Why on earth would you be talking in such endearing terms about the use of management technologies which are twenty or thirty years old in a book on contemporary corporate governance . . . . Things have moved on Henry . . . . I ask you, the reader, would your company use a computer to run your business if that computer system was designed in 1965 ?!!!!] Incidentally, this quotation has not been plucked from his book in isolation. Out of context. And in order to make some cheap point. The quotation encapsulates the neo-classical establishment thinking which is portrayed in his book. Sure, Henry states that 'no set of objectives or strategies can be laid down as fixed for all time' and that changes may be needed *'even between annual reviews'* but, in keeping with neo-classical thinking, he indicates that 'some managers, even in large and sophisticated organizations, resist anything that they see as restricting their freedom of action' as though he has no perception of virtual or real-time management. Whilst he then proceeds to state that 'by insisting that clear goals are set, and plans for achieving them laid down, the board can make a significant contribution to the performance of the organization' thereby questioning, if only by implication, even the possible existence of paradigms of vague management. There would, indeed, appear to be little room for the on-line real-time management of strategies in the world as seen by Henry Bosch. Henry then goes on to state that directors must 'check that the detailed budgets and specific actions of management are consistent with the corporate plan' being just another indication of the assumption of more or less stable environments. He also states, and categorically, that 'the most common, and most important, performance indicator is the annual budget which, at its simplest, sets milestones for income and expenditure as well as profit or surplus' and thereby, in expressing such a view, he well and truly encapsulates the essence of establishment-think. This is not to say, however, that his book does not provide, amongst its many pages, valuable information; for indeed it does. But with regard to corporate governance it basically addresses third, fourth, and fifth level stuff; and in static mode. Even the 'workable system' which is described therein can hardly be called a system. Its components may, in total, be described as an ad hoc collection of more or less remotely related matters. But a system? And not just a system. But a corporate governance system? Please Henry. And this is after he has quoted from the Tricontinental Royal Commission that '. . . . a board should ensure that it retains effective control over management . . . . to do that there must be *workable systems* which result in the board monitoring accurately the operations of the corporation. It is not enough merely to pronounce upon policy. There is a need to be satisfied properly that the policy is being implemented fully and efficiently. To put it at its simplest, the board needs to know *what is really going on* . . . . The board must retain effective control, but with that, of course, comes corresponding responsibility and accountability.' [Just for your information I have never met Henry Bosch, so there is no personal dimension, as such, involved here, whilst my comments are, at least in my opinion, objective and analytical, and emanate from my own philosophy concerning corporate governance and my underlying paradigm with regard to business management or, put alternatively, if you write a book I suppose that you have to be prepared to accept both the praise and the criticism.] The establishment mindset is further espoused by Henry, and in his book, with his statement that 'the board's single most important responsibility is to take whatever steps are necessary to protect the organization's financial position' and which statement is presented as being the most important conformance requirement of a board of directors. This statement of responsibility, however, has little or nothing to do with conformance and much and everything to do with one's views with regard to what makes a person appropriate to be a director. This protective focus would appear to rank way above the positively active role of directors and which role is that of *embracing and crystallizing appropriate opportunities and delivering the benefits of those opportunities to shareholders* and which fundamental responsibility does not seem to get too much of a mention in the book. [Look, I could continue deconstructing Henry's book almost indefinitely, but the outcome would only reinforce the obvious, which is that Henry has presented the traditional neo-classical establishment view of corporate governance, and thereby he has further confirmed the drastic need for quantum leaps and order of magnitude changes in that vital area of management.] To avoid, as best I can, any misunderstanding in relation to remote corporate governance, which I referred to above as third, fourth, and fifth level stuff (and it is noted, by the way, that the *actual* choice of matters for inclusion in a corporate governance regime is, indeed, yours and not mine) I am implying that the particular components of corporate governance, as are recommended by the neo-classical establishment, are matters which are remote from the cutting-edge of business reality. It's the difference, one may say, between embracing naked reality (that is, life in the flesh) and dressing-up a shop window dummy. The neo-classical establishment have, indeed, a wonderful wardrobe to choose from and, it would seem, they have chosen some wonderful clothes with which to adorn *their* dummies; whilst the dummies themselves look most beautiful. [The word 'dummies' could, of course, be interpreted as being a pun targeted at neo-classical establishment controlled companies.] Despite this, and unfortunately for the neo-classical establishment, *a dummy is a dummy is a dummy*, and it will never be a living body; the real thing. Living bodies, whether they are adorned with beautiful clothes, or are merely dressed in rags, have many favourable characteristics and attributes. They are creative. They do things. They are productive. They are reality. The dummy in the shop window may look wonderful. [You should look in a Coles Myer shop window some time . . . . or, there again, perhaps you should just look at Coles Myer itself now that the establishment are actively dominant . . . . for I wonder about its future.] But the dummy is not, and never will be, reality. The accountability and compliance corporate governance regime will never be as relevant, or as beneficial, to business, to shareholders, to stakeholders, and to society in general, as is that of the active management regime. Checking that the surgeon's knife is made of the correct steel, that it has been appropriately sterilized, and that it is as sharp as a razor, can itself never replace the incision or, indeed, the reality of the operation; for the operation (whether for good or for bad) actually achieves something !!!!!

[It is noted, as a matter of fact, that the damage which was inflicted on society by the delinquent entrepreneurs of the 1980s (and which entrepreneurs were, without doubt, aided and abetted in their activities by the establishment) eventually became obvious and gross. It is also noted, however, that the damage which was inflicted, and which continues to be inflicted, on society by the establishment, and which damage is also real but less obvious (for it is submerged and by the establishment itself) was, and is, just as debilitating to society. The damage which has been and is being inflicted by the establishment, however, is based on ignorance and it is inflicted, whether cognitively or otherwise, by stealth. It wears the clothes of respectability. That is why we need a book like this (being a forthright condemnation of ignorance in high places and an entreatment for fundamental action) for once again, at some point in time, the innocent will suffer, possibly by graceful but debilitating degradation, and the establishment will, without doubt, yet again disclaim their share of responsibility. Now, therefore, is the time to act. Not when the blood is on the carpet. Being anybody's blood. And anybody's carpet. As long as it's not their blood. And as long as it's not their carpet. For the establishment will not accept responsibility for their wrongdoings. That is why they institutionalize wrongdoing. There is then no-one at whom to point the finger. And there is no-one who feels personal concern or guilt. For, by their very act of institutionalizing actions (in, say, world's best practice) shame no longer attaches to wrongdoing; and nor does it attach to damage.]

These observations with regard to the establishment and its approach to corporate governance should not, in themselves, disturb Henry, or you for that matter, for you can be assured that the approach which is described in Henry's book is very much in keeping with the approach which is taken by the anglo-saxon branch of *the boring order of international establishments* and which approach is discussed in a report that was published in July, 1995, and which is entitled 'Who Holds The Reins?' and which report is an international survey of corporate governance practices. The approach to corporate governance which has been taken by the anglo-saxon countries included in the report (being Canada, the UK, and the USA) correlates quite well with the largely remote approach to corporate governance which is set out in Henry's book, and which approach is recommended for Australia. A copy of the aforementioned report may be obtained, at a small charge, from the International Bar Association which is based in London, England . . . . or perhaps you would like to borrow my copy !!!!!

The aforementioned report, the full title of which is 'International Corporate Governance - Who Holds The Reins?' was prepared by a task force which was set up by the International Capital Markets Group in July, 1994. It examined corporate governance structures in Japan, Germany, France, Canada, the USA, and the UK. The task force found that in the UK, the USA, and Canada, being anglo-saxon based countries, the corporate governance emphasis was on the shorter-term, whilst in Germany, France, and Japan the longer-term view was of more importance. The opinion is expressed (and which opinion is actually taken from an article which was written by a task force member and which article is based on the report itself) that 'no system of governance should be allowed to become so bureaucratic or restrictive that it stifles innovation and entrepreneurship . . . . a system should seek to improve and not impede performance . . . . enterprise needs to be dynamic and progressive' whilst integrity (being the qualities of honesty, fair dealing, and truthfulness) is also stressed as being important. Corporate governance, it indicates, is about providing investors (and, presumably, potential investors, stakeholders, and society in general) with useful information on which they may make important decisions with regard to the integrity of their investments. Doubtless this expressed purpose should have embraced decisions with regard to not only actual but also proposed investments; as well as business-based decisions. It would appear that another task force has now been established, subsequent to the publication of the 'Who Holds The Reins?' report, and which task force is charged with developing the various recommendations that are contained in the initial report. This task force has been established under the auspices of the Federation Internationale des Bourses de Valeurs (FIBV). I guess some of us will eagerly await the findings of that particular body.

It is noted that further reference to the content of the corporate governance 'Who Holds The Reins?' report is made below, rather than at this point, in order that greater relevance may be obtained from such comments and in the context of what is, at that point, the particular matter or matters under consideration.

Given the above, it would seem that the Institute of Chartered Accountants of Scotland has again taken a prominent position at the forefront of intellectual contribution to the profession; on this occasion in relation to corporate governance. It had previously issued a sixty (60) page discussion document which was entitled 'Auditing Into The Twenty-First Century' as well as having issued another report which was entitled 'Auditor's Liability' and which report itself (based on the social justice dimensions of joint and several liability for damages) took a very different stance to that which has been taken by the Big Six firms. [I guess all this activity must have something to do with the heather and the haggis !!!!!] A Past President of that Institute (himself a mover and a shaker) was chairman of the aforementioned task force (representing the International Federation of Accountants) whilst a Director of that same Institute was project director of the task force. Both were active in preparing the report 'Who Holds The Reins?' for the International Capital Markets Group. I was pleased to see that the Chairman of the Committee of Representatives was a partner and Chartered Accountant from a Big Six firm in Adelaide, Australia. Thank goodness that there are some members of the accountancy profession, around the world, who are prepared to do something worthwhile for society (and this despite any constructive criticism which may emanate from, and in relation to, their particular efforts) for thereby we can all make progress and hopefully secure otherwise unattainable benefits.

At this stage we should perhaps revisit the stance which has been taken on corporate governance by that most prominent of neo-classical establishment bodies, the ASX, and not least of all because of its de facto adoption of the role of surrogate for AIMA, for it is essential to business success that the dead-weight of the establishment be removed from its present *prominent* position in the determination of the future direction of corporate governance in Australia. [The establishment calls out to be challenged (few even thought of confronting Lloyds of London prior to its grand debacle) for, despite delivering benefits, it inflicts much damage on society.] The ASX has spent much of its effort in relation to corporate governance delivering to shareholders, to stakeholders, and to society in general, that most unacceptable of balls : the underarm. They know, and we know, that by default AIMA has become the 'Australian Corporate Governance Regulator' and that the ASX has been spineless in its limp-hand approach to corporate governance. It has pandered to the powerful investors, and at the expense of business, and for its own purposes. It is essential, as both a quasi and a pseudo law-maker, that the ASX embraces its responsibilities with responsibility. It must change its attitude and approach to corporate governance and also, indeed, it must change its attitude and approach to the specifics thereof. The ASX must be seen to be independent of AIMA. And it must become more eclectic in its approach to matters of corporate governance.

[It is noted that the ASX may well claim that it did, and indeed does, take an eclectic approach to corporate governance and that this is evidenced, not least of all, by the development of its listing rule. There were apparently seventy-six respondents to its request for submissions in relation to its proposed initiative. But with submissions of the quality of that which was made by the Institute of Chartered Accountants then it is, perhaps, hardly surprising that we got the quality of listing rule which we did, or that AIMA was so easily able to exert de facto control over the corporate governance agenda. It is pointed out, however, that the existence of an eclectic perspective does not necessarily depend upon the number of submissions which were considered by the ASX but, rather and amongst other things, it depends on the range, or the variety, of paradigms and philosophies (whether submissions or otherwise) that are genuinely considered, and in dialectic mode.]

Given the written material identified above, let's just wander off for a few pages into the human dimension of the neo-classical establishment, and so take some time out to look at certain of their messages and hype.

The then current chairman of the ASX, when defending the ASX corporate governance listing rule at a seminar which was hosted by the Chartered Institute of Company Secretaries in March, 1996 (the establishment, it is noted, have plenty of opportunity to massage minds) stated that '. . . . overdoing protective regulation can actually encourage more risky behaviour than would otherwise be indulged in both by financial institutions and by shareholders.' The chairman claimed that a prescriptive corporate governance rule would carry a number of inherent problems and '. . . . could encourage directors *not* to innovate or even to think very much about their company's corporate governance needs.' He went on to stated that '. . . . not ticking a box, even with a good explanation, could be taken by investors as prima facia evidence that the company was doing something wrong when, in fact, it could be doing something better than the recommended practice' whilst conversely ticking all boxes could be '. . . . wrongly taken as endorsement of the company's corporate governance.' Despite the defence of a disclosure-based approach to corporate governance, the chairman refused to rule out the introduction of a prescriptive regime; and which, by default, is what has been done by AIMA.

There are several messages in the preceding paragraph and not least of all the one which says that the ASX is hedging its bets on the 'prescriptive versus non-prescriptive' approach to corporate governance and basically, and in my opinion, because they don't know, for sure, which way to go. There is also inherent in the paragraph a fair amount of insinuation and innuendo, and not least of all in relation to that of 'risky behaviour' and encouraging directors 'not to innovate' in the area of corporate governance. The paradigm is, indeed, quite interesting as, although it may suggest connotations of depth, the actual perspective of the paradigm is quite superficial. The alternatives are presented as a dichotomy (being, that is, one or the other) and the status quo is supported by implications of unspecified fear. The fear is, on the one part, that companies will indulge in *more risky behaviour* than may otherwise be the case (with risk having connotations of badness) and with the source of risk being left for your own imagination to conjure up and to crystallize whilst, on the other part, the implied threat of *impeding innovation* (innovation being an event which we often assume to have connotations of goodness) and, through the inferred existence of such impediments, it is also insinuated that alternative approaches to corporate governance could not be as beneficial (to whom one may ask) as the approach to corporate governance that is currently recommended by the establishment. [Surely he jests.] Perhaps someone should tell the stock exchange chairman that neither risk nor innovation are, in themselves, good or bad, but that they are (as he knows) useful political weapons.

The justification for the corporate governance listing rule, as stated by the chairman of the ASX in its defence, is hollow and worth no more than a 'penny dreadful' itself. The establishment, being as boring as hell, have failed to come to terms with the fundamentals of what they are addressing; being the function of corporate governance. What, they should ask themselves, is the purpose of corporate governance ?!!!! The establishment, having established this, may then decide not to spend its time on silly argument regarding the merits and de-merits of prescriptive and non-prescriptive approaches. They would then have time to recognize that their own listing rule is, in practice, nothing less than a compliance-based regime and that, by utilizing AIMA guidelines and similar frameworks as de facto standards, that its application is also extremely deficient. Indeed, the regime can, at best, only manage to secure the underwhelming benefits which may be obtained from third, fourth, and fifth level initiatives whilst, at one and the same time, it sacrifices the overwhelming benefits which could be secured from first and second level initiatives. The absolutely underwhelming gains which may arise from the present impoverished actions of the establishment will, and at best, fall significantly short of the overwhelming gains which have now been, and which will continue to be, foregone (and for some time into the future) because of the blind initiatives of the neo-classical establishment. The clawback of this shortfall will be slow. And the debilitation will be great. In the meantime the ASX, by following the course of action which, in reality, it has followed (even though the actual listing rule itself is quite ethereal and anaemic in its requirements and, thereby, is everything to all people) will have done a great deal to both retard and to damage Corporate Australia and, as a consequence, society in general.

I guess we must always try to remember who their constituency is, down at the ASX and, despite misconceptions to the contrary, who their constituency is not. You will recall that the ASX did damn-all to mitigate the debacles and the debilitations of the last decade. They failed miserably to insist, in relation to the big players, that appropriate meetings of shareholders were called, or to effectively demand information and explanations with regard to various matters. So why would it do anything which is itself contrary to the wishes of its real constituents, and with regard to corporate governance? Elites, remember, talk with elites, and for the benefit of elites. And they make decisions, in our interests, and for their benefit. The establishment are not very good at looking after our interests. And sometimes, believe it or not, they're not very good at looking after their own interests either !!!!!

A few days later the managing director of the ASX made a pronouncement and which pronouncement was, of course, totally in keeping with neo-classical establishment thinking. He indicated that the accounting standard setters in Australia needed to dramatically fast-track moves to internationalize local accounting standards. This utterance was in response to the Australian Accounting Standards Board policy statement which re-affirmed its commitment to harmonize local standards with international standards. The thing is, there's nothing wrong with this as long as harmonization is in the best interests of Australian society, in the best interests of Corporate Australia, and, thereafter, in the best interests of the profession in Australia. The view of the ASX was that 'unless we are prepared to move to link up with what is happening elsewhere in accounting standards we will lose business to other markets' which is quite in line with the type of 'set in concrete' causation pronouncements from that source. Is the whole of corporate life, one may ask, intended to focus on maximizing benefits for the ASX ?!!!! It is claimed that standards released by the FASB (being the Financial Accounting Standards Board) in the US should provide the benchmark which all other standard setters themselves should follow. But who said that they are the fount of all wisdom? Who said that they get everything right? The establishment like (and, indeed, actively encourage and acclaim) conformance with the views and opinions of the establishment; and if that happens to be conformance with the views and opinions of the international establishment, they like that even better. Their mindsets are locked into conformance. It is the nature of the people in those positions. Conformance with the leadership set is applauded. [I wonder if the ASX is the only member of the establishment that doesn't seem to know that the FASB is under potentially terminal assault; being accused of being out of touch with business realities.] So when the ASX throws in such phraseology as '. . . . when trillions of dollars a year of equity investment flows between nations' then you can be sure that such colourful language is being rolled out as purposeful insinuation in order to impress us (and to steam-roller us into believing that we must, unconditionally and willy-nilly, rush into adopting these best practice international accounting standards {and to assist the development of which the ASX has donated $100,000} or else we're dead cabbage) and this despite the fact that such phrases are absolute rubbish; at least, that is, in the context of Australia.

Trillions ?!!!! There may well be trillions of dollars of equity investment flowing around the world somewhere. But when last did anyone invest a trillion dollars of new equity capital in an Australian company (remember, we already have the existing stock of capital and, admittedly the market value of that stock fluctuates, as it does anywhere, but incremental additions thereto are relatively small) or, indeed, when last did anyone invest a trillion dollars of new equity capital in *all* Australian companies and *in total;* being all the listed and all the unlisted companies (that is, the whole damn lot put together) and, for that matter, cumulatively over the last two hundred years since James Cook, another Yorkshireman, arrived on our shores. Even our largest company, BHP, in all its glory, is only worth $40b. Well I'll tell you when a trillion dollar investment of new equity capital last happened. Never !!! In reality, we'd need some twenty-five BHPs hanging around the place to even tot-up just one trillion of those trillions of dollars. The whole thing is pure hype to achieve poorly considered establishment ends. The managing director even went on to say that moves to embrace International Accounting Standards Committee standards could see the number of foreign listings double in the US. I presume he meant the number of Australian companies. Some are already in America. The New York Stock Exchange currently lists more than two hundred (200) foreign companies. Their entire market capitalization is about $330b. So what would be our share of that figure? And where's all this trillion dollar stuff. The whole lot, and from everywhere, only totals one-third of a trillion dollars. I think we must stop the hype and look, not so much at the trillions of dollars which may or may not be invested in equity around the world, and concentrate on the lower billions of dollars, indeed, the very much lower billions of dollars which impact Australia. And we must then look at that in terms of the big picture and the broad sweep of things; and not just in terms of some skewd hype from the ASX. [At this point I'll step aside for a moment so that you can reflect on the constant hype and pressure which seems to characterize contemporary existence (you know the sort of thing . . . . you just don't stand a chance in life if you haven't traded three dozen derivatives in the last hour; made four hundred connections, via internet, in twenty-five countries, in a fifteen minute period; have loaded, unloaded, and re-loaded your latest copy of Windows 95 to check that you're still connected to everything and everywhere; and have received a score of calls on your mobile; and all this before breakfast . . . . and which breakfast you haven't got time to eat anyway !!!!!) being hype and pressure that is typically applied to achieve obscure benefits from doubtful actions; and which mode is now being used by the boring establishment to achieve *its* own purposes. At this rate we'll all end up belting round like spinning tops, splurting out colourful flames like catherine wheels, and then exploding like a roman candle in a shower of sparks; having a heart attack or two; and wondering what the hell life was all about anyway. Yes, I wonder when last it was that you took time out, I mean real time, to gaze at the moon, the stars, and the universe, to ponder thereon, to relate the magnificence of creation to your own reality, and to contemplate your own future or, on a more earthly scale, when did you last set aside quality time to really appreciate the beauty of art, the enchantment of the theatre, and the splendour of music; or to just spend a reasonable amount of time with your family. Yes, I wonder when you last stopped and considered the mindless pursuit of emptiness.] Do you remember that recent election campaign about privatizing one third of Telstra, and how it would be way beyond the biggest new capital raising in the entire history of Australia. Well all that talk was about a mere eight billion dollars ($8.0b) of equity capital. That's all, relative to a trillion dollars of new capital. And that was suppose to be massive. [For comparison, the recently failed British Telecom / Cable & Wireless merger in the UK was to have been some $60b in total.] So where the hell does this trillion dollar stuff come in? Well that's simple. Very simple. It's all part of the push by the establishment (and this doesn't imply anything about conspiracy theories because I don't believe in them) to peddle their views and opinions, their convergence and conformance paradigms, and their perspective of the world. Convergence and conformance are indeed high on the agenda, whilst, implied in their world uniformity belief, of course, is the view that out there, somewhere, is an international committee of masterminds [just like that archetype of its kind . . . . the United Nations . . . . and we've all seen their applied brilliance over the past decades . . . . obviously the UN does a great deal of good . . . . nothing is all bad . . . . but it's the monumental screw-ups that concern me] and which committee of international masterminds have the answers to everything and who, for our benefit, are forever making divine utterances; and not least of all in order to correct their previous divine utterances. You know the type of mindset. If we get it wrong, then we all get it wrong, so don't worry. You'll be protected by claiming world's best practice. Like the rats, and then the children (on reflection the analogy is quite good) we follow the Pied Piper with glee as he plays his enticing tunes, but all end up, like the proverbial Lemmings, at the bottom of the cliff; shaken, stunned, crippled, or dead. I acknowledge that there's some degree of convergence correlation in almost everything.

That's how you get the big picture. But remember. You can view the big picture from many different locations. From high up. From low down. From in between. Or from somewhere else. And with the particular views often being quite dissimilar from each point.

Convergence. That's what they like. But convergence is typically only a first or a second level approximation. And it may well be a motherhood-type view of reality. Such a view is portrayed by the statement that most people in western countries have access to a television or telephone. This tells us some important information. But to really understand what is going on and, in most cases, to utilize that information to its best advantage or, at least, to a realistic extent, then you need to know a great deal more about the detail. In any case, I remind you that the reciprocal of the propensity for convergence is the propensity for divergence. Or, if you want to look at it another way (and in reverse) there's lots and lots of cascading levels of convergence, each of which explode outwards and from each and every point, until you find that you've really got divergence, and in abundance; and that the propensity for divergence is itself, and after all, very large indeed. Meanwhile, of course, common sense alone tells us that there's no single answer to virtually anything and that this is so not least of all in turbulent environments.

Let me return for a moment to 'Who Holds The Reins?' being the excellent study of international corporate governance which I mentioned earlier. That study pointed out, and as one of its main findings, that there are big differences in corporate governance between the anglo-saxon based countries and each of the other countries which were studied by the task force and, further, that within the anglo-saxon based set of countries and the non-anglo-saxon based set of countries there were also large differences in corporate governance practices. The report stated that the task force concluded 'that it was not appropriate, given the need to respect diverse cultures and legal structures, to prescribe an international standard for corporate governance' whilst it also stated that 'international prescription of corporate governance and over-regulation and bureaucracy at a domestic level need to be avoided' and went on to say that 'international investors may not have the right to demand that corporate governance practices in companies in which they invest should be the same as those in their domestic jurisdiction' but, *at one and the same time,* the task force still trotted out their belief that there is a natural process of convergence; supporting this view with, amongst other things, the development of audit, remuneration, and nomination committees, the tendency to separate the roles of chairman and chief executive, and the presence of non-management directors on boards. The task force do, indeed, seem to be somewhat schizophrenic in the context of their findings when compared with their supporting views. One is, and as a consequence, left to wonder whether these so-called *trends* are really worldwide trends (I wonder what the correlation coefficients are) or whether they are merely culture-based trends, or whether, in fact, they are just local trends; or even whether they are trends at all (as opposed to say happenings or something) and, even if they are trends, whether those trends will, after a first blush of, shall we say, enthusiasm, be reversed; or, indeed, whether the evidence for the incidence of such trends will (in the short, medium, or longer-term) become more sparse or even fragmented; and possibly spurious in nature. Or whether, in reality, the aforementioned dimensions of corporate governance are the essence of sound corporate governance and, if they are not of the essence, then whether it matters whether these national, multi-national, or transnational observations of these perhaps less relevant matters (and irrespective of whether or not they are indeed trends) matters at all. Finally, and in relation to this particular aspect, the report seems to forget the basic differences between Japan and Germany and yet other differences between Germany and the UK (as well as the differences which exist between each of everywhere else in the world) and states that 'nevertheless we believe that a degree of convergence will come about naturally' whilst then proceeding to state that 'fostering an understanding of the divergences between different corporate governance practices is central to these developments' and to which developments the report was referring I was not quite clear. The report, thereby, seems to take a 'two bob each way' bet on what is happening and which position, I would suggest, may have less to do with confusion, indecision, or any tendency to shilly-shally (and with regard to which latter term there would appear to be no tendency) and more to do with the underlying politics of the report; whatever may be those politics.

The problem with convergence views is that its supporters may be looking at the wrong dimensions or for things which are helpful but which, in the end, are not that helpful. In simple terms it's a bit like saying that there's men and there's women and that they all converge to form the human race. But that type of convergence doesn't tell us much about the race, the religion, the intelligence, the education standards, the thought processes, or the creativity of human beings or, for that matter, a whole host of other things. Sure, we can look at those different aspects both for men and for women. And they could then be combined. But has something fallen between the cracks? Did we really capture the personality, the motivation, or the very spirit of reality? So when we look at a country in relation to convergence and corporate governance, we must ask whether we have really discovered what we wanted to know when we examine characteristics in Japan, in Canada, or somewhere else? Of course we should look. We would be foolish not to look. For we will learn something. But we must consider whether the approach which is taken in practice actually does address the potential for success in business, and this irrespective of how that success may be defined; for business success depends on many variables and relativities. Perhaps, after all, convergence is only a mindset and that in reality things are just different, very different, being very different indeed, and that perceptions of convergence have little to do with real causation; even though, albeit spuriously, a high correlation coefficient may well exist.

In practice both concepts have their place in the sun and may well be utilized (it is noted that convergence and divergence may co-exist and need not necessarily be some synthesis of actuality) but I think there is a real problem, in general terms, when it comes to peddling one dimension in preference to the other dimension, and not least of all by predicting, as does the aforementioned report, that 'it favoured a natural process of convergence' presumably over a divergence of corporate governance practices; and with this itself being based on some pretentious language about such a circumstance flowing 'from an informed global debate' and which language is, without doubt, heavily value-laden. That is, if your particular practices don't converge with the *preferred* practices (and one may well ask, preferred by whom, and on what basis) then it must be because you're not well informed. Look, simply there are just too many multi-faceted variables, and with values which are also in a relentless state of change, to even think of supporting the convergence statement outright. That's not the way of the world. And in any case, the discussion itself begs the question 'what are we really searching for?' with regard to corporate governance. Is it, in fact, a *comparison* between and within countries, of their corporate governance practices (and the identification of some convergence theory and the establishment of 'world's best practice' when it's not the best available anyway) or are we really looking at the *effectiveness* of what we call corporate governance; and this, irrespective of the practices which are actually utilized? The end result may well be that, between countries and within countries, and within countries but between and within industries and, further, between and within industry segments, etc, etc, and so forth (and along many and various other dimensions including, not least of all, intra-company behaviour) a divergence of practices is truly the vehicle for the achievement of a convergence of relevance. That is, a convergence of effectiveness in the area of corporate governance. Yes, the naivety of corporate governance as it is practiced and promoted today, and not least of all by the neo-classical establishment, will be revealed in years to come, and this will occur as future developments and advancements in that field of management unfold before our eyes, for those advances and developments will be as astounding, and even more rapid, than the advances and the developments which have taken place in the computer industry over the past quarter of a century; and almost all of us can relate to those almost unbelievable happenings.

[In passing, may I also note that 'practices' themselves may be both present or absent, albeit usually in positive mode but with, for example and in negative mode, the threat of some occurrence or happening also being available for use either in an internal or an external context. That is, there may not be any specific applied practice as such which addresses some particular thing, but the practice itself may be the outcome, or the result, of one or more other activities or happenings. This may be illustrated by the fact that one of the most significant benefits delivered by an external audit of the general purpose financial reports of a company is the moral deterrent which is inherent therein. The overall outcome of various activities which are carried out (or, as the case may be, are not carried out, but which may well be assumed by others that they have been, or will be, carried out) to achieve other specific purposes (and which activities may be many and varied and not necessarily uniform in substance or in form; and which may alter {divergently} from one occasion to another occasion) have, in themselves, a reasonable high probability of delivering a moral deterrent benefit. It is evident that corporate governance practices, whether targeted or not in their delivery, whether concrete or ethereal in nature, and whether present or absent in themselves, and whether in essence they are negative or positive in mode, may likewise deliver significant benefits to a business enterprise.]

Look, in a global economy there will, naturally, be international agreements and partial convergence. But committees of eminent or distinguished people are not to be relied upon for their innate wisdom. They cannot be relied upon at all. No-one, nowhere, gets it right for ever. You're lucky if you get it right for just a short while. And that is when you are dealing with your own situation and not the world. The rest of the time (which, to me, seems to be most of it) is spent *trying* to get it right and, if successful, then *endeavouring* to stop it going wrong. And that's before invariably moving onto the next iteration in the search for either solutions or resolutions to, what would appear to be, almost everything. No, a very different approach is required to business management than the approach that is currently being peddled by AIMA, the ASX, and much of the rest of the neo-classical establishment.

It's like the ASX listing rule. You can do what you like as long as, in effect, it conforms with AIMA's views. It's the AIMA members who have massive investments in the large companies (but remember, on our behalf, for it's our money they play with) and it's their views that have become the de facto standard (thanks to a lack of thought by business journalists and the media in general) and this is so even though the AIMA recommendations aren't very good. Although you can, in a rhetorical sense, report what you like (that's one of the main deficiencies of the listing rule) it's as though there's something wrong if you differ from the AIMA agenda. You know . . . . Why haven't you got a non-executive chairperson . . . . And why aren't the majority of your directors non-executive . . . . I don't care that you're the most successful company in the world . . . . you still need a fully documented ethical code . . . . A nomination committee . . . . A remuneration committee . . . . An audit committee . . . . As well as a committee to look after the committees . . . . And so on and so forth.

[Funnily enough the majority of Corporate Australia doesn't have a strategy committee whilst, almost for sure, none would have a strategic management committee (look, I am prepared to concede that there may well be a white blackbird somewhere, but the chances are that it's not present today in our corporate world, and in the form of a real strategic management committee) and the reason for this is twofold. The lesser problem is that 'the powers that be' tend to think components (audit committee, ethics code, etc) and not systems. The greater problem, however, is that the elite, although they may talk about strategic management, and with ease, few of them actually know what it is : that is, to date they haven't, so as to say, been able to grab hold of it in their hot little hands. Yes, strategy is a bit like beauty; everybody knows what it is, but it always seems hard to nail down. So when it comes to strategic management and strategic management systems, they all manage this thing that they can't quite nail down, being strategy, and many of them are convinced (if only by themselves) that they manage it systematically; that is, if only they knew what a strategic management systems was if they fell over one. Just for clarification it may be useful to think of the two concepts, strategy and strategic management, first in static mode and then in dynamic mode . . . . for strategy *the thing* can so easily be confused with management *the process* . . . . for strategy itself is also a dynamic process. Strategy is only a thing when you think of it in static form. You could perhaps think of these closely related multi-modal concepts, strategy and strategic management, as looking at a photograph of yourself (or someone else if you would prefer) and then immediately viewing yourself on a video. You're the same person. But you definitely see yourself differently in dynamic mode. Likewise, strategy committees (and boards of directors) will make some pronouncement or other that this is our strategy. It's like that photograph. It's a thing. It's static. Whilst sometimes the photograph is in black and white. And sometimes it's in colour. Even those two mediums make the same thing look different. But they're both in static mode. Strategic management committees, however, come at the same thing, strategy, but from a very different angle. Its perspective is far more enlightening and relevant. The coloured video can be nailed down in static form. Nearly all of us, at one time or another, will have held a video in our hands. We're holding a dynamic event in static mode. When we play it we see it unfold. Strategic management, however, is a little bit different to playing a video. In fact, it's a lot different. For when we are endeavouring to strategically manage we are playing the game in on-line, real-time, mode. Whilst most boards of directors, whether consciously or otherwise, are only applying off-line, batch-type, strategic management. Incidentally, in the end real-time strategic management, and strategy per se, become the same thing. But that's addressed in a previous book and which book is reserved for discussion with those who really do want to take strategic management seriously. The point worth noting is that in the end it is *strategic management* that boards of directors should address and, as a consequence thereof, strategy itself.]

Committee-wise, every listed company should follow the AIMA recommendations; otherwise the reality will be, *please explain*. In fact the guidelines for investment managers go further than this in stating that . . . . 'The AIMA's Corporate Governance Guidelines should be made available to companies and clients and *applied consistently across all companies on all issues*. The loss of credibility from selective application *would not be acceptable* to corporates or external observers. Clients of members should be informed of the AIMA's Guidelines. Companies should be informed that the Guidelines are consistent with responsible investment management' . . . . almost as though anything else isn't !!!! The real problem is, of course, not necessarily the wording of the Guidelines but more the content and substance of what occurs within the boundaries of those Guidelines. AIMA, in terms of its guideline on communication with companies, and in relation to matters of corporate governance, will be promoting its own views on that subject; and this will be so no matter how flawed its philosophy and the application of that particular philosophy. This is, indeed, the tyranny of excessive power. [And that reminds me, Henry Bosch, in his aforementioned book, states with regard to board committees that 'even though it is possible for a board to perform well without them (that is, committees of directors) they have become important outward and visible signs of good corporate governance' . . . . and that . . . . 'it can now be expected that listed companies that do not establish such committees will encounter growing difficulties with their institutional shareholders'. This particular superficial, fad-driven, justification for having a board committee whatever may be its function (and I actually support the establishment of strategically relevant board-level committees which report to and make recommendations to the board of directors) is absolutely pathetic; but it is typical of establishment-think.] As strategists, we'd actually be seeking out differences, even small differences, with which to create the most dramatic of strategic advantages. It's from people, circumstances, and things that are different (and not just the things which are the same) that we can learn so much about business. [This book in itself is different and I am sure that its contents will provide an alternative view of the world of business and the accountancy profession.] The *Convergence, Conformance, and Compliance* mindset (being the three 'Cs' of establishment-think . . . . and which are not to be confused with the three 'Ks' . . . . being those far more wholesome icons of Australian life, *Kookaburras, Kangaroos, and Koalas*) even when only in implied form, is crippling and wicked. Life, and business, is wonderful because of its many differences (I've never seen a Platypus, or a Tasmanian Devil, although I did see an Echidna crossing the road once. Each of those creatures is very different. They're not just your usual run-of-the-mill cats and dogs and things) and even differences *within* species are important; as with a peculiar type of flower, or a deformed spider, or a human mutation; and this is so irrespective of whether the differences are microscopic or macroscopic, or blatantly obvious. Yes, differences are important. Indeed, they are very important. [In their own eras of success IBM, Apple, Compaq, Microsoft, and Sausage Software (who?!!!) each knew that.] So we should be consciously aware that the corporate governance conformance-type recommendations of AIMA, where they *impinge on strategy itself*, actually constrain the degrees of strategic freedom of a company. This is exemplified in their recommendation that the majority of directors on a board should not only be non-executive but also, within that category, they should also be what are termed, independent directors. That is, the majority of board members should be independent, non-executive, directors. So if AIMA's recommendations constrain a company's degrees of strategic freedom, those recommendations are either *potential-impeding* or *potential-debilitating* in relation to strategy; so they really do need to be revisited. And if they don't impinge on either corporate enterprise or business entity strategy, then why the hell are we acclaiming them as the best thing since sliced bread. Yes, why indeed are their alleged virtues being so loudly trumpeted, and by so many both inside and outside the business media, as though those business enterprise strategy-constraining AIMA recommendations encapsulate the ultimate in salvation for Corporate Australia ?!!!!

No. Let's just stop and think. Why on earth should we bring in any international accountancy standards that are not in the best interests of our society? And why on earth shouldn't we introduce accountancy standards which are not international standards if they just happen to be in our best interests, that is, in the best interests of Australia. The bottom line is that no-one, and that includes investors from the US and the UK, is going to rush in to save any one member of Corporate Australia if it goes kaput; and definitely not because we adopted some screwball international standard which wasn't appropriate to us anyway. The reality of the overseas money is simple. The rest of the world own over thirty percent (30%) of the equity capitalization on the ASX. That ownership has little or nothing to do with accounting standards. Equity transactions move in like lightening and they move out like lightening. Corporate Australia is, on the whole, a speculative play thing for such investors. If there's a dollar to be made, and its appropriate to the overseas investors, then they'll make it; and it won't depend on whether or not some international accountancy standard is being applied. International accountancy standards may, or may not, be good for Australia. But let us ensure that we first of all look after our own interests. Not necessarily in a selfish way. Or purposively at the cost, expense, or loss of some other country. And we need to do that 'looking after' wisely. Without doubt, we do have a responsibility to look after our own best interests, being the best interests of our society, for when our companies crash, or are debilitated, you can be quite sure that it will, overwhelmingly, be our shareholders, our stakeholders, and our society that will suffer whilst, at one and the same time, that such suffering will be underwhelming for those equivalent parties in the USA, the UK, and elsewhere in the world.

Look, I may be using an overstatement by the managing director of the ASX to make a point; in fact, several points. He may well have got confused with the derivatives market when he used the term trillions. After all, the entire annual value of equity turnover on the ASX is only about one hundred and twenty billion dollars

($120b) (but increasing rapidly) and with a total domestic (foreign companies apart) equity capitalization of three hundred billion dollars ($300b) or so; this being less than the market capitalization of the two hundred or so foreign companies (domestic companies apart) that I referred to earlier and which are listed on the New York Stock Exchange. Simply, whatever the managing director of the ASX was referring to, I think it's time we dumped the mindset which says that we've got to be puppets and perform in a way in which others would wish us to behave. The market will invariably find its own level and that level will not depend upon the adoption of some 'popular' international accounting standard. We must look after our own interests. America does. So does the UK. And so does Germany. And France definitely does. Oh yes, and Japan and Korea also do. As do a whole host of other countries around the world. So let's wake up. We happen to be in the correct region of the world, geographically speaking. And that is so for the next fifty years and more. And we have masses of potential. Statements, pronouncements, and rulings, as made by the ASX, may sound good. And they may make us feel as though we're part of the whiz-bang main game; even if, as yet, we're not. But please, let's not jump up and down for the ASX when it comes to what is in the best interests of business and society in general. They, like everyone else, have got to make their own way forward. It may suit them to pursue one course of action. But that's not necessarily in the best interests of business. Money is a very tradeable commodity. It can, almost at one and the same time, be extremely differentiated and very undifferentiated. Securing company listings or trading dollars for the ASX may well be enhanced by having convergent accounting standards. But the ASX must not endeavour to gain an advantage for itself at the expense of Australia. What the ASX should do is to take a good hard look at how it can help to improve shareholder value and through improved corporate governance. And it could make a very good start by requiring strategic management practices to be disclosed by all listed companies. And also for each and every material component of those companies. And it could require that the disclosure be specific. No need to tick boxes or anything. Just state clearly what you do ?!!!! That way it's not the wishy-washy airy-fairy stuff which *may* or *may not* be disclosed under the present rule. Sure, they will argue that such practices can be disclosed now. But they won't be. Not unless it happens to benefit the powerful. And what's more, the non-disclosure will be so not least of all because the strategic management practices of major companies are, in reality, dismal. A requirement, as is suggested, would focus attention on the strategic management practices of listed companies, as well as on the fundamental underpinnings of those business enterprises. This, in itself, would eventually lead to a Corporate Australia which is built on more solid foundations than is the present situation and which, in total, would deliver better quality profits than at the present time. This, being a positive and an active approach to corporate governance, would benefit shareholders, stakeholders, and society in general. What is required in relation to our accountancy and corporate governance practices in not the convenient adoption, carte blanche, of foreign standards but, rather, it is the institution of a persistent and never ending search for non-permanent solutions and resolutions which will facilitate the achievement of practical optimality in business outcomes for shareholders, stakeholders, and society in general, in relentlessly turbulent environments; and with such solutions and resolutions being a practical, but forever changing, optimality which suits Australia. This on-line, real-time, virtual resolution to the business challenges of our times would, of course, be somewhat traumatic for those in the establishment who continue to view external environments as essentially stable, businesses as being centralized monoliths, and 'world's best practice' as being basically convergent.

When we eventually bring in new and meaningful corporate governance requirements, and when we come to accept that such corporate governance requirements are to be mandatarily audited by the accountancy profession, and that this will be carried out in accordance with appropriate accountancy standards (and that this will be so irrespective of whether or not those standards are agreed to internationally and which standards, despite the views of the worldwide affinity of establishment members, will well and truly suit *our* business environment and *our* society) then we, here in Australia, will be setting the pace; we will be at the leading-edge in corporate governance and accountancy practices; and the different parties overseas, who will then themselves be laggards, can announce their own standards, and in an effort to catch up with our standards. So, in order to save a lot of time and trouble, let's get real now, and dump the neo-classical establishment view of corporate governance (as is promoted by AIMA and which has secured de facto compliance from the ASX) for something real. After all, the greatest contribution to our society which is obtained from the establishment's version of corporate governance (at least at the moment) is to actually impede the introduction of a more positive, active, and beneficial, management-focused corporate governance philosophy and which philosophy, as a result of its introduction, will provide the very real potential for facilitating a permanent, and an on-going, fundamental enhancement in the performance and success of Corporate Australia.

At this point let's just step aside again. May I just say that you may feel that the preceding criticism of the ASX is harsh. The point to remember is that, although the ASX only earns $12m and on assets of $136m, its 500 plus members have much influence in the business world. The ASX has credibility. It has integrity. It has respectability. But that doesn't mean that it knows best in relation to corporate governance. Or that it is using its best endeavours (it definitely is not by compliantly accepting AIMA's pedestrian, follower-based, and philosophically flawed views) to ensure that a most appropriate approach to corporate governance is actually developed for Australia. Why, in any case, would we rely on the ASX to create the best solution to the wants and needs of society.

[May I interject here and just remind you that not everyone who 'poohs' on you is your enemy and that not everyone who gets you out of the 'pooh' is your friend. For those of you who know the tale you will recall that, during its winter migration, the bird fell to earth exhausted, but fortunately for the bird, rather than freezing to death, the cow provided warmth for the bird by 'poohing' on it, whilst the cat, upon extracting the bird from that most unpleasant of situations, ate the bird. (I guess that, given the contents of this book, then I personally must be a cow.) You will recall that, in reality, it was Corporate Australia that fell to earth. Everyone seemed to 'pooh' on them . . . . having at first marvelled at its sheer beauty. And the establishment (and not least of all AIMA and the ASX) then, so as to say, pawed its way in, with a view to getting them out of the 'pooh'. The real danger of course, as you will appreciate from this apocryphal story, is the neo-classical establishment. For they are once again looking after themselves. So watch that cat . . . . for everyone's sake !!!!!]

Resuming now where I left off within our, so as to say, stepping aside, the point is that the stakes are so high, they are so great, they are so astronomical, that it is essential we find an appropriate approach to corporate governance, quickly. The establishment are, without doubt, hampering that outcome. The ASX must, therefore, be challenged, and in a forthright and continuous way, in order to secure a structural change in corporate governance practices; for such a change will undoubtedly bring massive rewards to Australia.

And while we're stepping aside (one can only wonder how many side-steps one can take before one falls off the edge of the planet) let me just reinforce this establishment thing. I raised it in relation to Bosnia earlier on in the book. You know, the thing about how the establishment can't be trusted to look after our well-being, but how they'll definitely endeavour to look after their own interests; even at great expense to everyone else. I raise it because it's so rampant throughout all parts of society. A prime example of this, and on an international scale, once again concerns the United Nations; but this time in terms of the blood-bath in Rwanda. [It's a bit like a corporate debacle really. The incompetence. The cover-ups. The disclaiming of responsibility. The degradation of both moral and ethical standards. And the devastation and destruction of the victims.] So what brilliance did the establishment deliver in Rwanda, where thousands upon thousands of Africans (the actual figure is around eight hundred thousand people) were brutally murdered, and others were mutilated beyond belief, as the UN stood by and watched the genocide. [It's all chaos theory . . . . worlds within worlds so as to say . . . . the international level, the country level, the corporate level; or whatever dimensions you may wish.] In fact, according to its *own* report (that is, a report which was prepared at the behest of the UN and others) the moral authority of the UN was fatally undermined by its own attempt to *pretend* that it did not know of the impending threat of genocide in Rwanda. Yes, its own report said it knew of the threat. It just pretended that it didn't know. [Does it sound familiar at the establishment and corporate levels . . . . the stock exchange, for example, didn't do its job properly during the corporate debacles of recent times, the auditors didn't do their job properly, the regulators went missing (God knows where the ASC, being the Australian Securities Commission, or rather its predecessor, the

National Companies and Securities Commission, was) whilst the business journalists got side-tracked and so forget to carry out their duties and responsibilities.] The UN (which is just another bureaucratic establishment body which, like many, has been more concerned with its own image than it has been with real and meaningful action) has since attempted to mitigate its failure to act, at least in its own eyes, by stating that it is now helping to redevelop that devastated country. I guess that the financial institutions could play the same tune. They failed gloriously when they opted not to exercise their shareholder muscle when things were wrong in the 1980s (they instead stuck their collective heads in the very pleasant sand and took those very nice profits; at least for a while anyway) but which same financial institutions are now claiming, through their mouthpiece AIMA, to be championing corporate governance. The UN report which, in one fell blow, demolished the UN, stated that the Secretary-General was not on top of the situation (I wonder how many managing directors can, if the truth be known, empathize with those words) whilst stating that the Security Council could not get its act together and, in any case, did not regard Rwanda as being strategically important. (Just a little bit more empathizing in the corporate world I would suspect . . . . Just a few more strategically important mishaps to remember from one's past . . . . 'at the time I didn't think it was strategically important' . . . . how such occurrences can come back to haunt the captains of industry; and others.) It's amazing what becomes strategic when you don't know what you're doing. With regard to Rwanda, well I'm sure that all those who are dead and who are in coffins (given of course that they had a coffin in which to be buried and weren't just bodies bulldozed into huge holes in the ground) will be very excited about the news that development aid is being provided by the UN. Perhaps they'll even manage a wry smile or two, as the maggots crawl out of their noses, into their mouths, and out of their ear-holes; which, of course, is very much the reality of being dead and in a hole in the ground. I guess it's much like the emotions and the internal fortitude of many shareholders and stakeholder; no doubt they also get eaten away and devastated.

[I thought that, in passing, I'd just mention that I haven't held shares in a listed company for over quarter of a century. Not since the great British Leyland 'the sky's the limit' float dudded me. I often think of that offer when I see the mums and the dads clamouring for the public floats of today. I wonder about Qantas, the sky, and its limits; and British Airways : perhaps its future saviour ?!!!!]

No, the establishment, together with its many tentacles, is no friend of ordinary people (be they shareholders, stakeholders, or society in general) and this is so no matter at what level its activities are observed. Just witness the Barings Bank whitewash as delivered by the Securities and Futures Authority in the UK. The self-regulatory code which can 'blackball' wrongdoers has now been reduced to a mere 'partial blackballing' if you happen to be at or near the top of your profession. A simple slapping of the hand for being naughty. Barings, however, is a classic case of the failure of strategic management systems (actually, on reflection, they probably didn't have any strategic management systems worth talking about) but nobody would have looked into that aspect. Investigators are so hooked on internal financial controls that they seem to miss the point about strategic management. [No, I'm no longer into passive compliance with the powers that be. They're an absolute disgrace. They may have power. In reality they appear to have power in abundance. But they don't have the knowledge, the understanding, or the insight in the area of strategic management. And they definitely don't have wisdom in that area of management. I mean. For crying out loud. What's more strategic than going bust . . . . And nobody looked into the strategic management systems. I wonder why. I guess those parties who investigated the matter are probably still wondering what they are. What they look like. And what they do. Well it's about time they started investigating the strategic management of these companies. That way they may then find out how poorly some of these companies are governed in reality.] No, I for one am no longer prepared to sit back and let the establishment (being the neo-classical variety or, for that matter, any other variety) get away with their corporate governance shams. And definitely not here in Australia. For sooner or later there will be even more shareholder blood on the carpet. Even more stakeholders who will be savagely debilitated. And even more skilful distancing of responsibility for wrongdoing. [And this is apart from all the benefits which are foregone by not appropriately addressing corporate governance.] No, this time round, instead of hiding behind its lack of competence, or what may well have been its actual incompetence, the accountancy profession can get its act together, embrace reality, and do a decent job.

So what is Corporate Governance?

Corporate governance may be defined as the actions of the board of directors of a company in managing a company, for and on behalf and in the best interests, of all of its shareholders, in total, through the continuous determination and active management of the strategies of the business enterprise.

This definition consequently addresses who does what, for whom, why (to secure benefits in the best interests of all shareholders, in total) and when. The definition, which requires a relentless and continuous frequency, accordingly embraces not only the off-line, but also the on-line, and sometimes the virtual real-time, as well as the actual real-time, variety of strategic management; and, synonymous therewith, on-line, as well as real-time, corporate governance. The definition thus implies the existence of relevant strategic management systems. This way there's no messing about with the fuzzy-wuzzy thinkers and their wishy-washy ideas and definitions. [As I think of one definition, I wonder where the hell focusing on *restraint* ever came from as a primary component of corporate governance. Business is about achieving things. In my opinion restraint isn't of secondary or even tertiary importance. Sure, it should be present. But it's not primary. It operates in background mode. And whilst I've raised the matter of the meaning of corporate governance, the definition which is referred to for guidance in the 'Who Holds The Reins?' report is two-fold, being on the one part 'a mode of living, behaviour, demeanour' and on the other part 'the action or manner of governing' and which first description tends to encapsulate the remote dimension of corporate governance and which remoteness is presently being vigorously promoted and crystallized by the establishment (because it didn't know what else to do in order to redeem itself for its massive historic multi-faceted failures; and it still doesn't) but which second description projects the more vigorous active-management dimension of fundamental corporate governance.] My particular definition, which is set out above, is both inclusive and exclusive in nature. Anything that is board-level strategic is in. And anything that is not board-level strategic is out. Whilst the ramifications of the definition, for the board of directors, are tremendous. Lead. Plan. Organize. Direct. Control. Carry out your tasks, duties, and responsibilities properly. We appoint you. We remove you. Whatever is required. Do it. Do it with integrity. And do it non-negligently. And you won't go too far wrong. In accordance therewith, corporate governance which is based on strategic management, unequivocally focuses the mind. It focuses the mind of each and every board member. The definition says, simply enough, do your job director. Make things happen on behalf of us shareholders, in total, and in our best interests. If, jointly and severally, you strategically manage our company appropriately . . . . and fail . . . . that's one thing. But if you fail, and you have failed to appropriately manage our company strategically, then that's a very different story. That's negligence !!!

Bob Tricker, who coined the phrase 'corporate governance' in a book which was published in 1984, offers the phrase 'the exercise of power over a corporate identity' as the definition of corporate governance. Almost any definition is open to both constructive and destructive criticism. His definition is powerful, as is that of my own definition, but, as with my own definition, his definition also suffers from erosion by multi-dimensional detail. In his case, one may ask, who has the ultimate power and who has the real power (the shareholders or the board, or some sub-set of either, management, in general, or some composite group thereof, or some other party or parties or, indeed, an amalgam that is drawn from these various sources) and does the real and the ultimate power coincide? And where, in its many omnipresent guises, is the inalienable dimension of countervailing power located? And what are the relative strengths of these often competing concepts of power and countervailing power, and on a static and dynamic basis? And where will power be located tomorrow? Also, the authority to exercise corporate governance, and the responsibility to exercise such governance, may well differ, and in a significant way, from the exercise of legitimate, and even illegitimate, power. Power, therefore, is but one dimension, albeit an important multi-faceted dimension, of corporate governance.

Bob Tricker also states that corporate governance, the work of the board, is not the same as that of management, and that it calls for additional knowledge and different skills. This knowledge and skills dimension, in general terms, is true; at least in normative terms. Corporate governance, however, and irrespective of how it is wrapped-up and presented, is itself both unequivocally and unavoidably, management; for it is clear that all the conceptual dimensions of activity, including that of leadership, which are executed by a director, and a board of directors, are also exercised by the substructure of management in a company. Management activity, together with its knowledge, abilities, and skills becomes, accordingly, a matter of emphasis. And this emphasis itself has overlapping, or blurred, characteristics and attributes which range from the activities of a director, at one extreme, through to the activities of an operational manager at the other extreme; and with operations being where strategic reality is delivered. Each component of management, wherever it is located, is accordingly concerned with strategy. For strategy, in its many and its varied manifestations is, of necessity, the plaything of management. The myth and the mystique of the superhuman director is, indeed, a mystique and a myth. The brutal reality of corporate history confirms that fact time and again. Both that myth, and the myth of the scarcity of suitable people to perform the role of director, are each put about by those who benefit from such myths; as well as the mindless. And those myths are also promulgated by their supporters, and not least of all the chief executive of the largest financial institution in Australia, AMP Society, which executive, subsequent to discussing his company's multiple profit increase to $1.9b for the year, stated in April, 1996, on the 'Business Sunday' program '. . . . I think it's driven by the fact that there just aren't as many candidates for directorships . . . .' whilst, contrary to this acclaimed fact, there are, of course, lots of potential candidates who would be ignored by his very own financial institution when it casts its shareholder votes for directors. In reality the drover's dog could perform better than some directors who reside on the boards of some leading members of Corporate Australia. The incestuous nature of the membership of those major boards is absolutely disgraceful. No. Business itself is so all-pervasive in our society that we cannot await the arrival of, or even rely upon, superhuman beings to be captains of industry and of commerce. In all practicality we must look to ordinary people to do extra-ordinary things. That is what has happened throughout history. And throughout the history of Australia. And those ordinary people doing extra-ordinary things include the Kerry Packers and the Rupert Murdochs of the world. Indeed, in continuing his protection of the establishment, and in response to a question concerning corporate governance, the chief executive of the AMP Society stated that '. . . . I'm not sure a lot's going wrong at board level. I think boards are responsible for oversight. Management's responsible for management. So the better question might be what's going wrong at management levels . . . . But I don't believe that it's the board's responsibility to manage the company'. [Well I too wouldn't mind picking up a big fat fee for *not* having to manage the strategic direction of a major corporate whilst, it may also be noted, that such statements can only confirm that some boards are even bigger 'wanks' than the 'wanks' that they were already thought to be.] The opinion of the chief executive of the AMP Society not only endeavoured to protect his establishment colleagues (being those on boards of directors) from responsibility for their actions, or lack thereof, but he also protected himself, and those like him (as they hide behind their institutional structures, their power, and their prestige) for his institution is a significant shareholder in Corporate Australia. It is the financial institutions that are instrumental in placing directors in the boardrooms of our major companies. So to proclaim a vastly different view to that which is expressed above would be to acknowledge their own lack of competence, or what may well be incompetence, in relation to that fundamental area of management. For they would, in effect, be proclaiming that directors, and boards of directors, are indeed responsible for the *management* of the strategic direction of the companies which they are suppose to serve and that, after all, their responsibility is not limited merely to some nebulous oversight function. The fundamental and the onerous responsibilities of financial institutions to our society (as is embodied in the strategic successes and failures of their many board appointees, in numerous major companies, and in various industries) would then be made most clear to us all. And it would also be evident that it is largely they, the financial institutions, who are, in the end, responsible for not bringing about, and in an expeditious manner, appropriate structural change in the strategic management of companies; and which quantum leaps and order of magnitude changes would vastly improve the strategic well-being of Corporate Australia. They are 'fat cats' for they enjoy what they have whilst blaming others (including the management substructures in the companies in which they have invested) for shortcomings, yet they seek only incremental improvements in the aggregate performance and success of Corporate Australia.

As I have indicated before, it is at the margins, at the cutting-edge, that reality is, in fact, revealed. For it is obvious that the reality of incompetence is well and truly hidden when it is mixed up with, and stirred into, the totality of the broth of business. And this is so when institutional shareholders, with all their might and power, deny that their own board appointees, along with other members of the board, *are responsible for the strategic management* of the companies to which they have been appointed. These financial institutions may provide massive benefits to our society (as they unequivocally should for they are indeed privileged) but they also provide massive impediments to beneficial structural change to the fundamental management practices of Corporate Australia.

For the record may I make it clear that, although I unashamedly criticize the neo-classical establishment, it is not the people themselves who I dislike. I feel sure that most of them will be quite pleasant folk. What I do oppose (and despite the 'heretical' nature of my observations) is what they stand for, what they promote, and what they perpetuate; for their duplicity is, indeed, great.

Returning now to the power of my own definition of corporate governance, it is obviously incumbent upon the board of directors of a business enterprise to ensure that the strategic management infrastructure of the business enterprise is both appropriate and sufficient to support non-negligent strategic decision-making and, thereby, to facilitate the creation, the development, and the active management, on an on-going basis, of the strategies of a business enterprise. It is also incumbent upon the board of directors to know how to utilize that infrastructure. And to understand what, indeed, it all means. As a consequence, wherever the tentacles of a business enterprise strategy reach throughout a company, the directors must also ensure that the strategic management infrastructure, at those points or locations, is well and truly appropriate; and that its use is clearly understood. In this way the wispy fuzzy-wuzzy stuff is removed from the centre of attention and reality can be crystallized. If the strategy requires an audit committee, a nomination committee, a remuneration committee, an ethics committee, or some other committee, then they can have one. But if the strategy doesn't require those committees, then they have very little to do with corporate governance; and this is so even though it may be decided that a company should have a 'such and such' committee because it gives comfort to some pressure group or other, for not everything in business is driven by profit maximization. Satisficing is far more prevalent. In fact, satisficing is the reality of business. Or committees may be created or maintained simply because the dummy (being, that is, the corporate dummy) looks nicer in committee clothes. But, as we all know, in the end you can't make a silk purse out of a sow's ear. So it really doesn't matter what on earth the superficial layers of committee clothing are that adorn these corporate dummies, for board committees (of whatever type) are not going to improve things, in a strategic sense, if they have little or nothing of consequence to do with corporate enterprise or business entity strategy. For it is reality that counts. Strategic reality !!!!

My definition of corporate governance can be expanded upon in order to provide further understanding of the scope of that term, such as including, for example, a statement which would also incorporate stakeholders, as well as society in general, within the sphere of corporate governance; but this would, in effect, only be adding further levels of detail to the preceding definition. An expansion of this nature may be useful in practice but, for present purposes, the above definition focuses on the fact that corporate governance resides with the board of directors of a business enterprise; or with those who execute that equivalent role. *The essential function of the board of directors of a business enterprise is to strategically manage the business enterprise.* All other relevant board functions, it is noted, are directly or indirectly derived therefrom.

The establishment, and all its hangers-on, can bleat till their heart's content. The fact is strategic management is the top, the bottom, the back, the front, the sides, and the inside and outside of corporate governance. It permeates every aspect thereof. Board-level strategic management is corporate governance for corporate governance is about managing the strategies of a company from creation, through rejuvenation, onto regeneration, and then recreation; or in any other way in which you may wish to look at it. Everything that is not derived therefrom, whether in static or dynamic mode, goes under, over, across, around, or behind it. Shareholders appoint the board of directors, and with a mandate to strategically manage their company, on their behalf, and in the best interests of all shareholder, in total. Shareholders want the reality of their business managed in order to deliver real benefits. Strategy is, in the end, Reality and Reality, in the end, is Strategy. It's that simple. We must never forget that fact. And we must be clear that everything else that happens is intended to make things happen, and in a practically optimum way, for shareholders. And this means not only applying strategies, but also changing, and creating, those strategies. So when the omnipotent neo-classical establishment (including the ASX, AIMA, some business bodies, professional institutes, other organizations, and various boards of directors of Corporate Australia) make their politically value-laden pronouncements concerning such things as the composition of boards of directors, the desirability of having a non-executive chairperson, the roles of executive and non-executive directors, remuneration committees, audit committees, and committees for forming committees, and even more committees for reviewing the committees which form committees, and much of everything else that they expound upon, you can be fairly sure that they don't know a lot about strategic management. In their own particular roles they may well practice the management of strategies. For strategy, after all, without doubt, and in the end, is reality. There is no escaping that fact. But when business enterprises heed the somewhat superficial recommendations of the neo-classical establishment, and they action their particular recommendations, then they are often applying strategy; although not in every case. Directors are practitioners of strategy. But as practitioners of strategy (being those persons who actually 'determine' business enterprise strategy) they do not necessarily allocate much time to thinking about strategic management per se. That's where the confusion may occur. They do things. They spend a significant amount of time doing things. And this doing may be for the better or it may be for the worse. But it's like driving a car. Just because you drive a car (you know, turn the key, press the accelerator, and make decisions about which way to go) that does not necessarily mean that, in reality, you know much about cars. Likewise, you may know a lot about making strategic decisions, about getting the money together, and about attacking the markets (that is, about driving) but it doesn't follow that you know a great deal about managing strategies. [That's where strategic management and strategic management systems come in . . . . well actually they come in a bit before that, but let's not get too involved.] When doing things (and remember, the job of a director is to cause things to be done or not to be done; and so *no decision* is, in fact, also a decision about doing things) there is one thing that is evident, the strategy which is caused to be actioned, whether passively or actively, may or may not be appropriate. And this may be the case not least of all when strategies are, themselves, contaminated by inappropriate AIMA-type recommendations.

Who said that non-executive chairpersons are always (or even overwhelmingly) in the best interests of shareholders. Or that it is always (or even generally) in the best interests of a company to have a board of directors which has a majority of individuals who qualify as independent directors. Who are these Merlins? These wizards of the business world !!!!! They may well trot out statistics, or survey results, and claim that the majority of the 'best' companies have these recommended characteristics. So what !!!!! Does that mean that those companies wouldn't have done at least as well, if not even better, had they had the reverse, or at least a different, strategic profile? Under different company conditions, or under different environmental conditions, or both, different solutions and resolutions would be appropriate. There may not even be just *one correct answer* to a situation or to an on-going circumstance (there usually isn't) and there may not even be an answer at all; that is, any answer. Also, just ask yourself what happened to many of those so-called 'excellent' companies which were named by Peters & Waterman as having been identified as possessing the eight success characteristics; and which companies were so readily glorified by all and sundry. We couldn't get the word 'excellent' off our lips and out of our vocabulary for years. Everyone was talking excellence; and about anything and everything. However, many of those companies weren't very excellent for very long. Indeed, some of them, would you believe, weren't very excellent at all. And between me and you (but don't tell anyone) some of them hadn't been strategically excellent for years. In fact, some of them even became corporate cripples. So why don't the establishment use their common sense; and learn from history. Well probably they haven't got much. They keep searching for the unfindable. The panacea for all ills. The ultimate answer. [Hell, do they never learn?!!!!] The manacled minds of the neo-classical establishment, as is evidenced by their very actions, are endeavouring to fit a whole new epoch (being that of the dynamic management of globalizing corporates which are embracing turbulent environments) into their superseded and dysfunctional frameworks. Their thinking is moribund. It does not embrace the emerging environment and the contemporary challenges of our times. Have they not noticed that there has been a quantum leap or two, and one or more order of magnitude changes, in the world of business. It's not age, in the ranks of the establishment, which manacles their thinking. Some of these people are quite young. Age, in fact, is almost irrelevant. It is their constrained debilitating mindscapes that are the problem; and the real menace. And, whilst the establishment touts its version of good corporate governance, the consultancy firms dart in like voracious piranhas (you will recall the bandwagon-effect which I referred to previously) and proceed to devour the hard-earned profits of companies by advising them in relation to the latest management fad; being that most dubious establishment version of appropriate corporate governance. These consultants, by the way, often have no cognitive paradigm or philosophical stance by which they operate. They really are the proverbial dedicated followers of fashion; and money. At the moment they're very enthusiastic about the 'accountability' based corporate governance regime. Next year. Or the year after. Whenever they note a change in the prevailing emphasis. The way the wind's blowing. They'll switch over to the 'management' based regime. And they'll talk to you, and with that implied air in their delivery, and in a way which will leave you wondering how on earth you could ever have believed that 'accountability' rubbish; and as though they, in their omniscient wisdom, had never actually had anything to do with that particular philosophy. It was so obvious that it was flawed. That is, it simply didn't grab the issue by the balls. That very failure was so very obvious. Yes, you really must have been daft to have actioned that 'accountability' stuff. Although I must say that I do wonder from time-to-time why they don't inform their clients, and at the beginning of an assignment, that both they and their clients have got it wrong? [In passing I may just say that corporate governance is a perfectly valid area of consultancy. It's just that what is being offered at the moment is so essentially impoverished. You should give me a call some time. I'd like to help.] Look, the simple fact is that the type of things which the neo-classical establishment have been recommending as corporate governance (given the appropriate strategic context) are, correctly, aspects of corporate governance. But, as I've stated previously (and given of course that they are, in fact, correct for a particular company in its particular circumstances) these things are, at the best, at level three, four, and five. They are so remote from the cutting-edge of reality that their promotion by the neo-classical establishment is undoubtedly impeding the real game. That is, the real game of implementing appropriate strategic management in companies. Sure, having an audit committee, or a remuneration committee, or a nomination committee, or a code of ethics, is part of a strategy (if, indeed, you wish those aspects to be part of your business enterprise strategy) but I think that you may be beginning to realize, perhaps due to my repetition, that these things are essentially components that are part of, or attached to, a strategy, and which strategy itself runs on an infrastructure and, further, that those components (imagine the ripples that are created in a pond when a stone is thrown in) reside on the third, the fourth, or the fifth ripple from the source of the ripples. And even the ripples disappear in the end. Only to be replaced by other ripples when the next stone is thrown in the pond. Business can be a bit like that. Except sometimes the stones seem to rain down like a never ending bombardment of asteroids. And the ripples can appear to be more like tidal waves. Although on occasions you may well be deceived by the calmness of the water.

[Look, before I proceed, let me say that I guess you've realized that you've already entered a veritable labyrinth of argument and consideration in relation to corporate governance. I just thought, at this point, that I'd let you know that there isn't that much further to go. Just two or three important dimensions. You'll then be able to appreciate the whole thing and make up your own mind with regard to whether or not there is, indeed, hope for the future. So perhaps if you can put your brains back into gear, at least for a while, I'll continue our little chat.]

Just for the record, the 'Nick & Nobby' show down at Coles Myer also failed to contact me (just like BHP didn't) and this despite the fact that they had done such an absolutely average job on their own corporate governance initiatives. They may have improved on what existed previously. Almost anything would have. But is it really what is required for that particular company. The changes do not amount to a quantum leap. And they're definitely not an order of magnitude change. They'd have been telling us all about them had that been the case. To concentrate on such superficiality, and at the exclusion of real substance, can only be of concern to shareholders. What are the Coles Myer directors doing? [I know it may be annoying to have someone tell you, and in a forthright way, how things are (whether good, bad, or indifferent) but that's my style of management consulting; at least you know where you stand, and you aren't then having to make strategic decisions based on some limp-hand input.] Meanwhile the media once again appears to be wetting itself over what may be, in effect, very simple corporate governance improvements. The motives of the media would, however, seem to be more related to damning the old regime rather than enhancing the new situation. [I wonder who upset them.] Once again let me spell it out. Administrative improvements and mindless compliance are not the kernel of good corporate governance. The core of appropriate corporate governance, and for any business enterprise, resides inalienably with appropriate strategic management. Coles Myer, for its sins, and despite protestations which we may hear to the contrary, has now managed (with the help of AIMA and its allies) to effectively subdue that all-important business dimension : entrepreneurial activity. Coles Myer is now dancing to the corporate governance tune as composed and orchestrated by those magnanimous members of the neo-classical establishment; and not least of all the financial institutions. [Oh, incidentally, I was reading the other day how the three institutions which had been the driving force behind the changes at Coles Myer, you know, the board changes and all that, have now been busily selling-down their investments in the company. I thought you may be interested to hear that piece of news. I guess we should always be alert to the fact that it's so easy, via the stock exchange, for valiant knights to be not so valiant when it suits them. And, in any case, someone else can always clean up the mess. Even if it's only a corporate raider.] Yes, of course Coles Myer will do entrepreneurial things. Almost every company does. At least in their own eyes. And profits may very well improve; or get worse. They may have improved, or got worse, anyway. That is, wherever they were going they may, in any event, end up there. No-one will ever know for sure whether profits are better, or worse, compared with what they would have been. We can't, in reality, have a dual time-warp, a ghost or shadow reality, to test the hypothesis; either prospectively or in retrospect. If we could then we may well choose a different profit outcome. Sure, you can run simulations, being of the Monte Carlo variety or otherwise. I agree with simulations. But in the end simulations are not reality. They're only models of reality. And reality itself is invariably different. What they haven't done, of course, is to fundamentally alter the structure of how they manage strategically. Of course I understand that they've altered the management structure. But that's not what I'm addressing. Big deal. So they now do it this way instead of that way. There's a few more checks and balances (which may or may not be good depending on the circumstances and what it is exactly you wish to achieve) but this is all lightweight stuff in the world of strategic management; and thereby corporate governance. You see, as with many companies, they're still managing profits; not strategy !!!!! Profit is a deceptive little devil. You know, you can have two different strategies and end up with an identical profit; being, say, the profit which you forecast. But the strategic underpinnings can be so very different compared with what you had expected; if, of course, that is, you'd actually set time aside to expect anything. You read about profit announcements in the media or you hear about them on television. And invariably they equate the profit, or the loss, and the size thereof, to success or to failure. We are now so conditioned by the institutions, the merchant bankers, the stockbrokers, the corporate advisory firms, and the business journalists, as well as everyone else who has anything to say on the matter, including the accountants, that we are quite prepared to accept that abstract concept, profit, in preference to reality itself; that is, strategic reality. When will they acknowledge that a company can have a really 'poor' profit outcome, and an adverse cash flow, but may have exponentially enhanced its strategic position; whilst the reverse can also be true. [Remember Westpac.] There's actually a lot more sophistication to the headline profit position to which I have just alluded, but it's a bit involved to go into here. I'll perhaps leave that for when I've been retained to consult to your company. Look, let me just mention in passing (now that I've raised the profit word) that when you start looking at things differently you start seeing things that you never saw before. Profit, for example, may be viewed as profit, or it may be seen as perhaps a strategic resource, or a significant strategic event. [And, by way of a note and a thought-provoker, you could, within profit for example, see the way in which goodwill is amortized (being a current and pathetic argument which is presently raging in terms of Exposure Draft 68 as well as having been pathetic in relation to previous ways of addressing this topic) as merely a component in calculating profit, or it could be seen as being an active part of the aforementioned strategic event. Or it could be seen as a strategic resource. Whilst it may even be seen as representing a strategic position itself. Although the way they address goodwill at the moment the propensity for the use of goodwill as a beneficially strategic opportunity is somewhat impoverished.] Oh yes, and getting back to the issue (I got carried away a bit there with the strategy thing, profits, and goodwill) they've cut the heart out of Coles Myer; with 'they' being the establishment. For my five cents worth, whenever you get a bunch of part-timers, sorry, absolutely independent non-executive directors, in control of a company, then in the end you're asking for trouble. Sure, I understand that non-executive directors, particularly of the absolutely independent variety, are, in the normal course of events, important. They're very important. In fact, they're very important indeed. And not least of all as one of the sources of countervailing power which exist vis-a-vis those 'bad' executive director types who use up board seats which non-executive directors could have occupied. (I've noticed that the term executive director seems to be getting as tainted as was the term entrepreneur a few years ago; isn't it silly !!!!) But when it comes to actually handing over *control* to absolutely independent non-executive 'remote from the action' directors, then you've got a real problem. It really is sad to see what was once one of our leading companies, in terms of strategic ranking criteria, being strategically debilitated by our very own, much loved and adored (at least, that is, by themselves) neo-classical establishment. The pendulum will, however, eventually swing back. It will be seen that handing over control to non-executive 'remote from the action' directors is no better than putting control in the hands of executive 'close to the action' directors. What we really need on boards of directors is talent; for we must be careful not to make the assumption, and by default, that non-executive, independent, directors are better at forming judgements which are in the best interests of a company, than other directors. On that realization the executive director will come back into favour, in a balanced way, and responsible entrepreneurship itself will then re-emerge as one of the most valuable strategic asset of Corporate Australia.

Ah well, I've got that off my chest, so moving on a bit, let's just ponder for a while on that wise old 'saying' which I noticed on television the other week. It was one of those quotations at the beginning of a film on SBS . . . . You know the one, the channel hardly anyone watches because it's in a foreign language and you have to read the subtitles, but which, in itself, is really great value.

'The eye you see is not an eye because you see it

. . . . It is an eye because it sees you !!!!!'

Strategy's like that. It's not so much what *you* are making strategy do but, rather, it's more about what strategy itself is *doing* to you. This is a very different way of looking at life; and strategies. It's more realistic. You're more likely to recognize and acknowledge reality; and act on it, whether pro-actively, reactively, or in some other way. And that fact, in itself, will probably produce more favourable outcomes than may otherwise have been the case. Sure accountability has its place. Of course it does. So does compliance. As well as conformance. Management, however, is pre-eminent. You, yourself, may perceive strategy. And you, yourself, may create strategy. And that creation may be embedded in one of the best prepared strategic plans in the history of the universe. But you can be quite sure that when strategy itself is encountered, its reality will be different, and sometimes very different, from that of your own anticipations; other than perhaps at motherhood level, or thereabouts. So you can be quite confident that . . . .

the strategy you see, almost for certain, you will never see

. . . . for, even if you saw it correctly to start with, which you probably didn't (there are simply too many variables, both in static and in dynamic mode, to achieve that outcome with any degree of accuracy, never mind precision) things will certainly have changed, and sometimes they will have changed beyond belief, and before you get there. That is one of the reasons why we need strategic management. Business enterprises need to manage strategies. Strategy is vision, but the vision invariably degenerates into action, whilst that action itself is typically remembered more gloriously than was its reality. Perhaps now you're beginning to see why nomination committees, remuneration committees, audit committees, ethical codes, and endless discussion with regard to executive and non-executive directors, non-executive chairpersons, and what have you, is basically a waste of time, no matter how important such matters may have seemed at the time. For they can only reside on the third, the fourth, or the fifth ripple. They have absolutely no claim to first or second ripple status. That status belongs to the cutting-edge of reality. Business enterprise strategy itself will determine what is and is not appropriate in terms of corporate governance. So you can see, some of those things which the establishment get worked up about may not even be relevant at all to appropriate corporate governance. The game's in play all the time. It's for ever changing. Yet the establishment (and not least of all AIMA, with its recommended list of committees tucked under its proverbial arm, and its demands for non-executive chairpersons and what have you) doesn't seem to appreciate that fact. What a surprise !!!!!

I will turn now to another important dimension and one which (more perhaps through ignorance, if the truth be known, than anything else) threatens, and due to emphasis, to misdirect and undermine the unfolding focus of corporate governance.

The focus of the corporate governance debate, as it unfolds, is now on management. The management of companies. The two competing conceptual philosophies are beginning to crystallize. It has become a matter of 'Management versus Accountability' in the field of corporate governance. The plethora of constraining factors which have developed and become a suffocatingly integral part of the accountability and conformance regime are de-emphasized under the 'management' philosophy of corporate governance. The management regime recognizes, acknowledges, and supports the natural state of business. Business is about striving to achieve things. It's about action. Positive action. Not negative compliance and committees. [Eagles find it hard to sore to great heights when they have balls and chains attached to their legs, and their wings are clipped.] The natural business dimensions, including those of responsible entrepreneurship, management performance, and business success, are positively enhanced by the 'management' philosophy of corporate governance. The management regime accommodates accountability, but correctly, in background mode.

Having realized the relatively low-added-value which may be obtained from the accountability regime of corporate governance (it may actually be low, moderate, or even high-subtracted-value) and having removed its boa-constrictor-like impediments and constraints from the spotlight, the matter to address then focuses on the appropriate *management paradigm* that is to be developed based on the 'management' philosophy of corporate governance.

There are always several paradigms that are compatible with any particular philosophy. You know the sort of thing that I mean. Capitalism is Capitalism. That's one philosophy. Communism is Communism. That's another philosophy. You pay your money and you make your choice. But which paradigm will you choose within Communism. Will it be that of Soviet Communism or will it be that of Chinese Communism? And within your choice there are, of course, all sorts of other choices. So, having now got the picture with regard to paradigms and philosophies, you can appreciate that it would be very silly to impose mandatory or even de facto 'pure form' non-general corporate governance requirements on any company. In the end it comes down to the choice of the shareholders, in total, with regard to how they want their company to be governed. Which philosophy (management, accountability, or some other suitable philosophy) and, based on that philosophy, which particular paradigm or framework. It's disclosure that's important. And it is important, not only for the shareholders of a company so that they may decide whether to change or to reinforce the philosophy and/or paradigm, but also for its stakeholders, and for society in general; and this is so for reasons which are fundamental to our society. A general level of mandatory requirements should, therefore, be issued and which matters are, mandatarily, to be disclosed by a company. If the requirements become too specific then business is unnecessarily channelled into certain directions and which directions may or may not be appropriate (for since when did those wise and wonderful members of the neo-classical establishment know what is best for a dynamic entrepreneurial company which is faced with the cutting-edge of reality in turbulent environments and in both the national and the international market place; even the companies themselves don't know, specifically, what is best) and which directions will, almost for certain, be inappropriate at some point (and possibly not too distant) in the future.

The important dimension which threatens to both misdirect and undermine the unfolding focus of corporate governance and to which I referred previously (and which matter falls within the 'management' philosophy rather than within the 'accountability' philosophy) is that of internal controls.

AIMA states, in its recommendations, that the board of directors of a company should assume responsibility for the integrity of the internal controls and management information systems of a company. That may be a good first step. AIMA, however, and beyond some brief comments in relation thereto, would appear to be silent on the matter. Its comments seem hollow and this is so, and not least of all, because of the general focus of the content of its recommendations document on what may be important, but remote, matters of corporate governance.

The Cadbury Code in the UK requires the board of directors of a company to describe the system of internal financial controls and to state that they have reviewed the effectiveness of the systems. The directors, however, are not required to report their opinion in relation to the effectiveness of the internal financial controls. One can only wonder what the point is in informing shareholders that the directors have reviewed the internal financial controls (which they should cause to have reviewed in any event, and irrespective of the matters that are under consideration here, otherwise they can only be negligent {even if damage is absent} in the execution of their responsibilities) if they are not then going to proceed to inform the owners, the shareholders of the company, whether or not, in their opinion, such internal controls are satisfactory and are, in fact, satisfactory throughout the entirety of the company.

One leading accountancy firm in the UK, in relation to reporting on whether or not the internal financial controls of a business enterprise are effective, wrote the following in their publication entitled 'Effective Corporate Governance' . . . . 'It is difficult to see how it will ever be possible to develop a sufficiently robust general benchmark for internal controls to enable opinions to be given on effectiveness, without creating expectation gaps. There are inherent limitations to the degree of comfort any internal control system will provide and these are exacerbated by variations in individual perceptions of what is, or is not, an acceptable level of risk. If further effectiveness reporting is to be contemplated, we believe that any such requirement should be deferred for several years. Mandating such reporting too soon will simply create pressure for the reporting standard to accommodate the lowest existing practice. Every company, after all, is going to report that their company's systems are effective; how could such a belief be challenged other than in extreme circumstances?' .... It would seem that here again the profession has opted for an easy cop-out in relation to business challenges. Could it be that this Big Six firm is saying that it is perfectly in order for the existence of internal financial control systems that are flawed (either in an important, a significant, or a fundamental way) not to be reported, in one way or another, to the owners of the company. [I wonder what those who lost millions in the Barings Bank debacle (and other, albeit less dramatic, system failures) would have to say in relation to this matter.] And, in any case, whatever happened to the review, by the auditors, of the internal financial controls of a company and which systems form the very foundations on which is based the preparation of general purpose financial reports. Is it perfectly in order for an auditor to rely on those systems, and to tell the world that everything is all right but, at one and the same time, find it impossible for the directors of a company to confirm the reliability of that position? Or does it really mean that the general purpose financial reports are, themselves, prepared on a different basis (being, for example, a static assessment of what reality is now, and a determination of the expectation that the company will survive for one year from the date of the audit report, but which company may well be hurtling dynamically, and because of its various systems, towards debilitation or disaster) and that, in consequence, an audit report isn't worth the paper on which it is written? Where, I wonder, is the value in such reports located? I seem to recall spending many a happy hour flow-charting and testing systems; and also doing other things in addition thereto. What, one may ask, has suddenly changed? It's a fairly practical and pragmatic decision whether or not a systems design is sound, and whether or not, in practice, it works. Isn't it then easy enough to provide an opinion in relation thereto? It is, accordingly, the mindset and the assumptions that are built into the above quotation which lead the person or the persons who are expressing the particular view to the conclusions which are expressed; and perhaps also a little bit of politics.

The preceding quotation, and the view expressed therein by that leading accountancy firm, correlates with the position expressed in the 'Who Holds The Rein?' report and based on the views of the corporate governance committee of the Toronto Stock Exchange. Its view was that 'all public companies should be required to report on the adequacy of internal controls on financial reporting' as part of their annual report. It was also stated, however, that before that particular proposal can be implemented 'a satisfactory framework of reporting on internal financial controls' has to be developed.

The mindsets of the neo-classical establishment are the same and they tend towards conformance with the views and opinions of other members of the neo-classical establishment. As long as they are all in it together (no necks to be stuck out) then they feel safe. A corporate governance opinion would not require that the systems examined are the best in the world but, rather, it would require a statement with regard to whether or not those systems are appropriate for the company. The convergence of systems design and utilization, in order to meet the standards of some predetermined benchmark or other, is irrelevant. Simply, do the systems work appropriately in the context of the company? Could you rely on accounts which are based on such systems? And if the board of directors form one view with regard to the systems of the company, whilst the auditors form a somewhat different view, and the difference therein is material, then one or the other, or both parties, ought to inform the shareholders of the situation; and this is so, corporate governance or no corporate governance requirements. Don't you think so?

Incidentally, before I forget, the publication to which I refer was well structured and most interesting. It covered many topics and definitely achieved its stated purpose of providing an overview of current developments in corporate governance. It also provided practical guidance; not least of all for non-executive directors.

The preceding discussion in relation to internal financial controls provides a suitable introduction to what is the most fundamental flaw that has occurred in relation to corporate governance.

Corporate governance has been defined in various ways and by different people. In unsophisticated language, those definitions, whatever their specifics, tend to agree that *corporate governance is about the board of directors 'running' a company for and on behalf of its shareholders* in total. The philosophical flaw itself was indicated on the very last page of the 'Who Holds The Reins?' report which was prepared by the International Capital Markets Group. This flaw has been addressed in implicit form in this book. In Australia the greatest culprit in relation to this flaw is AIMA and then, by the de facto adoption of the AIMA recommendations, the ASX.

The flaw itself has occurred, in my opinion, as a result of the type of organizations that have, to date, seriously addressed the issue of corporate governance. Let me quote from the last page of the aforementioned report. 'The International Capital Markets Group (ICMG) is a cooperative venture of the International Bar Association's Section on Business Law (IBA-SBL) the Federation Internationale des Bourses de Valeurs (FIBV) and the International Federation of Accountants (IFAC) each of which carries on its activities in the private sector and has an interest in the well-being of the world capital markets, including how those markets are regulated.' It goes on to state that the three organizations have entered into a memorandum of understanding in which they agree to cooperate for, and amongst other reasons, the following purposes:

> to consider developments within their areas of concern in the world capital markets, proposals for the regulation of the markets and, in general, matters which affect opportunities for transnational investment and transnational acquisition of capital; and

> to promote investor confidence internationally and the enhancement of investor protection.

The ultimate goal, as stated by ICMG, is an efficient and effective capital market. And therein lies the philosophical flaw. Corporate governance has not been viewed holistically. Overwhelmingly it has been viewed from the perspective of *financial capital markets* and with *fundamental business realities* having been addressed underwhelmingly. This is why, at this particular stage, corporate governance has crystallized in recommendations that are remote from the cutting-edge of business reality. Third, fourth, and fifth level stuff. Capital markets are a derivative of strategic reality. If there was no real business substance then the capital markets wouldn't matter. You could have all the money in the world. If, in the end, reality isn't there then the money isn't worth the paper on which it is printed. Yes, the two dimensions of financing and investment do go together. They are inseparable. But without fundamental business reality (being the substance of a business and strategic activity) or the anticipation of those dimensions, then investments and capital markets are irrelevant. The business of BHP is not borrowing capital. It's making profits. And through real activity. Its shareholders, being the owners of the capital, want a return in one form or another; and typically in the form of dividend payments and capital appreciation. To achieve that the board of directors must manage the reality of the business and (in the normal course of events) on an on-going basis, in order to derive those returns. They must strategically manage the business for and on behalf of all of its shareholders. Likewise, the board of Coles Myer strategically manages its retail activities in order to secure its returns for its shareholders. Yet corporate governance, in practice, has failed to embrace an holistic approach. And, in my opinion, this has occurred not least of all because the champions of corporate governance are overwhelmingly biased towards financial perspectives and capital markets. Even when, as was indicated previously, corporate governance ventured into the 'management' as opposed to the 'accountability' philosophy of corporate governance, and in the form of a statement by the board of directors that they had reviewed the effectiveness of the internal financial controls of the business enterprise, such controls were specifically described as the internal *financial* controls. The mindset is financial. Yet, as was indicated previously, there are three basic system types on which a company relies for the conduct of its real business. These, to refresh your memory, are the strategic management systems, the management information systems, and the operational control systems. What is significant also is that the *strategic realities* of the business enterprise should, in practice, determine the profile of those three fundamentally different types of systems. In the aforementioned publication, 'Effective Corporate Governance', the essence of what was being reported was largely financial or financial-related, whilst the suggested deficiencies in reporting, and which were addressed therein, included the identification and evaluation of risks and control objectives; financial and management reporting controls; as well as detailed operational controls. The preceding titles do not necessarily convey the content of each section with, in the case of the second section, a deficiency which was noted being that externally focused management information (such as that relating to markets and competitors) although themselves being essential elements in strategic decision-making, were typically excluded from company disclosures. From my perspective I would need to consider the specifics that the author of the suggested deficiency had in mind before deciding my own stance and this would be so due to the fact that certain types of disclosure may be strategically sensitive and would almost never, other than unintentionally, be disclosed. The emphasis in this section of the document, however, was on the negative dimension of controls and was not on the broader positive concept of management. I will say, however, that I do recognize and acknowledge that controls in this context are a negative dimension within a basically positive concept and that they are neither a positive nor a negative (or indeed neutral) dimension in a basically negative concept. The major deficiency of the section, at least in my opinion, was yet again the focus on reporting in relation to components and sub-components (the general emphasis on item-specific solutions and resolutions, in the literature, is almost unbelievable) as opposed to, say, reporting in relation to systems and beyond; whilst many of the suggestions for improvement, whether they were drawn from external sources or not, were basically matters of improved hygiene.

Further, Henry Bosch's in his book 'The Director At Risk' provides little more by the way of insight into this area of disclosure, suggesting that formal controls are likely to be established in four areas. Operational controls relate, he suggests, to the achievement of the organization's objectives. He then goes on to use foreign exchange controls as his example. Financial controls, he states, relate to the reliability of financial reporting. Compliance controls relate to adherence to the law and regulations. And other controls may be establish such as those which relate to an organization's code of conduct or ethics. He then proceeded to explain (and as evidenced by examples) how, in the area of compliance, some companies now even use questionnaires. All riveting stuff !!!!

Generally, and with regard to all contributions, the overwhelming focus has been on the financial, structural, organizational, and administrative dimensions, and with little of consequence being presented with regard to what directors, and boards of directors, should address in the area of *fundamental business realities* in order to satisfy, in a non-negligent way, their responsibility to exercise appropriate corporate governance, in a relevant mix and executed to a sufficient level, on behalf of shareholders.

Business enterprises address their fundamental business realities; their financial, structural, organizational, administrative, and such other considerations; and the inter-relationship of the company with financial capital markets, by means of strategic management. The appropriateness, or otherwise, of that strategic management is, of course, another matter. There will, indeed, be many and varied approaches thereto including, not least of all, a sincere belief by some parties that their particular approach to strategic management, and thereby corporate governance, is appropriately addressed (such parties may well be sincere . . . . but they will be sincerely wrong) and with many approaches being impoverished. Canada, it would seem, is the closest to an understanding of reality apart, that is, from its 'faux pas' in relation to disclosure requirements, and with regard to which it states that companies should make reference to, but are not bound by, the stock exchange guidelines, but should provide an explanation of the differences therefrom; and thereby with the requirement to report deviations giving the aformentioned guidelines quasi-mandatory status. Almost without exception the strategic management of a business enterprise is not explicitly addressed in the context of corporate governance. Indeed, it would appear that any reference to various dimensions of strategic management are mentioned almost in passing and as though strategic management is merely a footnote in the history of management practice. Perhaps, and given an impoverished cognition with regard to the particular role of strategic management in corporate governance, then some of the companies that exist today, and that do not pay appropriate attention to the strategic management dimension will themselves, sooner or later, become footnotes in history.

AIMA also addresses *fundamental business realities* but in what may be seen as an indicative guideline. It says some of the correct things in its 'Respective Roles of the Board and Management' section in that it states that one of the purposes of the guidelines is to ensure that 'the board can competently and efficiently monitor management in the organization and conduct of management's functions' but no real feeling of depth of understanding is conveyed. It does, however, refer to the AWA case (by way of a note) to reinforce its views. Strategic management itself (either as a concept, a construct, or a process) is not addressed by AIMA. Look, with regard to AIMA (and I hope I can dispose of further comment in relation thereto) let me say that because a powerful body like AIMA (but not only AIMA) does something, and it works, that does not mean that other actions which are different would not also have worked and, indeed, have been even more beneficial to the target beneficiaries than the actions which were actually taken. In this light, it may be stated that the corporate governance discussion is not necessarily about 'something good versus something bad' but that it is more about comparing one package of possible 'pluses and minuses' with another package of possible 'pluses and minuses' and with a comparison being carried out in both static and dynamic mode, and with regard to the entire population of companies. Unfortunately the AIMA recommendations have become the de facto standard and, as a consequence (as with other de facto standards) any omissions or variations in relation thereto will be viewed with caution; even though that pseudo mandatory outcome may not have been the intention of AIMA. If the influence of the de facto standard becomes too strong then corporate governance innovation may well turn into a bureaucratic negotiation process. It is my belief that when AIMA prepared its recommendations it had little idea with regard to other relevant corporate governance philosophies and paradigms; and not least of all the 'management' philosophy or the strategic management paradigm. If this is not the case then AIMA itself must be challenged in relation to its own competence. I also believe that the realities of business will, in the end, devalue the AIMA recommendations. Standard setting bodies, including AIMA, may be suitable for stable environments, but their actions are too slow in turbulent environments. Also, and worse, when the first major cases of corporate debilitation occur that are clearly connected to the present corporate governance recommendations of AIMA (such as where the new gods of the boardroom, those independent chairman and their merry band of non-executive directors, bungle the governance of a listed corporate, and others suffer) faith in that regime, whatever the excuses, will falter. When this devaluation occurs it may well reveal that the powerful financial institutions are deficient in intellectual contribution and, indeed, are even lacking in business wisdom; for just because financial institutions make large profits it does not mean that their recommendations necessarily equate with what is, in reality, in the best interest of either themselves or our society.

In the aforementioned report, 'Who Holds The Rein?', and which report is an excellent synopsis of the state of corporate governance internationally, its recommendations state that the key areas for disclosure initially might include:

> the respective roles, responsibilities, and methods of appointment of management and non-management members of the board;

> the responsibility for strategic direction, day-to-day management, and internal controls;

> the control over, and degree of disclosure of, the compensation and benefits of management members of the board; and

> the respective roles, responsibilities, and methods of appointment of internal and external auditors in relation to financial reporting and internal control systems with particular reference to the use of audit committees.

Although there is scope, in the first point which is set out above, for inclusion of a general declaration in relation to the strategic management of a company, being the 'roles and responsibilities of board members' there is, in essence, little real (or, for that matter, even implied) indication in the body of the literature that such is the intention, whilst the second of the aforementioned four points is itself conceptually important, but very limited, and can hardly be intended to satisfactorily address the strategic management responsibilities of a business enterprise.

In the section of the report which addresses the situation in the UK, and under the heading 'Board And Management' it is stated that . . . . 'It is the role of the board to determine the strategic direction of the company and to ensure that management operates within guidelines appropriate for achieving these objectives. Accordingly, the board both allocates resources and monitors the company's progress in the light of the strategic and financial goals it has set.' . . . . but the report, despite alluding to grander things in the preceding quotation, fails to reveal any substance in the area of strategic management in total or, indeed, in the more specific area of strategic management systems.

In the same section of the report, but in relation to the USA, it is stated that the overarching issue is that which is concerned with the effectiveness of boards of directors in carrying out their monitoring and oversight functions. My impression from reading the contribution relating to the USA was that the *zing* had, to some extent, gone out of the issue and that their brain-power had reached its limits on this iteration of activity. The report itself states that . . . . 'Usually the CEO, in collaboration with other senior executives, will develop the company's strategic plan and present it to the board for approval. While the board will discuss it (in varying degrees of depth) generally it will approve it substantially as proposed; one of the frequent criticisms of boards is that they are not sufficiently involved in that process.' . . . . and states elsewhere but under the same heading . . . . 'the ability of non-executive directors to become involved in strategy in US companies is limited because of (what the report describes as) the importance of *management consciousness* . . . . management has close control over what happens in the company.' One would surely think that these quotations alone could only reinforce the need for the appropriate strategic management of a company by the board of directors and on behalf of its shareholders. Isn't it the business enterprise strategy of a company which delivers value to the shareholders? Are these boards of directors purely 'Manets' or the work of some other impressionist? They look good from a distance but, when viewed close up, they can only be described as being terrible. [My favourite works of art are by Manet, Renoir, Degas, Morisot, and others, so please do not think I don't like the work of Manet.] One can only question the protection which is afforded directors by the 'business judgement' principle which indicates that if a director has acted in good faith and in the interests of the company, having been adequately informed, and their decisions are not totally lacking in business justification, then they are somewhat protected from liability. How on earth can any company director (whether executive or non-executive) be adequately informed if the board of director does not manage the strategies of the company appropriately. There is a massive weakness between what is stated in relation to the preceding principle and appropriate strategic management. There would be a need, as an absolute minimum, for appropriate board-level strategic management systems; not to mention related matters.

When a company goes bust, and the shareholders become aware that it was because the strategies weren't managed correctly, then the shareholders would have every right to know why the board didn't know that the management of the strategies was deficient or, indeed, disastrous. Likewise, when a business enterprise fails to seize opportunities (even by merely failing to recognize such opportunities) or it fails to crystallize such opportunities and to an appropriate extent, and for the benefit of all shareholders in total, then shareholders have a legitimate right to seek recourse from the board of directors; and this despite the 'business judgement' principle. For strategic management embraces and encapsulates all dimensions of corporate enterprise and business entity strategy; and this includes, amongst other things, the creation, the design, the development, the implementation, and the utilization of those strategies. The 'business judgement' rule may protect directors from liability if they have acted in good faith in the interests of the company, have been adequately informed, and their decisions are not totally lacking in business justification. But when a director is aware of fundamentally improved approaches to strategic management relative to the practices of their own company, but fails to embrace such practices, then one can only wonder to what extent the 'business judgement' principle would protect such a person in reality; not least of all if it were felt that the board avoided familiarizing themselves with such matters.

Strategic management, in its basic form and in its narrower sense, addresses the management of the strategies, as those strategies are perceived by the board, and their actioning at the coal face. This alone is a multi-dimensional challenge. However, in its more encompassing mode, strategic management addresses all dimensions of strategy. Given these particular comments (and which comments require no great depth of knowledge, understanding, or insight to be able to intuitively appreciate what has been stated) it is clear that a board of directors should, of necessity, know, and be able to appreciate, that the strategic management of the company is either appropriate or inappropriate and, thereafter, whether in essence it's application and utilization is satisfactory or unsatisfactory. To do this a board of directors needs to know, at the very least, that the strategic management systems meet this challenge; as well as much much more in the domain of strategic management. The board of directors cannot, by default or otherwise, simply *opt out* of the active strategic management of a company, for otherwise they are acting recklessly, careless of the consequences; and they may well be negligent. Many neo-classical establishment based boards have failed, and in a glorious way, to embrace leading-edge strategic management practices. The on-line strategic management of a company by its board of directors (preferably with real-time aspects) is at this time desirable; and it will, in the not too distant future, become necessary, albeit not sufficient, as that expectation becomes the norm.

The way directors govern companies for and on behalf of shareholders will change dramatically in the ensuing years. Directors will either lead, or they will be led, in that new direction. A company does not need to go kaput for damage to have been negligently inflicted. It is almost for certain that the business world has now entered the era of 'corporate morbidity' when many companies will succeed beyond belief and others will fail. That is, through the negligence, incompetence, or the lack of competence of boards of directors (and not least of all the boards of directors of globalizing corporates) business enterprises will be seen (or not be seen) to have missed out on opportunities; they will have failed, in a material sense, to crystallize benefits; or, for one unacceptable reason or another, they will have inflicted disadvantage on shareholders. Companies in that category will be the *walking wounded*, the *corporate cripples*, and the *living dead*, of the business world; with the nature and extent of their wounds, crippleness, and death having their own degrees of variation.

The rate of 'company debilitation' in the 'corporate morbidity' era will, indeed, be high. And the culpability of directors for such debilitation will, indeed, be great. The incidence of debilitation by stealth (caused not least of all by a distinct lack of competence, incompetence, and negligence at board level) will not be unusual; whilst those responsible will often continue to flourish, being appointed to other influential positions in the corporate world or to even higher status roles by governments; or for their services, so as to say, they may even be awarded the Order of Australia.

Canada, of all six countries in the 'Who Holds The Rein?' report, and over and above Australia itself, would appear to come the closest to addressing *fundamental business realities* and the issue of corporate governance, by embracing strategic management; but it would seem that it, too, cannot help falling back into neo-classical establishment thinking type modes. Canada, although it definitely does not embrace strategic management per se, and possibly so (as with other countries) because they are not as familiar with that subject as should be the case (strategic planning does not equate with strategic management) its write-up in the aforementioned report is more convincing than is that of either the UK or the USA. The contribution on Canada defines the principal objective of the direction and management of a business to be 'the enhancement of shareholder value' but it then goes on to provide somewhat appealing, but weak, support for that assertion. Canada, based on the aforementioned objective, and together with perhaps its more practical recognition of the realities of business, would (possibly unknown to them) seem to be, at least potentially, the nearest of the anglo-saxon-origin countries to (although still some distance therefrom) embracing a 'management' philosophy and a strategic management paradigm upon which to progress its corporate governance practices. Let us hope that the powerful parties there recognize and seize on this situation and particular opportunity to advance Corporate Canada.

In summary it may be stated that those who have embraced the challenges of corporate governance have failed to address that subject in a holistic way. They have largely focused on the capital markets; the financial, the structural, the organizational, and the administrative dimensions (and some specifics of which may well be irrelevant to corporate governance) and other considerations; whilst, at one and the same time, they have failed miserably to address the requirements for governing the business realities of a company at board level. This situation may well reflect the relative abundance of knowledge in the former area (and which knowledge is encapsulated in those persons who were or who are participants in the development of corporate governance and who have exercised their influence or power in that arena) and their relative dearth of knowledge in the latter area. The fact that the various participants, in total, and who have exercised their power and influence in the determination of the current corporate governance requirements, may themselves hold significant board appointments, and across many and various industries, or be involved with such companies in other capacities, or are, indeed, well and truly part of the neo-classical establishment, gives them little credence in the area of corporate governance. Such business status does not, in and of itself, convey relevant knowledge, understanding, and insight with regard to the actual realities of business, for simply, the reality that is incorporated in the current corporate governance recommendations (and its lack of indicative substance) clearly gives the lie to such a claim. Image, reputation, prestige, and connections, may well provide one or more seats at the boardroom table, but it does not confer skill, ability, integrity, credibility, talent, vision, or business wisdom; and that, if the truth be known, and of itself, is a real problem throughout not only Corporate Australia but, no doubt, also the world.

So where are we now on this hope thing . . . . This hope for the future. Well I think that perhaps we should now return to seeing a world in a grain of sand. And maybe heaven in a wild flower. And I think we're more or less ready to hold infinity in the palm of our hand. And enjoy eternity, at least that is, for an hour.

I have now discussed certain dimensions of corporate governance, and I have related that activity to the strategic management of a business enterprise, whilst I have noted, and in addition thereto, that the strategic well-being of a company is fundamental to both the preparation and the audit of general purpose financial reports.

In doing this I have also indicated that out of this relationship, this very trinity, can emerge the resurrection of the accountancy profession. This opportunity for the profession to embrace its own future, and a relevant future at that, emanates from one basic singularity, being the recognition and the acknowledgement that

the strategic management of a business enterprise determines whether or not it is a going concern

and that this actuality is so, and not least of all, for purposes of preparing and auditing the general purpose financial reports of a company. The aforementioned statement is very powerful, and so absolutely fundamental, for it indicates that the very existence of a business enterprise cannot be separated from the ubiquitous concept of strategic management. It is an inalienable dimension of a company. It underpins management's sovereignty. And in all its guises. It provides both the static and the dynamic foundations for every type of accountancy. And in its many and varied forms. For it is strategic management which determines the success or the failure, and the actual performance, of a business enterprise; this apart from the dimensions of misfortune and of serendipity.

For the accountancy profession to embrace its own future it must, however, become more relevant to shareholders, to stakeholders, and to society in general. It must move away from its parochial going concern assurances and inform the shareholders, being the owners of a business enterprise, with regard to the strategic well-being of their company. And this may be achieved through one of several forms. The profession, when preparing and when auditing accounts, could state, in simple form, that in their opinion

> the strategic management of the business enterprise is appropriate or is inappropriate for the company and that it has relied on that assessment in the preparation and the audit of the general purpose financial reports

whilst, and in a far more relevant and indeed challenging form, it could also provide an expanded opinion which would address the

> the degree, level, or extent of the appropriateness or inappropriateness of the strategic management thereof

and which additional information could provide fundamental benefits to shareholders, to stakeholders, and to society in general. A variation on each of the aforementioned categories of opinion may parallel, somewhat, the present situation (and, in so doing, pander to the accountancy profession) insofar as either of the preceding types of opinion could be presented in a context which

> addresses specifically the ensuing twelve month period or also and in addition
> addresses the period subsequent to that twelve months

and which particular format could thereby be used to address the expression of an opinion in either constrained or expanded form.

The performance and success of Corporate Australia is essential to our society for business is the engine that delivers the standard of living and the quality of life of our nation; and that is so both in present form, and into the future. The allocation and the use of the tangible and intangible strategic resources of a nation determines, and to a significant extent, the strategic direction of a society. In Australia this allocation and use is amongst sectors such as those of mining, fuel, and mineral resources, farming, manufacturing, services, and everything else. Within manufacturing, for example, allocation and usage will occur amongst low, medium, and high technology businesses. Whilst within the service sector allocations and usage will occur at least amongst companies in the tourism, education, telecommunications, and financial services sub-sectors. Each of these sub-sectors may themselves be exploded to identify even more areas of business activity and with the vehicle for the delivery of the derived (positive or negative) benefits being that of business enterprises; government activities apart. This overview, even though it is indeed simple in the extreme, conveys the reality of resource allocation. For resource usage, which includes human resources, indicates what type of society we are at the present time and what type of society we may become at various points in the future. Accordingly, it is essential that we, as a society, are sufficiently aware of the appropriateness, or otherwise, of the strategic management of companies, and not least of all when those companies are competing for critically scarce resources, for, and to repeat, it is the strategic management of all of our business enterprises which contributes, and in a significant way, to the determination of the present and the future standard of living, and the present and the future quality of life, of all Australians.

In the aforementioned 'Who Holds The Reins?' report it was noted that 'The amount of capital accumulated in companies around the globe is enormous. The efficient and responsible use of these resources in large measure determines the propensity of nations with market economies and of those seeking to develop market economies (to perform and succeed). Thus the mechanisms and processes by which companies are governed become a matter of vital importance to nations. If the companies in which wealth is accumulated are poorly governed, if their resources are inefficiently used, if their managements are inept, or if the power of management becomes channelled in a way which conflicts with the company's interests, all stakeholders and society suffer, not just the owners of the enterprise. It is therefore important that within every company there are means of ensuring that resources are used efficiently and in a manner that ensures the achievement of the company's objectives and its ability to contribute to the common good.' Many of the glorious technicolour examples of the 1980s reveal the spirit of this message. When companies such as Bond Corporation, Bell Resources, Tricontinental, National Safety Council, Hooker Corporation, Ariadne, Quintex, Elders, Linter Group, and Adelaide Steamship were debilitated or ruined, we suffered. Many billions of dollars of value simply evaporated in what seemed like no time at all. Often this value had not been very productive for years. Much of it was wasted. And someone, somewhere, was left holding the baby. In the end it was Australia. Had we examined the strategic management of these companies, together with many more companies, we as a society would not have suffered in the way and to the extent in which we have, and from many negative dimensions; whilst, in compound mode, a whole host of positive aspects would have benefited Australia.

As a country we can learn from the experiences of other countries, not necessarily on a like-for-like basis, but rather, conceptually and beyond. We should not, however, endeavour to apply or just replicate the behaviour of other nations because they perform well or are successful. We are Australia. We are not Germany, France, Japan, or some other country. We have our own culture, and our own national anachronisms, and we should utilize those, and other developing characteristics, to our advantage. No we are not Japan with its sense of family and a desire for consensus, with its long-termism, its inter-locking shareholdings, its dependence on bank finance, its myriad of informal communications amongst business enterprises, its low litigation emphasis, and its 'lifetime' employment for the thirty-five percent of the working population who are 'fortunate' to be employed by the elite companies and the sixty-five percent of other workers who obtain no real benefits of consequence from such a system. We are not Germany with (for an economy of that size) its relatively few listed companies, its emphasis on long-term bank as opposed to equity financing, the legislative albeit also cultural requirement for the codetermination by management and employees of the future of their company, the relative (for western countries) longer-term commitment of executives to their companies and, generally, the responsibility of a company towards 'all stakeholders' of the company. Neither are we France with its overt concentration of power, and not least of all in the president of a company who, as the occupier of that office, is far more powerful than any counterpart in the anglo-saxon-type regimes, and with its absolute plethora of family-based companies, its debt financing, and its domination of the equity market by individuals, and by inter-corporate investors. We are Australia. And our benefit is obtained from knowing how others operate. Not merely Canada, the UK, and the USA, or France, Germany, and Japan; although knowledge of their particular practices is important. We should also understand corporate governance practices in Korea (being one of the real drivers in our region) as well as Taiwan and Indonesia, how it works in the Middle Eastern countries, in Mexico, and in Chile, Argentina, Venezuela, and Brazil, and also in Russia, and various of the Eastern European nations, and many other countries. For if we can understand how other countries address their corporate governance challenges then that, in itself, may help our country to become even more successful than it is at the present point in time. But we don't have to converge as such. You see, what is best practice for any one of those countries may not be best practice for another of those countries. You may, by now, already appreciate that there is a vast potential for a wide range of corporate governance practices amongst countries and which practices may be very successful in the context of each of those countries. Practices in one country may seem to be the same practices as those which are practiced in another country, but the critical realities, and not least of all many of the cultural dimensions, will differ. Convergence, it is noted, will eventually create mediocrity.

[Utilizing computers as a different but a generally understood analogy, an assertion of computer convergence could be made because many firms use computers. It is evident, however, that with the vast array of hardware, software, and firmware (ranging from laptops, through desktops, and onto mainframes) and their combinations, and the use of local and wide area networks, the internet, and the world wide web, as well as constrained internets, being intranets, it is evident that it is specific divergence, and not general convergence per se, that has meaningful significance; for specific divergence resides in particular environments which have had their tendency towards general convergence differentiated.]

By way of illustration, and on a country basis, may I say that having lived for several years in South Africa (and which country is indeed blessed by being one of the most magnificently beautiful places on earth) I was once asked whether South Africa was *better* than the UK. I replied that it wasn't better or worse but, rather, that it was *different* to the UK. Likewise it may be stated that having lived in Australia for some years, Australia is also different to both South Africa and the UK. Whilst it may be noted that no doubt South Africa yesterday is different to South Africa today. There are at least two points which should be noted from this brief discourse. The first point, as was noted previously, is that differences are usually far more revealing than are likenesses; and this may be so at the first, the second, or the third difference. [The first difference, using the above countries for illustrative purposes, may be the differences between the UK and South Africa; and between South Africa and Australia; and between Australia and the UK. The second difference would be the differences between the differences of the first comparison and the second comparison and then the second comparison and the third comparison. With the third difference being the differences between the two aforementioned sets of differences . . . . whilst and in a somewhat different vein . . . . a change may be noted, the rate of that change may then be noted, and the rate of the rate of that change may also, and in addition thereto, be noted. The illustration is getting a little bit complicated for purposes of this book, but the point is that the generic level, or the absolute difference or change level, may not be the critical dimension that should be considered; it may be a derivative thereof. The second point which emanates from the aforementioned illustration, and which has also been alluded to previously, is that we cannot assume that we do know, or can know, everything about now or the future. This was indicated previously when it was stated that you may create strategy, and that creation may be embedded in one of the best prepared strategic plans in the history of the universe, but you can be quite sure that when strategy itself is encountered, its reality will be different, and sometimes very different, from that of your own anticipations; other than perhaps at motherhood level, or thereabouts. To accept that a strategic plan will unfold as it is set out assumes that all initial conditions are known, that there is some degree of sensitive dependence thereon, and that all inter-relationships and happenings are not only known, but are also understood. That assumption would itself tend to indicate that the execution of a strategic plan is, in essence, mechanistic, and that all intermediate and final outcomes are deterministic in nature. Reality, however, is different. There are things that are known. And there are things that are unknown. And there are also things that are unknowable. Not only is the present known, unknown, and unknowable but, likewise, the future itself is also known, unknown, and unknowable. Even if things were to progress for a while as we expect, or as we predict, they will not progress for ever along that course, for not only can the *known* change things, but the *unknown* and the *unknowable* will also change things; whilst, and from time-to-time, some of those unknowable changes (when they do eventually crystallize) will be beyond imagination. The dynamics of reality alone will defeat determinism. By the time you get there you can be quite sure that things will have changed. In accordance, and this may have become more and more evident from the preceding discourse, the appropriate strategic management of a company is truly critical to the achievement of sound corporate governance. And this is so for, in reality, strategic management is corporate governance.

Turning now to the expression of an opinion by the accountancy profession with regard to the strategic well-being of a business enterprise, let me commence by stating that we should be quite clear that the preparation of general purpose financial reports demands the same requirements as that of their audit; for they are two sides of the same coin. One is the creation. The other, for want of a better term, is the checking of that creation. Both the board of directors and the auditors form an opinion in relation to the accounts which are prepared. Both parties are appointed by the shareholders. And both parties report to the shareholders. It is, however and without doubt, the responsibility of the board of directors of a company to cause to be prepared and, thereafter, to present the general purpose financial reports of a company, and the information which is contained therein, to shareholders.

Given this, it is evident that the company shareholders, in total, should instruct both those who are responsible for the preparation of the accounts, and those who audit those accounts, that it is no longer acceptable to present what have invariably been relatively low-value-added financial reports to the owners of the business enterprise. The shareholders, in total, must tell both their board of directors, and the external auditors, that they wish to be supplied with general purpose financial reports that deliver to themselves significant value. That they the shareholders, unequivocally, want high-value-added reports and opinions. *And they must make it clear that the mandate of the board of directors and of the external auditors is to deliver information which is relevant and of substance and that, at one and the same time, technocratic superficiality is no longer acceptable as a substitute for fundamental information and meaningful professional opinions.* The accountancy profession itself ought not to object to such a requirement but should, indeed, positively support that move. In their role as professional accountancy bodies, neither the Society nor the Institute own the listed companies for which their members prepare the accounts and conduct audits, and so they should follow the instructions of those who engage their services or retain them : the shareholders. Whilst typically, and for large listed companies, nor do the directors own those companies. For it is you, the shareholders, who own your company. Your company belongs to you. So you can instruct your board of directors and your external auditors to do your will. And this you should do !!!!!

The objective of an audit of a general purpose financial report is 'to enable the auditor to express an opinion whether the financial report is prepared, in all material respects, in accordance with an identified financial reporting framework' and which statement has been quoted from the Handbook of the Institute. None of the strategic management reporting initiatives which were indicated previously contravene the boundaries of the preceding quotation.

From this point on, however, it is all down hill; with the above quotation being as good as it gets. What is perfectly feasible is, in reality, qualified out of existence by the profession; and you are left to wonder what on earth an audit report actually tells you. Why do the shareholders of BHP pay around five million dollars ($5m) for an external audit? Why do Coles Myer shareholders pay nearly four million dollars ($4m) for their audit? Why do many other companies pay one million dollars ($1m) or more for their external audits? And why do many many more companies pay hundreds of thousands of dollars for their audits? The Institute Handbook states that 'although the auditor's opinion enhances the credibility of the financial report the user cannot assume that the opinion is an assurance as to the future viability of the entity' and this is so despite its claimed lending of credibility, or otherwise, to the preparation of financial reports. *Does this mean, then, that an external audit report tells us what it tells us, but that, in truth, it doesn't tell us much at all ?!!!* Could the accountancy profession at last have managed to sever spirit from body? Could it be that we have fortuitously stumbled across the very meaning of Dante's words which are so indelibly inscribed above the entrance to the head office of the Institute of Chartered Accountants in Australia? It would seem, and without much doubt, that the fundamental work content of an external audit does, indeed, require a radical transformation and, in addition thereto, that a thorough review is required of the underlying basis for the preparation of the general purpose financial reports of a corporate enterprise.

The Institute Handbook sets out illustrative audit reports ranging from an unqualified report, through 'except for' and 'subject to' audit opinions, onto an 'adverse' opinion, and finally it gives an illustrative opinion which could be applicable to situations where an 'inability to form an opinion' is actually encountered. The most common audit opinion would, of course, be the unqualified audit report, or otherwise the recommended standards would not, in general terms, be located within or on the boundaries of business reality. Any differences of opinion that are encountered between the preparers and the auditors of accounts are, in practice, reconciled where differences in opinion are either important or significant. This, therefore, leaves only unreconciled fundamental differences of opinion for disclosure in an external audit report.

A critical aspect of the *scope* section of each of the aforementioned types of audit report is that which states that 'our audit has been conducted in accordance with Australian Auditing Standards to provide *reasonable assurance* as to whether the financial report is free of material misstatement' and which section then goes on to state that 'our procedures included examination, on a test basis, of evidence supporting the amounts and other disclosures in the financial report, and the evaluation of accounting policies and significant accounting estimates' before then further indicating 'that these procedures have been undertaken to form an opinion as to whether, in all material respects, the financial report is presented fairly in accordance with Accounting Standards and other mandatory professional reporting requirements .... so as to present a view which is consistent with *our understanding* of the company's financial position, the results of its operations, and its cash flows' etc, etc, and so forth. But do these standards provide the fundamentally relevant information which would be required by even an ordinary 'mum or dad' shareholder (never mind the financial institutions, investment bankers, stockbrokers, merchant bankers, etc, etc.) so that, on the balance of probabilities, they can be satisfied that their company is being appropriately governed?

The Institute Handbook also states that for an audit report to be *relevant* 'the information included in the audit report should relate to the needs of those to whom the audit report is addressed, including an explanation of the nature and extent of the auditor's work, and the degree of *assurance* provided' to the shareholders.

With regard to 'assurance' the Handbook of the Institute states that *assurance* is 'the satisfaction as to the reliability of information provided' and in relation to which it goes on to state that 'the degree of satisfaction achieved is determined by the nature and extent of procedures performed by the auditor, the results of the procedures, and the objectivity of the evidence obtained' in relation to the matters under consideration.

The term *reasonable assurance* which is identified above, and which term is included in the scope section of an audit report, is used when there is 'a high, but not absolute, level of assurance on an accountability matter' according to the Handbook of the Institute. The term is used 'in recognition of the fact that absolute assurance is rarely attainable due to such factors as the need for judgement, the use of testing, the inherent limitations on internal control, and the fact that much of the evidence available to the auditor is persuasive rather than conclusive in nature' . . . . whilst the aforementioned Handbook continues . . . . 'the concept relates to the accumulation of audit evidence necessary for the auditor to conclude whether there are any material misstatements in the subject matter taken as a whole . . . . reasonable assurance relates to the whole audit process . . . . reasonable in any given situation will depend on the facts of that situation and is determined by what evidence could reasonably be expected to be gathered and what conclusions could reasonably be expected to be drawn in the particular situation' under consideration.

So what's the problem? Well perhaps first of all we should remind ourselves that the very essence of being a professional is the necessary requirement to make judgements and, thereafter, to express professional opinions. Almost everyone in their own particular occupation, trade, vocation, business, or profession makes judgements. It is, however, the type and nature of those judgements which helps to determine whether or not a person is exercising a profession. And then, amongst professions, and for want of a better term or three, the degree, ranking, or status of a particular profession. Whilst within a particular profession there is also a further differentiation of the degree, ranking, or status of the specific specialities of that profession. [If you are in doubt with regard to these assertions then consider the professional status that you afford a doctor compared with a teacher; and then consider the professional status that you afford a brain surgeon or a heart specialist (particularly as a patient) when compared with the status that you afford your general practitioner or, and alternatively, you may prefer to compare the status which you afford a kindergarten or primary school teacher compared with that of a university lecturer or a professor. You may not like such differentiation but it is, indeed, a reality.] What has happened with the accountancy profession, in total, is that its professional status has diminished over the years. This is so on a relative basis and it may also be the case on an absolute basis. The advances in the world of business have outstripped the advances in the accountancy profession. And this eventuality has occurred as a result of both active and passive behaviour; and by default. We, as a profession, have failed to embrace the challenges of our times whilst, and at one and the same time, we have also established, or have endeavoured to establish, protective barriers or buffers around our activities; and we have failed to redefine our tasks, duties, and responsibilities, and our fundamental role in society. The accountancy profession has, by default or otherwise, abdicated responsibility for the basic business dimensions of its activities and this abdication, at the major corporate level, has been in favour of management consultants. Yet some of the tasks which are (actually or potentially) undertaken by management consultants truly belong in the domain of the accountancy profession. They are absolutely accountancy based. They are fundamental to the practice of accountancy; and this is so both in relation to those who prepare and those who audit accounts.

The status of a profession correlates with the nature of what it addresses, its inputs, its activities, and what it delivers. The well-being of a profession is very much affected by its moral, ethical, and intellectual realities. The values of our society have changed but the establishment, and not least of all the broad leadership of the accountancy profession, has not acquiesced in those changes; at least not to the extent to which society itself has internalized such changes. Society has been hurt and it is rightfully angry. Almost everyone knows someone who has suffered as a result of the recession. Many people are concerned that they may not have jobs or even an income. Parents are worried about the future of their children. The massive victory of the coalition parties over the long serving government in the recent federal elections showed one dimension of that heart-felt pain and concern. That massive victory was not so much about embracing the policies of the new government but, rather, it was more to do with running away from the past. The government has no mandate other than that of removing the lingering trauma of the recession from our society and to create what may be perceived as a new and a secure future.

So what is the role of the accountancy profession in relation to this particular objective; this creation of a new and a secure (albeit not predictable) future? Well, as I have already indicated, we as a profession have failed miserably during the past decade or more. We have failed to embrace, and in an appropriate way for our times, the things which we do whilst, and in addition thereto, we have also failed to embrace new and emerging dimensions. Instead of being bold, we have used politically correct language to convey the impression that we are doing the correct things for our society whilst, at one and the same time, the leadership of the profession have endeavoured to distance our profession (and thereby their own firms) from its fundamental failings, and its ineptitudes. It was mentioned earlier that the Handbook of the Institute states that the objective of an audit of a general purpose financial report is *'to enable the auditor to express an opinion whether the financial report is prepared, in all material respects, in accordance with an identified financial reporting framework'* and, consequently, it is pointed out here, and with regard to the fundamental initiatives which are suggested in this book, that the existing framework and the possible emerging framework (and which new framework is partially incorporated in the draft pronouncement that is included in the 'Statement of Principles' as was recently issued in the UK and which statement has evoked much invigorating discussion) are each compatible with the suggested fundamental initiatives addressed in this book. It is the nature and the substance of the work which underpins whichever framework (apart from any framework deficiencies which may also exist) that is deficient; and sometimes those deficiencies have resulted in appalling outcomes. It was also mentioned previously that due to the reconciliation of views which occurs when differences of opinion exist in relation to accounts (for general purpose financial reports are not finalized and then audited but are, in practice, held open for adjustments) it is often only the differences of opinion in relation to things which are fundamental that, in reality, elicit something other than an unqualified audit report. The real problem arises, however, when the accountancy profession itself does not know when a particular issue is fundamental and this is so because the profession doesn't always know what it is looking at; as was previously exemplified by reference to knowing or not knowing the difference between a diamond and a piece of glass. As a result of this phenomenon fundamental deficiencies themselves cannot be resolved, or even reported, for, and due to our own professional inadequacies, we don't actually know that the fundamental deficiencies even exist.

Actual reported deficiencies may include many things such as being unable to verify the existence of a material asset or liability, or they may be purely technical matters, as with non-compliance with an accounting standard, and which may be epitomized by the non-standard disclosure of goodwill. Reported deficiencies, in consequence, may not be what may be termed 'business matters' at all. They may include the appropriateness of the accounting policies selected, particular accounting estimates, and compliance with relevant statutory requirements. Yet it is business matters which the shareholders should know about and this is so in order that they may make their own decisions with regard to, say, their board of directors and its strategic management of their company. The actual realities of business have not altered because goodwill is written off on the inverted sum of the digits basis instead of on a straight-line basis over twenty years, or whatever the specifics may be these days; for nobody seems to be able to make up their minds anyway, and what is arrived at is typically pathetic. Sure, the particular treatment of goodwill may well affect the view of some investment manager somewhere, but that is in the context of the worldview of that particular manager; or maybe a whole gaggle of such managers. Any positive or negative happenings that are derived from a non-standard treatment of goodwill, and the responses thereto, are arbitrary and contrived. They do not affect the substance of the business per se but, rather, the whole issue boils down to the way goodwill, and the business itself, are being viewed. A mining company will still extract its gold, or its copper, or its iron ore, and it will still sell it, and this will be so irrespective of the arbitrary amount that is attributed to the value of goodwill. That is reality. Distortions in reported profits, or in assets and liabilities, will occur because of standards, rules, and conventions which distort reality. And impacts, consequences, and outcomes will occur due to the specific distortions which are inflicted on reality and according to how critical the deviations which will or do result from those distortions may be viewed by various parties. But this doesn't get away from the fact that the accountancy profession itself (consciously or otherwise) is playing games with reality and that those very games, in some cases, may be used by both acquisitive and non-acquisitive entrepreneurs (and this is the way life is under the present accountancy regime) to their particular advantage but, at one and the same time, to the disadvantage of some or all of the shareholders of a company.

The real challenges, and the overwhelming benefits to society, are located, however, in even more fundamental dimensions. And the failure to crystallize those benefits has been due to the abject failure of the accountancy profession to report to shareholders, in total, in relation to the strategic well-being of their company. This revelation and crystallization of shareholder, stakeholder, and societal benefits, as was indicated above, can be addressed along three dimensions. The first relates to the appropriateness or the inappropriateness of the strategic management of a business enterprise; the second is embedded in the degree, level, or extent of that appropriateness or inappropriateness; whilst the third addresses the duration of the aforementioned situation.

An audit report, according to the quotation from the Handbook of the Institute of Chartered Accountants and which quotation was set out above, is suppose to be *relevant* and the information that is included in an audit report is meant to relate to the *needs* of the shareholders; whilst it is suppose to provide *reasonable assurance* (if this is, in fact, the case) that the general purpose financial reports, *in all material respects,* and *as understood by the auditor,* are indeed *free of material misstatement* when viewed as a whole.

It may be noted that the Institute Handbook defines *relevance* as meaning 'that quality of financial information which exists when that information influences decisions by users about the allocation of scarce resources by helping them form predictions about the outcome of past, present, or future events; or confirming or correcting their past evaluations; and which enables users to assess the discharge of accountability by the management or governing body of the entity' in question.

Where is *relevance,* one may ask, when the strategic well-being of a business enterprise is *not* addressed by either those who prepare accounts or those who audit those accounts? It is clear, from this fundamental omission, that neither *needs* nor *relevance* are being addressed in the context of shareholders in total. Their relevance and their needs, along that dimension, are being largely ignored by the accountancy profession; and this is so both in relation to the preparation and the audit of general purpose financial reports. [This is not to say that there is not a great deal of work dedicated to the preparation and to the audit of general purpose financial reports, for clearly there is much time, effort, and skill applied thereto; and this is so despite the aforementioned fundamental omission.] However, given the preceding observations, which are indeed correct, then the *assurance* which is provided (other than by coincidence) is, and to all intents and purposes, a fiction. Of course any assurance which is provided should, without doubt, be what is termed *reasonable assurance* for no reasonable person would ever expect absolute assurance; after all, we are relying on the professional opinion of someone who is suppose to know and understand what it is that they are examining. With regard to the term reasonable assurance, and as mentioned previously, the Institute Handbook states that 'reasonable in any given situation will depend on the facts of that situation and is determined by what evidence could reasonably be expected to be gathered and what conclusions could reasonably be expected to be drawn in the particular situation' which is under consideration. *But when you don't know what evidence could have reasonably been expected to be gathered then how do you know what conclusions could have reasonably been expected to have been drawn?* The insulation of the accountancy profession from appropriate leading-edge strategic management thinking when preparing and auditing general purpose financial reports (as well as in relation to other professional work) has resulted in fundamental emptinesses, or voids, in the application of professional practice. The very foundations of such work are at least weak and, in all truth, are possibly flawed. By the time the constraint of *'as understood by the auditor'* is overlaid on everything else (for the auditor may never understand reality if the applied practices of the accountancy profession do not change in order to embrace strategic management) then one is only left to wonder whether shareholders will ever have their *relevant needs* satisfied and which *needs* and *relevance* appertain to the basic fundamental realities of their company. Well chosen words which are included in various accounting edicts needlessly protect the accountancy profession whilst, at one and the same time, they mask business reality; for every accountancy practice (including the Big Six firms themselves) could outsource this specific aspect of their work, being that of strategic management reviews, by retaining what the profession terms 'experts' but who are described as 'specialists' by myself, to carry out such work and on their behalf; whilst all large companies (including not least of all globalizing multi-national corporates) could adopt an equivalent practice in the preparation of their own general purpose financial reports.

There is, and I stress, absolutely no need for any accountancy firm or for any listed company, together with its derived entities, not to actively address the fundamental needs of shareholders, in total, in the area of the strategic management of their company. For all shareholders, and not merely the financial institutions and other powerful shareholders, are entitled to know whether or not the strategic management of their company is appropriate. This is so basic to all shareholders that they have a right to that knowledge.

The Institute Handbook states that 'accounting policies must be selected and applied in a manner which ensures that the *resultant* financial information satisfies the concepts of *relevance* and of *reliability* and thereby ensures that the *substance* of the underlying transactions and other events is reported' in the general purpose financial reports. The use and juxtaposition of the terms *resultant* and *reliability* in the preceding quotation conveys the impression, and in a way which is obvious, that the very source from which the resultant financial information emanates should be reliable. The term *reliability* has been defined in the Institute Handbook as meaning 'that quality of financial information which exists when that information can be depended upon to represent faithfully, and without bias or undue error, the transactions or other events that either it purports to represent or could reasonably be expected to represent' and which information contributes towards the totality of the general purpose financial reports.

With regard to *substance* the Handbook of the Institute states that 'if financial information is to be both relevant and reliable, it is necessary that the *substance* rather than the *form* of a transaction or other event be reported where substance and form differ' whilst it goes on to state that 'reporting the substance of a transaction or other event requires that the information reported reflects its *economic* effect' and further that 'in accounting, the substance of a transaction or other event is reflected in the assets, liabilities, equity, revenues, and expenses (being the elements of financial statements) resulting from or altered by the transaction or other event' which is entered into by the business enterprise.

The contention with regard to the *economic* effect is, of course, an overstatement insofar as, in practice, that term really refers to portraying the immediate *monetary* or *dollar* effect of a transaction or other event in the assets, liabilities, equity, revenues, and expenses, as may be relevant, whilst it does not necessarily refer to the *economic* effect in the context of the strategic value to the business enterprise of a transaction or other event. The use of the term *economic* effect, and in relation to fundamental matters, may therefore only be a *quasi* economic, or worse, a *pseudo* economic effect; being, in reality, an *apparent financial effect* which may not coincide with either an *economic* or a *strategic* effect when the *real* substance (in relation to what is happening) is embraced. The use of the word *substance* in concert with the term *economic* effect is, accordingly, pretentious, for the term *substance* as used in the aforementioned sense is itself somewhat remote from reality; it being pitched at, in practice, a superficial level of substance when examining the form of a transaction or other event and not at the *real* source of that substance. Substance, in the sense in which it is used in the Institute Handbook, would seem to refer to recording the honesty, the truthfulness, or the genuineness of a particular transaction or other event, and not necessarily its substance in the context of the business enterprise in total. This is reinforced by the statement which was quoted previously that 'in accounting, the substance of a transaction or other event is reflected in the assets, liabilities, equity, revenues, and expenses (being the elements of financial statements) resulting from or altered by the transaction or other event' and which form of accountancy simply does not record the substance of the *economic* effect (for when last did the accountancy profession ever account for goodwill on an economic basis) whilst it definitely does not account for *economic* effects in the context of the *strategic management* of a business enterprise; yet both acquisitive and non-acquisitive entrepreneurs, and whether consciously or otherwise, invariably make economic or strategic evaluations with regard to their own actions. [Is a similar exercise beyond the inherent capabilities of the accountancy profession?] The aforementioned approach to accountancy simply endeavours, and admirably so in the context in which it is addressed, to record the truthfulness of a transaction or other event. It is misleading, however, to suggest that this change of emphasis (if indeed it is a change at all) focuses on substance rather than on form alone, for when it comes to expressing *reasonable assurance* in relation to general purpose financial reports (which should be a fundamental happening of great moment) the substance that is being addressed is, other than by coincidence, only an *apparent* substance.

There are, and in relation to a business enterprise, three general dimensions of substance, being the financial, the economic, and the strategic; each of which may well give a different result. The accounting standard dwells on the *financial* dimension whilst lending apparent credibility thereto by referring to the *economic* effect. It uses, as one of its examples, the sale and the lease back of an asset. [Could it be that the search is, in fact, now on for that elusive *seventeenth* way in which to present a lease on a balance sheet?] The financial portrayal that would be obtained by basing an approach to recording transactions and other events on the information which is contained in the Institute Handbook would be fine at a simple level. However, for going concern and other strategic assessments the preceding financial approach would not necessarily give the correct result. For a correct outcome to occur then all three dimensions would need to be addressed; being the economic, the strategic, and the financial. It is, and without doubt, that the *real substance* of a transaction or other event is necessarily encapsulated in the *strategic management* of *economic resources* and it is that dynamic happening which may then be viewed in terms of its *financial* effect.

Bearing this in mind, there is one thing for sure, what is being addressed in the Handbook of the Institute has little to do with the real *needs, relevance, reliability, or substance* of anything when each of those concepts are themselves considered in the context of the entirety of a business enterprise and from the perspective of all of the shareholders, in total, of a company. Further, given the use of the Institute Handbook information to determine the going concern status of a business enterprise, and in the manner in which it is practiced by the accountancy profession, and not least of all when determination is itself based upon the general premise of *'as understood by the auditor'* then it is clear that the outcome could be very misleading indeed: given the general intellectual impoverishment of the accountancy profession in the field of strategic management. Is it any wonder, rhetorically speaking, that during the past decade those who prepared accounts and those who had audited those same accounts seemed to express what amounted to 'utter surprise' when those companies that they had so ably examined went bust. Simply put, these people didn't know what they were looking at and so, in accordance therewith, it is also clear (other than perhaps in the presence of duplicity or perhaps even, to coin a word, multiplicity) that those same people couldn't spot a corporate disaster, year-after-year-after-year, even when it was staring them in the face !!!!!

[Now let me see, I wonder if our all-time favourite Australian genius 'Blind Freddy' has returned from his trip to Ok Tedi yet (he's been up there having a little swim in the river sludge and giving that 'non-existent' tailings dam the eye) if he is, he may be able to help us out here : he's pretty good at the old education and training routine, especially in the area of strategic management.]

The *going concern basis* is an accounting policy. As such it is an essential dimension in the preparation and the audit of general purpose financial reports. It is also critical to the understanding of such reports. It is stated in the Institute Handbook that 'the going concern and accruals basis of accounting are so generally adopted in the preparation of financial reports that their use can be assumed in the absence of any statement to the contrary' in any general purpose financial report. The *going concern basis* is defined as 'the accounting basis whereby in the preparation of the financial report the reporting entity is viewed as a going concern : that is, the entity is expected to be able to pay its debts as and when they fall due and continue in operation without any intention or necessity to liquidate or otherwise wind up its operations' and which definition is, in practice, usually coupled with a twelve month timeframe which commences from the date of the signing of the general purpose financial reports.

Given the *needs, relevance, reliability, and substance* considerations which have already been discussed above, and putting aside the fact that the general purpose financial reports of a company do not present fairly (outside of the non-business-oriented financial framework with which the accountancy profession insists upon working) the position of a company in a business context (and this is so due not least of all to the pathetic way in which goodwill is treated by the accountancy profession) we should then seek to satisfy the *needs, relevance, reliability, and substance* dimensions of general purpose financial reports through the accounting policies which are used by a business enterprise. Perhaps in that location we can help to justify the four million dollars ($4m) which is spent by Coles Myer on its audit fee and the five million dollars ($5m) that is spent by BHP on their external audit. Perhaps it is in that specific area that we can, after all, locate (or at least endeavour to develop) the provision of high-value-added accountancy services.

The myriad of edicts that were recently issued by the accountancy profession (many of which are effective from the 1st July, 1996, or earlier) provide little comfort for shareholders who are seeking any reassurance with regard to whether their company is a going concern; or, indeed, how going it really is in reality. The discourse entered into above in relation to this matter is based on the new pronouncements. The accountancy profession, by its actions, has bluntly refused to provide anything of relevance in this area for shareholders : being the parties for whom both the preparers and auditors of the general purpose financial reports ultimately work.

The specific edict on the *going concern* uses a somewhat different definition of that concept when compared with the definition that was quoted previously. In the second part of the aforementioned definition the wording states that a business enterprise is a going concern if 'in the absence of evidence to the contrary, the entity is expected to continue in operation without any intention or necessity to liquidate or to curtail significantly the scale of its operations' when considering this situation at, presumably, the date of signing the general purpose financial reports. This is a very different definition to that of the first definition and which former definition was really pitched at a technical level in terms of the ability to pay debts together with some more obscure and, perhaps, residual technical matters. The second definition is broader (and thereby more acceptable) but is simply wrong in the area of its last criterion; being the significant curtailing of the scale of the operations. Whether a company significantly expands or curtails the extent of its operations is, in itself, irrelevant with regard to whether or not it is a going concern. The strategic well-being of a company may be much improved after a curtailment of operations than it was prior to such a curtailment; whilst a major expansion (recall CSR in the 1980s) may jeopardize the company. There is, in fact, no a priori case for the making of such a categoric statement with regard to curtailment and the going concern basis;

or with regard to the strategic well-being of a business enterprise. The edict also states that 'when planning and performing audit procedures, and in evaluating the results thereof, the auditor should consider the appropriateness of the going concern assumption underlying the preparation of the financial report' but then *incorrectly* limits this statement in relation to the time-frame that it imposes on the assessment of the going concern principle.

The present approach to determining whether or not a business enterprise is a going concern is fundamentally deficient in its basic philosophy. And the paradigm is riddled with component-type assessments. These components may also be examined under a different philosophy (although not all such component matters will be included in an examination under a different philosophical approach due to their irrelevance in the determination of the use of the going concern basis) but, when used in terms of the present philosophy, they are not going to provide sufficient comfort for sophisticated shareholders who are knowledgeable in the area of leading-edge strategic management. The accountancy profession, under its expressed (albeit implied) philosophy, relies on evidence which is remote from the substance of the strategic management of a business enterprise. Forward budgets and cash flows may sound intuitively appealing as evidence for or against the use of the going concern basis; as may basic deficiencies in management information systems; as, indeed, may an assessment of the undue influence of a market dominant competitor (and which examples are each taken from the aforementioned going concern edict) but each one of the examples that are contained in the relevant appendix to that particular edict are at least twice, and probably three or more times, removed from the very substance of what we are addressing : being the fundamentals which underpin the use of the going concern basis in general purpose financial reports. Whilst the very edict which supports the aforementioned going concern edict, being the particular edict which deals with the knowledge of the business, although adding further discussion, is likewise also at least twice removed from the crux of the issue.

Until the accountancy profession changes its attitude, and in a significant way, towards the shareholders of a business enterprise, then it is delivering little worth having in terms of any reasonable assurance that it can provide shareholders in relation to their company. Even in the age old area of internal controls (and upon which controls the profession places considerable reliance for the soundness of the general purpose financial reports of major corporates) the relevant professional edict categorically disclaims responsibility, stating that 'an audit of financial reports conducted in accordance with Australian Auditing Standards is not designed to, and therefore does not, provide sufficient appropriate evidence on which to base an opinion on the adequacy of the internal control structure' but that edict itself refers to another edict which would facilitate that finding, if it were applied. The edict also states that 'an auditor engaged to report on the financial report has *no responsibility* to understand and evaluate the internal control structure beyond the level sufficient to plan and develop an effective audit approach *unless* there is a specific statutory, regulatory, or *additional contractual requirement* to the contrary' in existence. It also states that 'in a financial report audit the auditor is only concerned with those internal controls that are relevant to the financial report assertions' and so, again, it is only examining the deck chairs, and not matters appertaining to its voyages.

It is also mentioned, in passing, that although performance audits may contribute to an understanding of the suitability or otherwise of the use of the going concern basis in any particular situation, the philosophy underpinning the edicts that have been issued, and which come into effect at the aforementioned date, are not altogether satisfactory; whilst other matters are also of concern. Performance audits are audits (other than the external statutory audits which have been referred to above) which examine all or part of the activities of a business enterprise in order to assess economy and/or efficiency and/or effectiveness in relation to some or all matters. Not only are the definitions of economy, efficiency, and effectiveness somewhat suspect (talking about, for example, minimizing inputs and maximizing outputs, rather than, for example, the practical optimization of matters in relation to strategies) the edicts also emphasize the assessment of risk, but relative to what, for there is very little indication in the edict with regard to any real knowledge or understanding of the strategic management of a business enterprise; although it does state that 'an attitude of professional scepticism' should be adopted. It may be that the aforementioned 'professional scepticism' should more correctly be directed at the 'professional competence and due care' of those undertaking this type of work; being one of the ethical principles, according to the edicts, that is required of those parties who undertake such activities. The general philosophy which is conveyed by the performance edicts that have been issued by the accountancy profession tend to suffer from the same deficiencies as do the relevant body of other edicts which have been so issued, being that of an impoverished knowledge and understanding of strategic management; and with this impression being gained, not least of all, when the edicts address, or verge on addressing, that particular dimension. This view is again exemplified, albeit to a lesser extent, in the edict which relates to prospective financial information, and which edict comes into effect, at the latest, in January, 1997. In addition to concerns with regard to the meaning of both 'best-estimate' and 'hypothetical' assumptions (the specific meanings of which, amongst other things, need to be cleaned up, including the potential confusion in relation to projections and forecasts, and which latter terms, in the context in which they are being used, should be dropped) the philosophical underpinnings of the edict itself should also be examined.

It has already been shown, in reality, that when the profession visited the cutting-edge of its own incompetence it was found to be wanting. Companies went bust and the profession wouldn't have known that such an event was, in reality, under way. The flagrant disowning, by the profession, of its responsibility to embrace business realities, is evident. Boundaries and buffers are, it would seem, far more important to the profession than is the embracing of the *needs, relevance, reliability, and substance* of matters that are important to shareholders when their directors present their externally audited general purpose financial reports.

The bottom line is that whatever the many and the varied edicts of the accountancy profession address (and they actually address many excellent matters) the expression of that most fundamental of opinions, being the opinion in relation to the use of the going concern principle in the preparation and audit of general purpose financial reports, is itself fundamentally flawed. The expression of a favourable opinion with regard to the use of the going concern basis is, without doubt, implied in unqualified audit reports. It may also be implied in certain qualified reports. The professional work which is recommended and which is applied, in practice, in relation thereto is absolutely deficient. A corporate enterprise may be heading for disaster, being a process which may take one, two, three, or more years to crystallize, yet the accountancy profession would still unashamedly report to shareholders that the particular company is a going concern. There would, in terms of the applied practices of the profession, be no indication given to shareholders with regard to the existence of this situation due to the fact that the profession does not, at the present time, examine and report upon the strategic management of a business enterprise and it, therefore, does not report on the state of the corporate governance of a company; whilst, in any case, its perspective is limited to a twelve month timeframe. By the time 'the profession' manages to convince itself that a corporate enterprise is dysfunctional, or has fundamental problems, its actual demise may well be confronting shareholders. As a profession, the recommended practices in the area of the going concern are both immoral and unethical, for we are willing to prepare accounts and provide an unqualified audit opinion in relation to a company which is alive, but dying, but provide little or no indication of that condition to its shareholders.

In the context of corporate governance, strategic management, and the accountancy profession, the practices of our profession must change. We must revisit our moral responsibilities towards our society, we must re-examine our ethical relationships with all shareholders, and in total, whilst it is imperative that we embrace quantum leaps and order of magnitude changes in the intellectual knowledge and capabilities of the members of our profession; and not least of all in the area of strategic management.

The accountancy profession must now embrace the realities of our times. We have now entered, as was indicated earlier, the era of corporate morbidity. The era when many business enterprises will succeed gloriously and others will suffer corporate debilitation. The glorious failures of the past decade, that litany of disasters, are, for now, behind us; although no doubt other spasmodic, albeit constrained but disastrous outbreaks, will occur. We have, in fact, well and truly entered the era of debilitation by stealth.

Westpac, once our biggest bank, was perhaps a marginal case in the heralding-in of this era, for Westpac was not, in reality, the *walking wounded* or a *corporate cripple* for it was more akin to a member of the *living dead* of the business world; being a company which was rescued due to the desires of a government, and the actions of the establishment, for neither dare risk the potential consequences of allowing the failure of a major bank. Westpac did not lose one thousand six hundred million dollars ($1,600m) in only one year; or even in half a year. That was a fiction of business politics and the accountancy profession. But that particular event encapsulated many of the fundamental problems in the way in which profits are determined in general purpose financial reports for purposes of their disclosure to shareholders, to stakeholders, and to society in general. And nor did the State Bank of South Australia and its subsidiary, Beneficial Finance, lose the three thousand million dollars ($3,000m) or more which, in aggregate, they reported in such a relatively short period of time. Financial loses, in the case of Westpac, were blindly stored up behind what amounted to no less than a 'dam wall' of imprudence, and when the 'dam wall' could not hold back the magnitude of those losses any longer (despite having, no doubt, opened the sluice-gates in the previous reporting periods, and to varying degrees, to release the unbearable pressure) they finally had to admit, and formally as late as in the 1992 accounts, that they had indeed lost, what was claimed to be, one point six billion dollars ($1.6b) in only *one* year.

Rubbish . . . . Absolute Rubbish !!!!

No, Westpac never lost that, or a similar amount, in one year. And nor did the State Bank of South Australia lose its money in one year. And nor did Beneficial Finance rock up its reported losses in only a year or so. The 'dam wall' phenomena, as with many of the catastrophic collapses which emanated from the decade of greed, had been well and truly with us, and at major corporate level, for an extended period of time. And those professionals who helped to facilitated the fiascos, the debacles, and the disasters of those times (whether overtly or covertly, actively or passively, or by default; and maybe in ignorance) had failed to examine the strategic value of those companies. They had allowed themselves to become actors in the play. They had failed their professions.

But perhaps these companies were forerunners to this new era, for despite their very real losses (being very real indeed) they 'died' to 'live' again; and mainly because they were financial institutions.

Perhaps the real harbinger of this period, this era of morbidity, is Brambles Industries, for that company experienced debilitation, and in its own right. Its loss was not part of the decade of greed. That time of lemming-like behaviour. Its strategic debilitation was actually caused by its own inept strategic management. Having acquired Environmental Systems Company Inc. in 1992, it wrote off three hundred and thirty-seven million dollars ($337m) in 1994 due to, according to Brambles Industries, structural change in the hazardous waste market. [It sounds more as though it was their strategic management that was hazardous and wasteful.] Let's be generous and say this loss represented, on average, about two year's consolidated net profits. The company won't go bust from that write off; at least not at the moment. It's capitalized at about three billion dollars ($3.0b) or thereabouts. But how long does it take to recover from such a waste of capital from such a strategic error, or series thereof? Brambles may well make lots of profits over the forthcoming years. That's not the point. There was no need for Brambles to waste its resources. Brambles, to identify the totality of its morbidity, could measure this debilitation, including its nefarious dimensions. The findings would be most interesting.

The 'morbidity factor' puts a company in the wounded, the crippled, or the dead category. It affects the rate at which a company can develop when compared with the rate at which it could otherwise have developed. It may well take Brambles, to all intents and purposes, five or even ten years to recover from this debilitation. It may never recover. [CSR was debilitated by self-inflicted wounds for much of the '80s.] The fundamental problem is impoverished strategic management. And you can be sure that Brambles is by no means alone on that particular dimension. Just think of TNT, Ansett, ANI, Goodman Fielder, Burns Philp, Pacific Dunlop, Ampolex (now part of Mobil) and Coles Myer. Each of these companies has its own degree of woundedness, crippleness, or deadness. [Forget the stock exchange as a measure (share prices go up, down, or stay neutral) for the share price doesn't tell you much about the strategic management of a company : investors were, in recent times, still innocently buying shares in high-profile companies shortly before they were to feature in some of the most notorious corporate disasters in history.] Some companies have been in trouble for years. Other companies have more recently achieved that status. Whilst yet other companies have been in and out of trouble time and again. Woolworths was once in trouble. Big trouble. But, by means of strategic wizardry, it managed to extract itself from that unfortunate state of affairs. Things, as Woolworths has shown, can be changed. Accordingly, for TNT, Ansett, ANI, Goodman Fielder, Burns Philp, Pacific Dunlop, and Coles Myer, there is hope. Whether changes are fundamental or just superficial (or somewhere in between) and whether they are enduring in nature is, however, a matter for deeper consideration.

Given the preceding discourse then, one may well ask, why isn't the accountancy profession reporting this debilitation or, indeed, absence of debilitation, to shareholders, stakeholders, and society in general? The accountancy profession reports on live situations. But it reports on those live situations as though those companies are static, or inert, and not as though their situations are forever changing. So why doesn't the profession embrace reality and acknowledge the dynamic nature of what it is addressing and on which it is reporting? Why doesn't it prepare general purpose financial reports that are based on relevant fundamentals?

Strategy is about doing things. It's about action. And it's about delivering reality. So let's be quite clear : strategy is *not* strategic planning and strategic planning is *not* strategic management. The practical problem in business, however, is that success tends to create a sense of invincibility and which condition itself provides a sense of ease, comfort, or cosiness. So in good times globalizing companies, domestic corporates, and virtually all others, typically don't pay much attention to the strategic management of their strategies; whilst in bad times they think that they can't afford to address strategic management. CSR didn't seem to think that they needed help in the early 1980s. I know. I visited them. And that was before it all went wrong. I also visited them a four years or so ago. And they still didn't need help. But between those visits CSR had managed to waste countless millions of shareholder dollars. Its morbidity was high. And it was debilitated. If only we could turn back the clock. Or, perhaps even better, if only we could time travel forward from now . . . . and then come back . . . . I'm sure companies would do things much differently. The contribution which could be secured by companies applying appropriate strategic management, based on the use of appropriate strategic management infrastructures, would be seen to be so valuable. I'm sure FAI would have done a few things differently over the past decade or more. And, of course, ANI may not be in the pickle it is in today had it smartened up its strategic management. I visited both FAI and ANI three or four years ago. You get plenty of talk at FAI. They're very receptive. But ANI were always too busy being too busy. So they were bound to catch a cold. That's the trouble with invincibility . . . . It invariably turns into vincibility !!!

The thing with business is that everything keeps changing and so you've got to keep on top of your strategies all the time. And that is what strategic management is about. It's all about managing strategy itself. And not least of all in turbulent environments.

Business, believe it or not, is not about money. It's about reality. Money is the common denominator. It's also not about profits. For profits are a derivative. An output. A measurement. At least, that is, when they are compared with something. BHP, according to its 1995 accounts, had an operating revenue of eighteen point five billion dollars ($18.5b) and an after tax consolidated net profit of one point two billion dollars ($1.2b) or so. The BHP shareholders received a dividend of less than seven hundred million dollars ($700m) in total. Eighteen and a half billion dollars of activity to make a one point two billion dollar profit and out of which a dividend payment of less than seven hundred million dollars was paid to shareholders. So what's it all about? Well business is about doing things, real things, and with real things, and this is so whether those real things are essentially tangible or intangible in nature. Companies are creatures of our society. Shareholders get their cut. Stakeholders get their cut; and that is normally a lot more than the cut which goes to shareholders. And society gets its cut. And these creatures of our society, and in aggregate, have an on-going existence. Business enterprises are, and without doubt, essential to our standard of living, our quality of life, and the way in which we live. They are essential to our whole existence. So why don't we tell shareholders, stakeholders, and society itself about the strategic well-being of these so essential corporates? The accountancy profession, of course, is at fault. I don't mean that it's the sole culprit. It's just a culprit in a big way. The profession hasn't so much got it wrong. It's just that it hasn't got it right. It's more to do with the fact that the way they look at things is not quite correct. It's a bit like this book. You may look at it as a mass of characters; as a collection of words; as sentences; as paragraphs; as pages; and as chapters. You may even stand back from it all, observe it, and correctly state that this is a book. That view is not wrong. It's just that it's not right. This book has little to do with words, sentences, paragraphs, and chapters, although they are indeed integral to its existence. This book, and contrary to the previous perspective, has everything to do with the thoughts, the ideas, the visions, the views, the feelings, the emotions, the values, and a whole host of other things which are encapsulated herein. Those dimensions will never be captured by the words or the sentences which are included in this book but, rather, they will be conveyed by a consciousness, an awakening, and an awareness. This book has endeavoured to explore a feeling or, rather, a whole set of feelings with regard to strategy and strategic management, and with regard to corporate governance, and the accountancy profession. It has also endeavoured to communicate views and opinions about moral values, ethical standards, and intellectual contribution in the world of business. It may well have caused apprehension or concern, raised sensitivity or sensibility, or perhaps even stimulated fervour and passion. There is a whole unspecified infrastructure which is critical to understanding this book, a whole emotional experience, encapsulated not least of all in philosophies, culture, mindscapes, assumptions, presumptions, inferences, dynamics, and many more spoken and unspoken, but imperatively critical, transitory, transitional, and transformational dimensions; and with each such dimension, both individually and in aggregate, being set in the context of, amongst other things, the reader's own characteristics, attributes, personality, and emotions. So to look at this book as just words and as sentences, or as an aggregation thereof, although it is not wrong, it is for sure not right. And that is what the accountancy profession does when it attempts to know and understand Corporate Australia. It focuses not so much on the wrong things as, perhaps, not quite on the right things. And being not quite right, in the world of business, is light years away from being fit for our times !!!!!

A new philosophy must be embraced in relation to reporting to the shareholders of a company in relation to the appropriateness or the inappropriateness of the corporate governance of their company. In a report entitled 'Corporate Collapses' which was issued by the Institute of Chartered Accountants in Australia, and which report was sub-titled 'Lessons for the Future' and which was published in March, 1994, various important matters were revealed. The report stated that 'more training of current and future chief executive officers, better planning, a stronger focus on determining strategic direction, and attention to quality and timely management information are major factors which can help to avoid corporate failure' and not least of all, that is, amongst major corporates. The report also stated that overall 'a greater investment needs to be made in readily available management skills and modern business tools for companies of virtually any size to minimize the potential for poor performance and corporate failure' or, in my words, there is a fundamental need for a major investment in advanced management technologies; and this is so whether those technologies are hard, soft, or pliable. The report, in addition, also stated that many of the root causes of corporate collapses 'are also relevant to the poor performance of many of Australia's companies which did not fail completely' and which companies did not, therefore, form part of the base of data that was utilized for the aforementioned report. In essence, in order to achieve a much higher level of performance and an appropriate degree of success in the world of business, on a national and on a global scale, there needs to be both a significant and a sustained investment in the strategic management practices and strategic management infrastructure of Corporate Australia.

For shareholders, stakeholders, and society in general to stop paying, in their blood, for the lack of competence or, indeed, for the incompetence (as well as the negligence) of others, boards of directors, those who prepare accounts, and those who audit those accounts must change, and fundamentally, the way in which they execute their respective responsibilities; and these changes must show through in what they deliver.

In the 'Effective Corporate Governance' report which was referred to previously it is stated, with regard to taking due care in relation to the going concern basis, that 'where there is no evidence of significant problems, it should be relatively straight forward to demonstrate that there is *reasonable assurance* that the enterprise has adequate resources to continue in operational existence for the foreseeable future (with the main focus on a one year rolling period) but the renewed emphasis on this subject by directors and auditors is likely to bring greater rigour to the consideration of this issue' by various parties. Although there is still this mindset of a one year view, as though this is a magic number, the general gist of the quoted statement is in the correct direction.

What was even more pleasing, however, was the clear statement in the annual report of the Institute of Chartered Accountants in England and Wales, issued in March, 1996, that the Institute itself is 'championing good corporate governance' in the UK. The original Cadbury Committee report, which was entitled 'Report of the Committee on the Financial Aspects of Corporate Governance' and which report was issued in 1992, underpinned many of the corporate governance initiatives which were actioned in the UK. The recent birth of *Cadbury's Child* being the 'Hampel Committee on Corporate Governance' has resulted in that committee being sponsored by, amongst others, the Institute. This has positioned the Institute to be able to play an 'active role in defining and improving corporate governance' in the UK and, of course, elsewhere. The annual report of that body goes on to state that 'by such involvement we have secured a central role for members in the corporate governance debate . . . . we will make a substantial contribution to the deliberations by drawing on the unique expertise of our members' in that field. Let us hope that both the Institute of Chartered Accountants and the Hampel Committee are prepared to take an eclectic approach to corporate governance, whether based on submissions or, indeed, other contributions, and that a whole range of paradigms and philosophies will be genuinely considered, and in dialectic mode. Let us also hope that, in this re-visit, we are not restricted by the boundaries of previous thought, and its paucity of content, for those boundaries and that content (despite having possibly being a necessary pre-requisite for further progress) were well and truly remote from the cutting-edge of reality.

It is understood that the creation, the design, the development, the implementation, and the utilization of leading-edge initiatives in corporate governance (and which initiatives involve quantum leaps and order of magnitude changes) will emerge not so much as the result of a sprint, but more from a marathon effort. And nor should any of the prevailing pressures be allowed to engender an impression of a race towards some final outcome, for there will be no final outcome; whilst the total process (despite the giant leaps that will result from my own inputs to individual companies) will be one of osmosis. Some benefits will emerge immediately, others will emerge over the next five years, whilst yet others will emerge during the ensuing decade and beyond. It is evident that in order for shareholders, for stakeholders, and for society itself to benefit from this new era in corporate management we must construct solid foundations, build sound infrastructure, and develop on-line and real-time management practices which will unequivocally propel boards of directors into far more relevant modes in which to execute, what will eventually be seen as, responsible corporate governance. The practice of corporate governance, without doubt, is irrevocably set to change beyond belief !!!!!

In this age of infotronics (this term is a composite of the words information and electronics) the accountancy profession has been left behind. It has failed to embrace its role as a contemporary, business-focused, knowledge-based, industry that is located in the information dimension of the infotronics era. One of our most vital assets, that of intellectual capital, is strategically debased; and with much of that capital being located in low-value-added areas. As a major profession we should be at the leading-edge of intellectual development whilst, in our own field, we should be developing that leading edge. And it should be from that edge that we should be propelling ourselves forward and onto greater achievements. It would seem, in metaphoric terms, that we know a great deal with regard to 'steam-driven-engines' but know little concerning the state-of-the-art in 'laser-guided-missiles' or, being more specific, we are significantly deficient in the emerging area of leading-edge, cutting-edge, corporate governance, and which discipline basically equates with that of strategic management, and which latter discipline provides the very foundations upon which the accountancy profession is based.

To address the aforementioned multi-dimensional fundamental deficiency, and in order to stake its own claim to its own future, the accountancy profession must gladly welcome (and must not spurn) its intellect-driven visionaries; being those members who have already anticipated a transformational change in the focus of accountancy and so, accordingly, seek-out, and actively develop, new and appropriate management practices. The contemporary demands of corporate governance (and not least of all those particular demands which will, both now and in the near future, emanate from the compelling need to appropriately manage the ever increasing myriad of globalizing business enterprises) and which demands fall within the recently reactivated domain of our professional competence (being the assessment of the strategic well-being of corporate enterprises) must be eagerly embraced by the accountancy profession. The profession must unhesitatingly come to terms with the fundamental knowledge which is required for the strategic management of corporate enterprises (it is no use avoiding this challenge by making a dash for freedom, so as to say, or being apprehensive in relation thereto) for the validity of everything else that is done in accountancy depends thereon. The accountancy profession must assess, in the preparation and the audit of general purpose financial reports, the strategic well-being of a business enterprise. This is unequivocal; for a financial based, twelve month, prospective assessment is both superficial and irrelevant. It is absolutely misleading. It addresses transactional superficiality rather than fundamental substance. Twelve month assessments are, in practice, overwhelmingly based on a tactical demonstration by a company that it can continue to exist for the duration of, what is, an irrelevant timeframe. Such evaluations fail miserably to identify fundamental strategic debilitation whilst, at one and the same time, they provide little or no real evidence of strategic durability. It is most important and, indeed critical that the accountancy profession delivers high-value-added services to general management, to boards of directors, and to shareholders. And it must achieve this level of service with the use of, amongst other things, state-of-the-art advances in the areas of information technology and telecommunications. It is not necessary for the purposes of this particular book to delve into why this is desirable for major corporates (especially globalizing corporate enterprises) for it is only important to know that these advances must play an integral part in the evaluation and determination of the use of the going concern basis by companies, the assessment of the strategic well-being of corporate enterprises and, indeed, in the actual strategic management of those business enterprise. Only when the accountancy profession has made several quantum leaps and various order of magnitude changes in relation to its own abilities with regard to the strategic management of corporate enterprises will we again reside at the leading-edge in the world of business.

Turning now to what should be done. Turning to the hope. Three factors were identified earlier which contributed to the decline of the accountancy profession. These were, seeing accountancy in a narrow perspective and as a financial-based discipline; having a membership, but in particular a leadership, with an impoverished business education; and embracing management consultancy, in the way in which it has developed, as the future of the profession.

It was indicated previously that the large accountancy firms, these multi-profession business enterprises are, in effect, in control of the accountancy profession and that it is they who are setting the fundamental agenda for the future of that profession; for it should be remembered that for power and influence to be exercised, the powerful partners (and such persons need not even officially be ranked amongst the partners of those firms) do not have to hold office themselves. They need only let it be known, to those who hold high official positions in the profession, which way crucial issues are to be addressed. And this may be done both cognitively and incognitively and passively and actively. There is, however, no conspiracy, for these professional businesses most definitely look after their own interests. They are very successful. And they stridently pursue the adoption or enactment of matters which promote their own strategies. It was also mentioned that control of the accountancy profession by the large successful multi-profession service businesses (and whose partners, in total, only represent around one percent or so of the membership of the accountancy profession) may not, in fact, be in the best interests of the accountancy profession, for the strategies of these massive professional service businesses, and not least of all those which have a tendency to become worldwide juggernauts, may not actually coincide with the best interests of the profession. This is so, and not least of all, because accountancy (although it is an important part of those firms) is only one of the professional businesses that are conducted by those firms and, further, that accountancy (and whether this is so absolutely or relatively) will eventually become a less significant part of those professional service businesses. The public interest may not, therefore, be served by the accountancy profession (and possibly by its own default) allowing those persons who hold appropriate credentials, but who have very different agendas, to control the accountancy profession; and this is so not least of all where that control is actually exercised (whether now or in the future) by parties who have little or nothing to do with that profession, but which parties may very well control the large professional service businesses.

At the moment the massive increase, worldwide, in management consultancy has focused attention on the probability of the very large accountancy practices becoming management consultancy businesses and therefore, in essence, not being accountancy firms per se. To be more specific with regard to what these professional service business are, in reality, it would be necessary to identify the particular type of management consultancy that is currently being delivered and the nature of that which will be delivered in the future. Even now, and at this stage, it may be relevant to ask whether the particular brand of 'management consultancy' that is practiced actually emanates from accountancy, management, law, engineering, information-technology, telecommunications, or in fact from some other specialization; or essentially from some combination thereof. It should also be asked, in dynamic mode, how this focus will evolve; for it is almost for sure, and at least in relative terms, that accountancy itself will decline in its inherent importance to these juggernauts. Indeed, the strategies which are pursued by the accountancy profession, due to the control of that profession by these multi-profession service businesses, will eventually be subsumed (if this is not already occurring) into the overall strategies of those, then mammoth, worldwide business enterprises. By that time the accountancy profession, and much like the massive transnational corporations of the world, will no longer necessarily act in the best interests of our society, for that profession will be a mere tool of the juggernauts; and which multi-profession service businesses themselves eat off the multinational and transnational corporations.

Yes, as was stated earlier, I do think that we need to seriously, and urgently, re-think the future of the accountancy profession, for I do not believe, and from observation, that the leadership of our profession have given it much independent thought at all; given, of course, that they even care. And yes, we do need a radical change in the profession of accountancy but we do not need a radical change in the accountancy profession. As was also stated previously, if the large professional practices wish to pursue their particular interests, then that is their choice. But it should not be at the expense of the accountancy profession. And nor should it be at the expense of our society. For that is what is happening. The two-pronged debilitation of the accountancy profession (occasioned by the de-professionalization of the profession and the failure of the leadership to enhance the substance of our professionalism in any material way) has, during the past fifteen years or more, been very effective. Change, however, is of the essence. And, as stated, the profession needs to be re-invented. But such re-invention should not be for what the profession is not but, rather, it should be for what the profession ought to be. The accountancy profession is very much a business-based profession and we are a profession which should address business. So let us do just that . . . . and re-create our own future !!!!

High on the agenda of the federal government is that of micro-economic reform. The waterfront may well be a problem. And so may industrial relations. And also the tussle over the sale of Telstra. But what about the so badly needed reform of business itself. The way it looks at things. The way it manages. The way it reports. Karpin may well have addressed certain matters. As did the competition policy as set down by Hilmer. But what of that colossal area which is concerned with how companies manage strategically and which area itself affects every single company, every single day, of every single week, of every single month, and of every single year; and year after year after year. What about the fundamental structural changes which cry out for improvement in the area of strategic management.

Times have changed and business has shifted the emphasis of its attention from that of operational matters, through management information concerns, and onto corporate governance. The focus of attention, although of course always addressing each of these matters, has changed. The strategic management of a company is critical to the on-going performance and success of a company. And it is in this realm that the accountancy profession itself has a potentially significant strategic advantage. The profession has of right (and, indeed, is bound by existing accountancy and auditing standards) to ascertain, on the balance of probabilities, whether or not a business enterprise is a going concern for the purpose of preparing and auditing general purpose financial reports. It is a non-negotiable activity. Not to carry out this responsibility in an appropriate way is, almost for sure, negligent. To be able to form a meaningful opinion in relation to this particular responsibility (putting aside the deceptive artificiality which has been imposed by the accountancy profession itself by means of its own very inadequate edicts) requires a relevant examination of the strategic management of a business enterprise and, thereby, the corporate governance of a company. Not to execute this function, and with a high level of professional competence, whether this particular omission occurs intentionally or otherwise, is to recklessly deceive shareholders, directors, stakeholders, and society in general; and this deception is so whether or not actual damage is inflicted. Even at the present time the financial position, as presented by boards of directors to shareholders, and which position is based on the professional competence of those who prepare accounts and those who audit those accounts, demands this reasonable assurance; otherwise the going concern basis should not be used as a basic accounting policy of a company.

For the accountancy profession to push out their own boundaries of disclosure in this area beyond their present somewhat artificial and irrelevant position (and then disclose what the accountancy profession should already know with regard to a company when it evaluates the basis on which it determines the appropriateness of the use of the going concern basis) is not asking a great deal. This is particularly so when it is borne in mind that the specific requirement of the accountancy profession itself is to provide relevant information to the shareholders of a corporate enterprise.

The profession, by pushing out its own boundaries to what would be a more relevant location, could disclose (and in the opinion of those who prepare accounts and those who audit those accounts) the state of the strategic well-being of a company. It has already been indicated that expertise in this particular field is available to the large professional service businesses who audit the vast majority of listed companies (if they are themselves deficient in that area of professional expertise) as well as to the major listed corporate enterprises; and this is so even if that knowledge, understanding, and insight happens to reside in small, but highly specialized, professional practices. The opinion which would be provided in relation to the going concern basis would not, however, be based on the definition which is effective at the present time (and which definition is, no doubt unintentionally, a deceptive construct for, when it was tested at the cutting-edge of its own reality, that definition resulted in much blood being spilt and on many carpets) nor would it be based on the definition which will be introduced shortly but, rather, the definition would embrace, and with greater relevance, the strategic management of a corporate enterprise. The profession may then begin to be more meaningful to shareholders, to stakeholders, and to society itself.

The goal, however, would be to provide an extended assurance with regard to the strategic management of a corporate enterprise, and this would arise by means of a disclosure, in general purpose financial reports, concerning the degree, level, or extent of that assurance. At that point the accountancy profession would deliver to shareholders, in total, fundamental high-value-added services; being professional opinions which would allow the owners of a corporate enterprise to take decisions which they themselves may considered to be appropriate in the light of the professional opinion expressed in relation to their company; and for which professional opinions shareholders expend large sums of money.

Would it not be of great value to the shareholders of TNT, Ansett, ANI, Goodman Fielder, Burns Philp, Pacific Dunlop, and Coles Myer, as well as to prospective shareholders (and this apart from stakeholders, such as financiers, and society in general) to be provided with *reasonable assurance* that the strategic management of their company is appropriate; or inappropriate. After all, the strategic management of those companies is fundamental to their existence, their performance, and their success. Whilst it is also fundamental to the value of the shareholdings of shareholders.

As a consequence of the relatively impoverished state-of-the-art in the area of strategic management in major corporate enterprises, it is evident that when deficiencies are drawn to the attention of a board of directors, then that act in itself would require that the appropriateness of the strategic management of the business enterprise be improved; for where fundamental deficiencies in the strategic management of a company are brought to the attention of a company, and those responsible for such management (in this case the board of directors) do not address such deficiencies, then they themselves would be negligent. Should loss subsequently occur as a result of the impoverished strategic management of the corporate enterprise, those directors may well become personally liable for the whole, or part, of that loss. Where the auditors, and this is the case even today, do not examine these matters (and it is almost for sure that in many cases they do not) and deficiencies in that area exist, and the auditor does not draw the attention of the board of directors to such matters, then they too may well be liable for the whole, or some part, of any loss which is occasioned by such impoverishment; for auditors cannot hide behind their impoverished knowledge, understanding, or insight of strategic management, thereby pretending that strategic management is quarantined from their assessment of the going concern basis.

This work in relation to the strategic management of a corporate enterprise is of extremely high value to companies. The benefits which can flow from improved strategic management and which can be secured by shareholders, in total, and from a fundamental structural improvement in the strategic management of their company, can be significant. The aggregate net benefits which could flow to Corporate Australia would be enormous. Not only would the 'morbidity factor' of companies, on a national basis, be reduced over time, but the actual 'success factor' would improve. To what extent a major redistribution of scarce resources would occur would depend on various considerations but there would, almost inevitably, be some degree of resource redistribution in the economy. Even if there were to be little or no real redistribution of resources amongst companies, which is unlikely, there would still be an improvement in both the effective use and utilization of resources. The benefits which would be derived by shareholders in total, stakeholders in aggregate, and society in general, and which benefits would be based on transparent knowledge (rather than on simple and deceptive opaque knowledge) with regard to the appropriate strategic management of corporate enterprises, would be tremendous. What is also of importance is that those benefits could be secured simply by the accountancy profession reporting their opinion, in the already existent general purpose financial reports, in relation to the strategic management of corporate enterprises and, as was stated above, with regard to the appropriateness or, indeed, the inappropriateness of the strategic management of a business enterprise; the degree, level, or extent of that appropriateness or inappropriateness; and, as relevant, the applicable prospective duration of the aforementioned situation.

The impact of this shift in reporting emphasis (being the reporting of the appropriateness, or otherwise, of the strategic management of corporate enterprises) on the way in which institutional investors, merchant bankers, investment bankers, stockbrokers, corporate advisory firms, and even 'mum and dad' shareholders see companies, will be significant. It will cause a re-evaluation and a redistribution of previous opinions with regard to the good, the bad, and the ugly companies which comprise Corporate Australia. What will be more easily identified is where the high-added-value and the low-added-value, on the one part, and, on the other part, the low-subtracted-value and the high-subtracted-value resides. Whilst companies themselves will focus on the improvement of their strategic management. The institutional investors, merchant bankers, investment bankers, stockbrokers, and corporate advisory firms may even change the way in which they evaluate corporate enterprises; and thereby be better off.

Whatever reality is within the profession, and whatever the views may be which are held by those who control the profession, the commitment to do the right thing, to be moral and ethical, must predominate. We must tell shareholder, stakeholders, and society itself about the strategic well-being of corporate enterprises. Expediency has been too prevalent, and for too long, and we have ended up with a bankrupt profession; and one which is unfit for our times. Fundamental change is now required by society.

For those accountants who are misty-eyed, and wish to cling to the past, the thought of fundamental change to the foundations of reporting may be traumatic. But for those in our profession who wish to embrace the future, and in the context of business itself, for those who are prepared to cross the rubicon of risk, then they, by now, may well be gripped with excitement; for they will recognize that the profession has a once in a lifetime opportunity to establish itself once again as a pre-eminent profession and, on this occasion, in a fundamental area of business activity.

In Australia the fee income which would be earned for providing these high-value-added accountancy-derived services, whether as auditors (for the going concern basis provides the underpinnings for the overwhelming majority of general purpose financial reports) or as business management advisors (being, say, the accountancy profession's version of management consultants) and in the area of strategic management, could be of the order of one hundred million dollars each year; whilst in the UK that figure could approach five hundred million dollars in total. In both cases these figures exclude the dollar amount of information technology and telecommunications inputs. These aggregate fees would be a small investment by corporate enterprises when compared with the potential for significant returns which would be brought about as a result of the quantum leaps and the order of magnitude changes in the corporate governance of corporate enterprises. It will be recalled that Brambles Industries lost almost four hundred million dollars itself; and in a brief period of time. The losses which, in practice, are undisclosed (whether they are hidden, accumulated, or offset against profits) are significant. The costs of strategic debilitation, each year, over a decade, and beyond that timeframe, are colossal for Corporate Australia. The investment in strategic management tools, techniques, practices, procedures, models, guidelines, frameworks, methodologies, and systems (being the essentials of a strategic management infrastructure) could only be productive. Their use, and their utilization, may well ensure not only non-negligent corporate governance, but also improved business performance and, thereby, enhanced corporate success. These benefits should, indeed, be secured for Australia.

Well .... enough of this frivolity .... I must away .... I've got things to do. Yes, he's back from Ok Tedi .... so 'Blind Freddy' and I are going star-gazing for a while. I find it so invigorating. But before I go may I say that this book has discussed corporate governance, strategic management, and certain moral, ethical, and intellectual dimensions which impact the accountancy profession. The future contribution of the accountancy profession to society is very much in the public interest. Once you have read this book, you should not praise it because it says what you wish to hear. And nor should you condemn it because it offends your particular point of view. You should first look at its substance; then examine its scope; and perhaps finally embrace its messages. For any fool can see what is wrong with it .... but it takes a wise person to see what is right. And then I would ask that you be just, fair, and equitable in the formation of your opinion.

Postscript

In a letter published in the April, 1996, issue of the international version of the English Institute's magazine 'Accountancy' it was stated that one delegate voiced her concern that the proposed merger (of various UK accountancy bodies) was opposed by the grassroots members. She stated that the Council of the Institute was not in touch with the views of its members. It is also claimed in the letter that the President of the English Institute responded by stating that those members who believed that the Council were not in touch with the views of its members were both naive and misguided. The aforementioned letter, which was not written by the lady cited above, went on to say that 'it is now apparent that the views of the naive and misguided are the majority views' for the Council's merger plans were subsequently scrapped. The Institute apparently believed that two-thirds of members were in favour of the merger but, when the pilot poll was counted, some two-thirds of the twenty-four thousand (24,000) or so grassroots members who responded didn't want to merge. The trouble, of course, was that the Institute had been talking to itself. They had talked to active members. To the, so as to say, enlarged in-crowd. They had made their judgements based on an unrepresentative body of members. The Institute wasn't listening to the grassroots, so when the merger proposal was presented, they quietly cast their vote : in the negative. No one, it may be noted, seemed more surprised at the outcome of the poll than the President himself. He stated that 'the Council had been encouraged by the strong level of support from many senior members of the profession' and therein, of course, lies the problem. He had spoken with many of the *senior members* of the profession; that incestuous group who are clueless when it comes to what ordinary members think about issues or, indeed, what their aspirations and visions are for our profession. Why, one may ask, is this so? Well simply because its all a waste of time, spending the time, to tell them what you think. They, the all powerful, are not going to do anything anyway. They've made up their minds . . . . so don't confuse them with the facts . . . . the opinions . . . . the views . . . . the aspirations . . . . and the visions of the one hundred thousand or so ordinary members.

So what can we, here in Australia, learn from this episode? Well the profession in Australia is probably controlled by one hundred or, at the very most, two hundred members. I don't mean there's only that many members on committees or what have you but, rather, that when it comes down to the critical things, the power and the influence of at least some sub-set of that one hundred or so members is very much present. You will recall that I did try to stand for election (and that I got nobbled from a great height for my willingness to participate) and in any case, it should be noted, who in the hierarchy listened to my point of view, as an ordinary member, when I voiced my views on what I believed to be the grossly immoral and unethical behaviour of our profession in relation to the capping of negligence awards (you will recall that I actually support proportional liability) but which views were contrary to the views of the power coalition .... so all I got was a letter from the President (which I treasure even to this day) to tell me to get my thinking straight .... and when it came to actually making an intellectual contribution to the fundamental substance of what our profession does (based upon the then latest version of my leading-edge reference work on strategic management and strategic management systems and which book eventually took four years to write) it was all too much for the cocoon brigade, so they shut up shop .... and I've had to spend another six months writing this particular book in order to draw attention to a few of the more fundamental problems, opportunities, and challenges which are faced by the accountancy profession.

It would seem, as evidenced by recent utterances, that at least the President of the Institute of Chartered Accountants in England and Wales has travelled the road to Damascus and, indeed, has himself seen the light, for he is now saying that 'we need to continue to ensure that the Council is tuned in to members views, is listening to what members are saying (and) more than that, we need some way of finding out what the silent majority really think' and want from the Institute. What was really encouraging, however, was what the President had to say with regard to education and training, and the future of the profession. To quote him 'the first area in which we shall be seeking members views is the crucial one of education and training .... I hope you will take the opportunity to get involved' so personally I'm hoping that the invitation extends to overseas members. He also stated (bearing in mind what was mentioned in relation to the failed merger attempt that was noted above) that it is essential to look at 'how to involve more members in formal consultation exercises, how to assess responses to consultation exercises (and) how to reach the silent majority' of members. 'I would welcome your views' he stated and then suggested that, in fact, members should 'contact your Council members . . . . telephone the Institute . . . . or write to me' personally in order to 'make your voice heard as we address the future of the Institute for the next decade' and beyond. Well, given that invitation, I thought that I'd send the President of the English Institute a copy of my book. It sounds as though the profession over there could be getting very serious about its future. And strategic management, being part of our own natural domain, could very well be part of that future. And if by chance, and at the present time, it's not part of that perceived future, then it should be placed on the agenda, and very soon indeed.

I hope that the Institute of Chartered Accountants in Australia and the Australian Society of Certified Practising Accountants also recognize and acknowledge the fundamental problems, opportunities, and challenges which are faced by our profession; some of which have been mentioned herein. I know that we have come a long way as a profession. But I also know that we still have a long way to go for, in relative terms, we need to re-establish ourselves as leaders in the world of business. I do hope, and given the content of this book, that the leadership of the profession in Australia have themselves travelled the road to Damascus and that, in a blinding flash, they too have also been converted to reality; for we really do have to get serious about strategic management. It's very much part of our future. So just in case they've got real about rescuing the future, by embracing reality, I've decided to send both the President of the Institute and the President of the Society a copy of my book.

With the emergence of corporate governance as a worldwide issue, and the fact that strategic management is an overwhelming and inalienable part thereof, and given the very real need for the accountancy profession to fundamentally realign itself with the world of business, perhaps it's the right time to get things moving; and in a big way. Actually, and upon its launch, I think I'll send copies of my book to various parties in six countries (being not only Australia, but also New Zealand, South Africa, Canada, the USA, and the UK) so I hope that someone, somewhere out there, enjoys reading it; and, having read it, actually wants to do something progressive. I also hope that we, here in Australia, will be able to address, and very constructively, the moral, the ethical, and the intellectual dimensions of our profession so that we'll be well equipped, that is, really well equipped, to move through the rest of this decade, and into the next millenium. I hope also, and as a profession which is vital to the well-being of society, that we really do become fit for our times and that, thereby, and as the accountancy profession, we are truly able to do our part to provide hope for the future. For in the end, when it comes down to it, corporate governance is strategic management, and strategic management is business and, after all, business is our business !!!!!

Just A Note

Well, I've really enjoyed having this little chat with you; this conversational soliloquy. You never know, perhaps one day I'll have a face-to-face chat with John, John Prescott that is, and maybe Sol and Nick, and the others from Coles Myer, as well as some of the people down at the ASX. And it's also conceivable that I could meet with AIMA. Or at least with some of its symbionts. And I mustn't forget those folk down at the Institute and the Society either, and the many many members of the profession. For all you know, one year the powers that be may even get a rush of blood to the head and invite me to address their annual convention, or what have you, and with a suggestion that I offer a controversial view on something or other. Oh yes, and to all those people who didn't make this particular literary encounter as, so as to say, actors in the play, and which people, and through their various contributions, have made my life so very interesting over the years, please don't worry (or, there again, perhaps you should) you may well make the cut-off in my next epistle. In the meantime, please feel free to write to me, or even to give me a call. As a management consultant, and as one who specializes in strategic management and the management of strategy itself, and also as someone who has created an approach to managing strategy through the use of strategic management systems, and not least of all for globalizing companies, you never know, I may even be able to benefit your company. Remember, the way you manage strategy is important to both your own future, and to the future of your organization, and it's also important to your work force, and to their families, as well as to lots of other people. And it's also important to our society. So please be careful when you manage it for, directly and indirectly, your strategy affects many people. Perchance we don't happen to meet, that is, failing a personal encounter, then maybe we'll see each other around. Whatever happens. Best wishes all the same. Regards.

Malcolm